STYLING JIM CROW

STYLING JIM CROW

African American Beauty Training during Segregation

Julia Kirk Blackwelder

TEXAS A&M UNIVERSITY PRESS

College Station

The paper used in this book meets the minimum requirements
of the American National Standard for Permanence
of Paper for Printed Library Materials, Z39.48-1984.
Binding materials have been chosen for durability.

Frontispiece: Beautiful Hair: Nature's Gift and the Beautician's Craft.
Advertising photograph, Franklin School of Beauty Records,
courtesy Houston Metropolitan Research Center,
Houston Public Library.

Library of Congress Cataloging-in-Publication Data

Blackwelder, Julia Kirk, 1943–
Styling Jim Crow : African American beauty training during segregation /
Julia Kirk Blackwelder. — 1st ed.
p. cm.
Includes bibliographical references and index.
ISBN 1-58544-244-5
1. Hairdressing of African Americans—History—20th century. 2. Beauty culture—United
States—History—20th century. 3. African American women—History—20th century.
4. Beauty shops—United States—History—20th century. I. Title

TT972 .B53 2003
646.7'2'08996073—dc21
2002153965

In memory of Robert A. Calvert

Contents

Illustrations

Preface

The writing of this book began with my uncovering the Franklin School of Beauty Papers at the Houston Metropolitan Research Center of the Houston Public Library. I began to piece together the stories of the Franklin School and of the Franklin-Jemison family from these records. My inquiry began as an interest in a family story that pulled me into a larger world. Studying the Franklin records led me to Marjorie Stewart Joyner, and Joyner led me to the Madam C. J. Walker Company. The history of African American beauty education has drawn me to see the wretched institution of racial segregation in a different way than I previously had understood it. Within black communities Jim Crow was a double-sided reality that contained the elements of its own death. Jim Crow fastened a badge of inferiority on African Americans that excluded them from opportunities and denied them rights established in the Constitution, but in segregated institutions such as the beauty schools black Americans built skills, financial resources, and self-respect that ultimately empowered them to destroy Jim Crow. J. H. Jemison's life and career as he preserved them in the Franklin Beauty School records have taught me an essential lesson about the political power of self-respect. I am grateful for the opportunity to tell the part of the story of African American beauty training that appears in the following pages.

Several people have assisted me in writing this book. Tara Wenger, formerly a research archivist at the Houston Metropolitan Research Center, both befriended me and helped me work through the Franklin records. Wilma Gibbs of the Indiana Historical Society and Michael Flug of the Vivian Harsh Collection at the Chicago Public Library also assisted me and took interest in this research project. My Texas A&M colleague Sara Alpern discovered the Randolph family of Indianapolis, which currently owns the Madam Walker company. Sara's determination to uncover new historical sources led to our meeting with the Randolphs and the discovery of a large body of Walker records that remain in private hands. I also appreciate the encouragement of Kathy Peiss as this project inched forward.

The College of Liberal Arts of Texas A&M University under the leadership of Dean Woodrow Jones, Jr., provided the funds that permitted this research. While working on this book, I had the opportunity to meet and talk briefly with Ronald Jemison, Sr., and I have benefited from Mr. Jemison's knowledge of the beauty industry and his recollections of his parents. Albert S. Broussard, Walter L. Buenger, and Cary D. Wintz read drafts of the book manuscript and offered suggestions and corrections. I appreciate their generosity.

This book is dedicated to the memory of Robert A. Calvert. Bob encouraged me to bring my first book manuscript to Texas A&M University Press, he was instrumental in my moving to the Texas A&M Department of History in 1993, and his friendship was true. Bob loved Texas: he fought to change its race relations, and he relished his opportunities to teach its history. All who study the state remain in his debt, as do I.

STYLING JIM CROW

Introduction

Styling Jim Crow is about enterprise and about race leadership. *Styling Jim
Crow* is about the business of training aspiring hairdressers, about teachers
who styled black grammar-school graduates into skilled workers and small
shop owners. The book centers on the careers of beauty-school managers and
instructors James H. (J. H.) Jemison and Marjorie Stewart Joyner, two African Americans who helped style the liberation of women of color from the
clutches of legal and extralegal segregation in the South and the North.
Through the first six decades of the twentieth century the grooming of
women's hair occupied an important place in African American identity politics, and employment in cosmetology, or "beauty culture," offered women of
color one of the few occupational options away from field, factory, and
kitchen. In the first half of the twentieth century privately owned black beauty
schools sustained an uncommon environment in which women learned to
survive under Jim Crow while their teachers worked patiently and tirelessly to
abolish the despised institution of racial discrimination. Cosmetology instructors trained eager matriculates to provide hair care for black patrons and
groomed their students to lead model lives as citizens and as tradespeople independent of white employers. Commerce, gender norms, politics, and culture all intersected inside the beauty school.[1]

3

Marjorie Stewart Joyner and J. H. Jemison stood at the helms of enterprises that brought self-reliance and pride of accomplishment to generations
of African Americans. Along with their peers, Joyner and Jemison developed
hair-care techniques, marketing strategies, and business associations that propelled the African American beauty industry from the Great Depression
through the 1960s. Joyner and Jemison embodied two differing models of business leadership, but both Joyner and Jemison enjoyed considerable success in
their undertakings. J. H. Jemison proved much more astute at business than
did Marjorie Stewart Joyner, but Joyner surpassed Jemison in shaping beauty
education nationally. Marjorie Stewart Joyner understood the importance of
the beauty industry in African American female culture, and she achieved national stature in the industry. Joyner traveled throughout the United States
and participated in multiple organizations that tied the beauty industry to the
larger black community. In contrast, the history of J. H. Jemison and his extended family is the story of beauty education at the local level and the inter-
woven nature of personal matters and commercial activities in a family business. The business records that Jemison amassed during his active leadership
in the industry also captured the aspirations and determination of prospective
beauticians. While Joyner had high visibility among beauticians, Jemison directly touched the lives of many more women through his daily work in the
classroom. The histories of Marjorie Stewart Joyner and J. H. Jemison illustrate the national impact of the beauty industry and demonstrate the important roles that beauty schools played in African American business and
politics.

Marjorie Stewart Joyner oversaw a Madam C. J. Walker beauty school in
Chicago, but her career flourished largely apart from her own school and
through her advice to other beauticians and beauty-school operators. Joyner
dedicated herself to racial uplift by working to help other women of color succeed in the industry and through her broad involvement in civic life. Joyner
conducted training seminars throughout the country and inspired beauticians
and beauty teachers with the potential to earn well. J. H. Jemison concentrated his greatest energies upon building a fledgling school into a successful
business, and in so doing he launched and nurtured countless African American beauty careers. Joyner's career opened the way to prominence in African
American women's clubs and to invitations to White House functions. Jemison led his race in a variety of business, civic, and political activities in Houston. His accomplishments engendered community-wide respect, and his leadership spanned racial lines in Houston and in Texas at a time when few African
American men played any role in Texas politics. While civil rights stood at the
core of their political concerns and commitments, Joyner and Jemison were

for-profit educators first and political activists second. Both educators devoted the majority of their working lives to improving women's opportunities to earn a living within racially segregated communities.

Both Marjorie Stewart Joyner and J. H. Jemison began their careers in Chicago's black neighborhoods, and they entered the business of beauty instruction before state law regulated hairdressing. Joyner opened her first beauty salon during World War I and shortly thereafter made the acquaintance of Sarah Breedlove Walker, the legendary Madam C. J. Walker. During the 1930s Joyner began to travel the country as the national supervisor of Madam Walker's chain of beauty schools. In the 1920s J. H. Jemison went to work as a beautician and instructor at the Madame N. A. Franklin College of Beauty in Chicago, and he soon took over direction of the school. Jemison moved the Franklin School to Houston in 1935, bucking the contemporary tide of African American regional migration. Joyner and Jemison strengthened African American beauty education, and they shared membership in the National Beauty Culturists League (NBCL), an African American association dedicated to elevating training standards and raising beauticians' earnings. Marjorie Stewart Joyner founded the United Beauty School Owners and Teachers Association (UBSOTA), an organization that Jemison joined and in which he stood out as one of the few active male members.

Joyner began her career as did most beauticians of her generation with virtually no capital and limited education. Although she never achieved personal wealth, Joyner headed a legion of African American cosmetologists who lifted themselves into the middle class through hair care and she contributed to the evolution of a multimillion-dollar industry in the process. Jemison continued to lead the Franklin School of Beauty through the 1960s. Through a lifetime in the beauty-school business Jemison helped shape the lives of the young women of color who passed through the school, and he contributed prudent economic and civic leadership to Houston's African American community. Under his meticulous management the Franklin School yielded earnings and profits that moved Jemison financially ahead of most Houstonians, black or white.

Both J. H. Jemison and Marjorie Stewart Joyner found that Jim Crow interfered with their business activities and frustrated their competitive drive. Both business managers fought segregation in the beauty industry and in American society. Adhering to deeply rooted confidence in classical liberalism and self-help, beauty educators such as Joyner and Jemison worked gradually but militantly for racial change. When change finally came in the decades after World War II, women of color gained new vocational options and entered more prestigious and better-paying occupations. Ironically the death of Jim Crow undercut black beauty schools' segregated service to women who previously had been bound for field labor, domestic work, or factory employment. The businesses of both educators declined after the 1950s, but Jemison and Joyner left behind legacies of leadership that their business records reflect. The successes that they enjoyed derived partly from the seriousness with which women of color regarded personal appearance.

In the segregation era carefully groomed hair and immaculate dress armed women against the arrows of racial insults. Beauticians thus played a role in undermining Jim Crow and styling its defeat. Historian Deborah Gray White opens her narrative of African American women's organizational leadership with a vignette that speaks of the importance of dress and hair styling among race leaders:

> On a sticky hot night in 1916, Charleston's black women met at Mt. Zion A. M. E. Church to hear Mary Church Terrell speak on "The Modern Woman." As recalled by Mamie Garvin Fields, perspiration dripped from the women, and the sweltering heat, their dresses clung to them. So many packed the sultry chapel that their hats touched and they were unable to move their pasteboard fans any further than a few inches from side to side without elbowing each other.
>
> It mattered little, for we were all eager to hear what this preeminent educator and first president of the National Association of Colored Women had to say. Terrell did not disappoint them. According to Fields Terrell spoke not only about the modern woman, but in her pink evening dress and long white gloves, with her hair beautifully done, "she *was* that Modern Woman."[2]

Today, as yesterday, dressing hair implies much more than the mere cleaning, trimming, and arranging of tresses. Sociologist Ingrid Banks has observed that "For black women, hair matters embody one's identity, beauty, power, and consciousness."[3] Banks argues that hair care remains central to women's understandings of who they are and what they can accomplish in their lives.

Both cosmetology teachers and beauticians of the Jim Crow era found a racial mission in their work. The African American beauty school emerged in the early twentieth century because women of color cared deeply about their appearance and because beauty salons had become a fixture of racially homogeneous black neighborhoods throughout the nation. Schools of cosmetology proliferated and thrived during the 1930s because states began to regulate hairdressing and the newly adopted state codes demanded formal training as a prerequisite for obtaining a beauty operator's license. Black-operated salons specialized in the goods and services preferred by their clients. Schools of cosmetology such as the Walker and Franklin enterprises particularized their instruction to the ethnic markets their graduates would enter.

The trained beautician of the first half of this century occupied a unique position in the occupational structure because so few wage-earning pursuits welcomed women of color. Many untrained women continued to dress hair part-time, but they seldom achieved the economic or social status accorded the licensed practitioner. While hairdressers often described their trade as a profession, they stood somewhere above domestic servants but below schoolteachers in social status. Writing at the end of the 1930s, Ruth S. Jones, state supervisor of beauty schools in Pennsylvania, noted that "Beauty culture cannot yet be classed as a profession. It is not yet a calling requiring an extensive amount of preparation; instead, it is a pursuit requiring manual or mechanical training and dexterity."[4]

Although informal beauty training has a long history, organized schools of cosmetology did not appear until the marketing of beauty products had been developed nationally. Cosmetic manufacturers and beauty-salon managers knew the dangers of employing untrained beauty operators. The treacheries of submitting to the untutored hairdresser far exceeded the dissatisfactions of an uneven cut or failed hair taming. Broken hair, hair loss, discolored hair, scalp burns, and scalp infections afflicted some women who trusted their heads to the care of beauticians. The rapid expansion of the beauty industry through the 1920s had led to the broad employment of untrained workers. Once licensing of beauticians and barbers was in place, both schools and licensed practitioners sought to drive "jackleg" beauty operatives out of business, both as a means to distance themselves from the less qualified and as a means of driving up prices. While unlicenced workers were never entirely eliminated, their numbers dwindled as they quit the business or completed instruction and submitted to state examinations.

The trials of Alabama beauty-shop owner Mrs. M. C. Crutcher, an African American businesswoman, demonstrate the perils of launching an enterprise in hairdressing in the absence of regulated cosmetology training. Crutcher opened a three-booth beauty shop in Alabama in 1937 and sought to enlist several hairdressers to be under her supervision. Only one woman answered Crutcher's employment call. The job applicant claimed knowledge of hairdressing and secured the job although she could furnish no evidence of experience in the industry. Crutcher later recalled that "It did not take but one head . . . to find out that [my operator] was not a beautician."[5] Rather than fire the incompetent worker, Crutcher undertook to teach her employee the requisite skills, her only recourse locally since Alabama lagged the nation in beauty education and licensing. Crutcher had learned firsthand the pitfalls of unregulated commerce in hairdressing.

Before World War I, beauty-salon owners trained their own employees through shop apprenticeships as Mrs. M. C. Crutcher did in the 1930s. By 1920 salons that trained hairdressers had begun to describe themselves as schools, or "colleges," but beauty instruction consisted largely of learning to groom hair through observation and practice, a system that differed from the shop apprenticeship only in that the training now carried an instructional fee. The 1930s movement to license beauticians propelled the organization of freestanding schools of beauty culture whose instructors also submitted to examination and licensing by state boards of cosmetology. Beauty colleges grew and prospered during the Depression, even while the sale of skin and hair products declined, because the industry itself had changed through government regulation. As skilled hairdressers who had already been teaching the principles of hair care to fee-paying students, Marjorie Stewart Joyner and J. H. Jemison were well positioned to advance to the status of licensed beauty instructors. Through the century men such as J. H. Jemison proved the exceptions in a field dominated by women.[6]

The period from 1930 through 1960 comprised the golden age of the African American beauty school, and Jemison and Joyner advanced with the industry. The success of beauty schools for whites and for women of color followed from the coincidence between the imposition of regulation on the hairdressing industry and the highly restricted educational and employment prospects of working-class girls. By the end of the 1930s nearly every state had a cosmetology code in effect. Although all state license laws required that hairdressers to complete a prescribed course of cosmetology, through the 1960s few states mandated that beauticians obtain a high-school diploma. Hairdressing thus provided a singular avenue to a satisfactory wage for girls who had left secondary school before graduation. Southern states adopted segregated cosmetology examinations from the beginning, and northern states gradually implemented differing standards by race. For poor girls generally but for African American girls in particular, beauty training held out the promise of economic mobility. African American beauty schools emerged to meet the demands of women of color eager to build hair-styling careers. Marjorie Stewart Joyner and J. H. Jemison, both of whom began their careers as trained hair stylists, turned their talents to training others just as the demand for beauty education blossomed.

The rise of the beautician, regardless of race, was tied to Americans' movement into towns. A 1980s exhibit at the National Museum of American History captured the significance of African American migration and also bespoke the considerable economic and social worth of the African American beauty industry in the early twentieth century. The Smithsonian Institution constructed a facsimile of the 1916 Chicago beauty salon of Marjorie Stewart Joyner and situated it at the center of "Field to Factory: Afro-American Migration, 1915–1940," an exhibition that recognized the accomplishments of persons of color who had left the South to build new lives north of the Mason-Dixon line. The African American beauty industry, like its white counterpart, emerged in urban centers where women had convenient access to small retail establishments and where door-to-door selling was feasible. The South comprised an especially important market for the African American industry because of the concentration of women of color in the region. The largest manufacturing concerns, however, were located in the Northeast and the Midwest where African American communities burgeoned as migrants fled southern poverty and sought redress from legalized segregation.

Between 1870 and 1930 more than 1.5 million men and women made their way northward, with the vast majority of these migrants of color moving in the second and third decades of the twentieth century. Detroit, Cleveland, New York, and Pittsburgh grew rapidly, but African Americans on the move favored Chicago above all other destinations. African American newspapers such as the *Chicago Defender* and the *Pittsburgh Courier* cast lifelines into the South and drew African Americans north with news of better economic and political prospects outside the South. These same journals helped African American entrepreneurs market their merchandise within and outside the South.[7]

While the Great Migration defined culture and politics among blacks in the North, the intraregional migration of southern African Americans was far larger and more important in reshaping the economy of the region and politics of the nation in the twentieth century. The urban transformation of the South both antedated and postdated the Great Migration of African Americans away from the regions of their birth. Beginning with the Civil War but taking on major momentum after the turn of the century, African American movement into the towns and cities of the South stimulated the emergence of compact commercial districts that fostered and nurtured small retail businesses throughout the region. Smaller and less grand than northern infrastructures, Atlanta's Sweet Auburn could not rival New York's Harlem. Nevertheless southern African American business zones were far more numerous than their northern counterparts. Medium-sized cities such as Hattiesburg, Mississippi, and Macon, Georgia, supported blacks' only commercial districts and smaller towns hosted the cafes, bars, and barbershops that legalized segregation required. These communities employed beauticians trained in the South and provided markets that supported northern manufacturers. Marjorie

Stewart Joyner built her career by traveling to African American communities in the North and in the South. J. H. Jemison built his enterprise by relocating from Chicago to a southern urban market.

In black communities beauty culture fit into a larger service sector that disproportionally drew the labor of African Americans through the century. Before the Civil War the capital deprivation of free blacks and the decisions of white slave owners had encouraged people of color to specialize in artisanal pursuits such as barbering and catering. Capital and property accumulation among African Americans grew after emancipation but proceeded slowly as racial discrimination closed one economic opportunity after another to blacks. The Freeman's Bank, created by Congress in 1865, had offered hope to thousands, but it soon proved a poor resource for African American entrepreneurs, and its failure in 1873 crushed the dreams of countless recently freed citizens. The history of the bank's mismanagement and collapse, however, served to remind African Americans of the necessity of relying on their own resources, a constraint that further encouraged racial solidarity. As Reconstruction optimism turned to Jim Crow realism, Americans of color built loyalty to African American enterprises despite the scarce resources and limited offerings of these businesses. The African American beauty industry successfully negotiated this rough terrain.[8]

The comparatively low capital investment required to establish service businesses encouraged African American concentration in such enterprises, and this pattern of specialization continued into the twentieth century. Tradespeople of color entered heavily into those pursuits in which they might reasonably expect to find white as well as black clients. In 1935, when African Americans constituted one-tenth of the nation's population, blacks operated one-third of the shoe-repair shops in the country and one-fifth of the dry-cleaning establishments. While African Americans also disproportionally maintained barbering and hairdressing businesses, they had less representation in these areas than in trades where patrons of both races sought their services without inhibition. While some white men continued to frequent African American barbershops in 1935, virtually no white women darkened the doorways of African American beauty salons.[9]

Before the turn of the century both the beauty salon and beauty instruction were rarities. Grace Garnett-Abney, whose memories were captured in a 1941 interview, operated a beauty parlor on Chicago's South Side in 1896. Beauty training at this time consisted of a brief apprenticeship in a beauty salon. Garnett-Abney trained in such a setting, the Burnham Beauty College, and was the school's first student of color. At the turn of the century, a handful of African American women gained admittance to loosely organized and unregulated beauty schools such as Burnham. These schools prepared women to groom and style the limp, straight hair that characterized many white patrons. The African American beautician not only faced discrimination in catering to white women, but also had to develop on her own the techniques that met the hair-grooming demands of women of color.

Garnett-Abney set up a shop in which she welcomed women of all races, but she soon found her practice restricted to women of her own race. She succeeded in attracting African American clients who paid her to dress their hair and to fashion natural-hair wigs for them. Garnett-Abney's business rested on her discovery "that their hair would grow by pulling it out with hair tongs."[10] The young beautician then saved the hair that she pulled or combed from her clients' heads to make the wigs that provided her major cash income. Garnett-Abney remembered that only two salons that served whites on Chicago's South Side had opened before she had inaugurated her business. She initially expected to attract white customers but soon found otherwise. Garnett-Abney's patrons, overwhelmingly women of color, came to have their hair straightened or to purchase wigs. The hair-setting methods she had learned at Burnham had no value in her business. As Garnett-Abney's history suggests, an enterprising woman faced relatively few barriers in entering the beauty trade at the turn of the century as no licensing or inspection agencies scrutinized these activities.

Garnett-Abney had contemporaries in cities throughout the nation, each of whom had developed their own products and techniques for hair care through trial and error or apprenticeships. Elizabeth Barker's grandmother and mother both dressed hair in Atlantic City, New Jersey, before the turn of the century, but most of their clients were white women.[11] As the twentieth century dawned, whites forced African American women almost entirely out of the field of serving white clients, and specialty shops such as Garnett-Abney's proliferated. Elizabeth Barker carried the family's Atlantic City business into the twentieth century, but her patronage was entirely African American. The Census Bureau recorded 514 African American women and 16,966 men in barbering and hairdressing occupations in the United States in 1890. Over the ensuing decade, the numbers of women entering the profession rose sharply. By 1910, 3,093 African American women had reported themselves to census takers as being gainfully employed in hairdressing while growth in the number of male barbers or cosmetologists failed to keep pace with the overall increase in the male workforce or the numerical increase in the number of women in the trade. The historian Robert C. Kenzer searched city directories of 18 North Carolina cities and found 29 hairdressing establishments and 369 barbershops in operation between 1909 and 1916.[12] African Americans operated the vast majority of the hairdressing salons and slightly more than half of the barbershops.

Given both the motivations to pursue beauty culture and the ease of occupational entry, women crowded into beauty care in American urban centers, especially in cities that were home to sizable African American populations. New York in 1920 had more than 800 beauticians of color, but Indianapolis, which headquartered the Madam C. J. Walker enterprises, had the greatest proportion of workers in the industry, with 11 percent of all working women of color engaged in beauty culture.[13] Chicago, which is still home to Johnson Products, one of the few remaining minority-owned cosmetic firms, hosted a plethora of African American beauty parlors and multiple beauty schools in addition to those that employed Marjorie Stewart Joyner and J. H. Jemison. Major growth in hairdressing occurred in the 1920s as electrified equipment for hair processing was introduced, and as beauticians promoted elaborate pressed and curled hairstyles that became the rage among American women of all races. By the close of the 1920s, the beauty salon was an ubiquitous feature of most American neighborhoods, and salons were more common in black than in white communities. In 1930 nearly 13,000 African American women worked as beauty operators while the number of men in barbershops, where some white patronage continued, had reached only 21,500.[14] A 1930s survey of black businesses in New Orleans turned up seventy-two beauty parlors, nearly equal to the number of barbershops and exceeding the number of African American restaurants, drugstores, and garment-pressing shops.[15]

Within African American and white communities, some beauty schools rose from the marketing schemes of cosmetic and hair-goods manufacturers while others evolved from the training programs of skilled beauticians who took on apprentices.[16] Manufacturers of hair-care products organized cosmetology instruction to elevate the expertise of their sales staff beyond the skills demonstrated by the competition. Producers of cosmetics and hair goods held clinics to instruct their employees or agents in the use of their sales line. These "beauticians" practiced their trade as representatives of manufacturers, earned commissions on the products they sold, and collected fees for the services they performed. Unlike the still-familiar "Avon lady" or Mary Kay representative, African American sales agents of the early twentieth century marketed their wares along with their services by demonstrating their products in salons that dispensed hair, skin, and nail care. In this unregulated environment, many women practiced hairdressing as a secondary line of wage earning and on the basis of lessons they had learned from friends or relatives. Through the early 1930s some beauticians continued to sell preparations they had manufactured in their salons or homes. The U.S. Food and Drug Administration (FDA) first regulated the manufacture and sale of cosmetics in 1938, and these regulations eventually ended legal sales of homemade products. The FDA continues to oversee the manufacture and sale of cosmetics while individual states regulate health practices in beauty salons and control the training and licensing of hairdressers.

Marjorie Stewart Joyner and J. H. Jemison climbed ladders that stood on the beauty-culture foundation laid by earlier industry pioneers, but their careers as teachers followed from the regulation of hairdressing and beauty-product manufacturing. Joyner's and Jemison's tutelage made paths for succeeding generations of African Americans who, in the face of seemingly overwhelming odds, freed themselves from a life of service to whites and advanced into dignified economic independence through skills that they and their clients valued. The first chapter of the narrative that follows describes the legacy of beauty culture that Joyner and Jemison inherited, outlining the development of the hair-care industry in African American communities of the Jim Crow era. Chapter 2 focuses largely on the activities of Marjorie Stewart Joyner, but it also explores the Madam C. J. Walker organization and the role of traveling agents in marketing Walker products. Chapters 3 and 4 relate the history of the Franklin School of Beauty and the J. H. Jemison family while also considering the dreams and frustrations of Franklin Beauty School students striving to enter the styling trade. The concluding chapter offers some observations on the contributions of beauty care and beauty education to the well-being of African Americans of the Jim Crow era and the roles of Jemison and Joyner in advancing and adapting to changes in American race relations.

CHAPTER 1

The Legacy
of Beauty Culture

During the first three decades of the twentieth century, African Americans built youthful enterprises in cosmetics manufacturing and beauty services into mature multimillion-dollar industries. These industries paved the way for beauty education and facilitated the careers of Marjorie Stewart Joyner and J. H. Jemison. Twentieth-century beauty culture emerged from a confluence of nineteenth-century beauty practices and the rise of consumerism in the United States. In the late nineteenth century women of color began to sell home-manufactured hair tonics and cosmetics to their friends and neighbors, and some charged fees to dress women's hair. Emerging to attend a niche market of unique tastes, the beauty industry grew rapidly into a major sector of the African American economy between 1900 and 1945.[1] White discrimination against persons of color located the beauty industry at the juncture where African American race pride and Jim Crow realities collided. Racial segregation limited the prospects of black enterprises, but racism also sheltered African American businesses somewhat from white competition within African American markets. White-owned cosmetic firms had little or no experience in meeting the needs or the market tastes of African American consumers, and white hairdressers refused to serve women of color.[2] Because Jim Crow checked minority access to credit, most African American beauty con-

cerns began from household enterprises, and successful business people gradually built their fortunes by funding expansion through their own profits.[3]

At the turn of the century beauticians with little or no training practiced
their arts as distributors of skin and hair products that they purchased or manufactured. The cosmetics industry antedated the beauty salon as manufacturers such as Sarah Breedlove Walker (Madam C. J. Walker) engaged in direct
marketing through advertisements in African American periodicals and later
recruited agents to sell their products. Manufacturers including Walker experimented with hair-treatment compounds and invited their friends into
their homes where they demonstrated for them the wonders their creams and
lotions could work. Home demonstrations evolved into household salons and
free-standing beauty parlors developed as home salons succeeded. As retail
distribution expanded, cosmetic firms increasingly demanded that beauty-
culture agents acquire expertise in employing the product line they sold and
that they treat customers' hair and skin as part of their marketing endeavors.

Despite the several disabilities under which African American entrepreneurs operated, some in the beauty industry succeeded handsomely.
Juliet E. K. Walker has described the first three decades of the twentieth century as the "golden age of black business," citing beauty culture as the leading
sector of economic activity.[4] Beauty schools, in contrast, reached the peak of
their prosperity after these decades of product development. Producers of cosmetics for white women marketed some of their products to the black community and developed specific lines for African Americans in the early days of
the beauty industry. Separate advertisement campaigns for the racially defined
white and black product lines of white companies appeared in white-owned
and African American newspapers, respectively. Marketing their products to
African Americans through newspaper mail-order campaigns, white companies were not easily distinguished from African American businesses that conducted similar marketing efforts. Nevertheless black firms were ascendant,
and African American entrepreneurs overshadowed white cosmetic companies in African American markets after World War I, a dominance they would
maintain until the end of the Jim Crow era.[5]

The African American industry of beauty culture capitalized on long-
expressed hair-grooming preferences. During the slavery era many African
Americans, bonded and free, adopted hairstyles that embraced African American definitions of beauty and that echoed African traditions, but some women
also experimented with hair-straightening and skin-lightening techniques that
reflected white American values.[6] In antebellum America women of color
stood in the constant shadow of white judgments that devalued their natural
beauty. White Americans commodified their notions of slave beauty as they

did the skills, talents, and physical strength of African Americans. Slave traders advertised light skin and straight hair to describe human merchandise more highly prized than ebony-skinned chattel with tightly curled hair.

African beauty skills traveled west on slave vessels and evolved in America. Irrespective of beauty standards slave women groomed their hair for health and convenience. African techniques of braiding and head wrapping helped workers keep their hair clean and out of harm's way through the strenuous labors of household and field, and slaves' hairstyles preserved aspects of the cultures from which their ancestors had been wrenched. Slaves dressed and groomed more according to personal tastes on the Sabbath or holidays that released them from some of their labors.[7] Free blacks living under white hegemony felt the stings and discriminations of racialized beauty norms, but free persons selected the hair and dress styles that pleased them. After emancipation the competing impulses to braid or to straighten hair persisted, but freedom opened the way for African American enterprises that encouraged the development of distinctive new beauty standards and of commercial hair-care products. Over time the African American cosmetic market developed in response to beauty standards, and beauty products were freely chosen within African American communities and adopted from an understanding of what Colored Methodist Episcopal bishop Lucius Henry Holsey, writing in 1879, described as "peculiarities of the hair."[8]

Women of color learned about braiding, wrapping, straightening, and conditioning hair from their grandmothers, mothers, and friends. Beauty secrets were part of a larger cache of folk wisdom that utilized common household products and plants to prepare a plethora of health aids. African American women of color experimented with recipes for skin and hair care that had been handed down through generations. In closely knit communities of color, word of a woman's skills in enhancing health or beauty spread quickly. A good reputation in hairdressing might easily develop into an after-hours occupation. Hairdressers of the turn of the century practiced several approaches to the grooming and styling of hair including braiding, straightening, and waving. Some hairdressers made wigs or wove additional strands of hair into the natural head of hair. To condition the hair, hairdressers prepared compounds composed of perfumes, bleaching agents, and solvents blended into bases of petroleum or animal oils. Manufacturers touted one category of products to stimulate hair growth, another to cure scalp ailments, and others to tame or straighten curly hair. Beauty agents promised that hair growers would produce a head of hair that was long and thick.

Hair growers had formed the initial basis of the success of African American beauty pioneer Annie Turnbo Malone and of Sarah Breedlove Walker.

A'Lelia Bundles has written that the efficacy of growers rested on "regular shampoos, scalp massage, nutritious food and an easily duplicated, sulfur-based formula" rather than a miraculous compound invented by either of the two beauty giants.[9] Interviewed in the 1970s, beautician Elizabeth Barker remembered that her grandmother had made a hair preparation based on castor oil that had been very popular with her white customers and that she had also used the product with her grandchildren. Barker concluded, "But all I can say is she used that product on all of her grandchildren's heads of hair and every single one of them had outrageously thick, healthy hair. So . . . I wish that she had lived long enough for me to learn what that product was."[10] Where hair growers more likely had beneficial effects was in conditioning hair to make it less susceptible to breakage from the abuse of straightening tongs, heated metal combs and irons, and harsh chemical compounds. As beautician Margaret Holmes reported, "Of course, in the cruder days—straighteners, they used to call them—there used to be terrible sores and loss of hair and that sort of thing in the early experimental days."[11]

Annie Turnbo Malone and Sarah Breedlove Walker reached broader clientele by adding conditioning creams, shampoos, combs, setting irons, and other products to their line of offerings. A third race business giant, Sara Spencer Washington, inaugurated her Apex beauty system roughly a decade after Malone and Walker had built sizable manufacturing plants. Washington added wigs and other hairpieces to the general line of hair products that Malone and Walker had marketed. Ultimately all three companies organized chains of beauty colleges to add an additional market segment to their enterprises and to further the distribution of their products. In the long run Washington's business proved the most successful even through she got a relatively late start. Beauty-marketing systems changed as product lines became more elaborate and as firms moved increasingly into wholesale activities and out of the direct-marketing approach.

As cosmetics firms vied for market share, manufacturers escalated their product claims through advertisements placed in the African American press. Cosmetic-marketing strategies frequently pivoted upon convincing the public that a "Dr. Fred Palmer" or "Dr. Delano, a noted Indian doctor,"[12] possessed special gifts and had invented secret formulas that fooled Mother Nature. African American newspapers, which had provided the major venue for entrepreneurs of the early twentieth century, remained an important marketing tool well after World War II. In 1947 the nation boasted more than 150 African American newspapers. The vast majority had circulations below 10,000, but the largest and most influential journals published both local and national editions and reached many more readers than the average urban periodical. The

Pittsburgh Courier had reached a distribution of 275,000 in the late 1940s. The second-ranking paper was the *Chicago Defender,* which claimed 130,000 national subscribers and a circulation of 62,000 local readers in 1947. Other major papers included the Baltimore *Afro-American* and the New York *Amsterdam News.* The Norfolk *Journal and Guide,* which claimed nearly 63,000 in circulation, was the South's leading African American newspaper, but no city in the former Confederate States published a journal that approached the North's greatest minority serials. The *Houston Informer and Texas Freeman,* which served as the central Franklin School of Beauty advertising venue, reported a circulation of 24,300 during the forties.[13]

Beauty product advertisers walked a slender line between racial pride in genetic characteristics and market demands for hair-straightening and skin-lightening agents. Some early manufacturers made no apologies for their catering to white-defined standards and appealed directly to some African Americans' wishes for fair skin and curl-free tresses. The marketing approach of the Strait-Tex Chemical Company with its Hair Refining Tonic and Bronze Beauty Vanishing Cream was hard to miss. The Hi-Ja Chemical Company asked, "Why have hair that you are ashamed of — nappy, kinky, stubborn hair — when it is easy to have hair that you are proud of? Have hair that falls in straight silky, soft, gleaming strands below your shoulders." Sarah Breedlove Walker and the Walker company consistently pitched their products as working to "glorify the womanhood of our Race" and avoided claims of fabricating the ideals of whiteness. Walker promised "long, luxurious hair and beauty-kissed complexion" but never mentioned whitening or bleaching skin. Eager to exploit the full range of the African American market, however, printed Walker advertisements included sidebars that noted the availability of Tan-Off for "freckles, pimples, tan, etc."[14]

Petroleum derivatives comprised the base of most skin and hair conditioners of the time, and similar products have persisted to the present day. Among the recipes of the 1940s is the following for taming hair and protecting it from drying:

>   Petroleum (Snow White), 1 lb.
>   Yellow Beeswax, 4 oz.
>   Venice Turpentine, 2 oz.
>   Paraffin Wax, 1 oz.
>   Castor Oil, 3 oz.
>   Boric Acid, 2 drams
>   Quinine Sulphate, 1 dram

Salicylic Acid, 1 dram
Oil of Lemon, 2 drams
Oil of Rose Geranium, 4 drams
Gum Camphor, 1/2 dram

The beautician prepared the hair cream by melting the solid ingredients, mixing in the liquid additives, and stirring the batch as it cooled into a soft solid. After a liberal application to the patron's hair, the hairdresser worked the cream into the scalp and then removed the excess oil with an absorbent towel.

Through the 1930s all major African American firms marketed petroleum-based preparations from scalp conditioners to oils employed to straighten or "press" hair when used in combination with heated combs. Similar to cold-cream conditioners, hot-oil treatments addressed various scalp conditions, particularly dandruff. The beautician heated a compound to a liquid state but took care not to get the oil so hot as to burn the client's scalp. Sectioning the hair with combs and clips, the practitioner applied the oil a little at a time and rubbed it into the scalp in a massagelike fashion. The hairdresser then toweled off the excess and styled the hair according to the client's preferences. While hair pressing also utilized a heated oil, the goal of pressing was to cover the hair strands rather than the scalp.

Hair pressing was more complicated than the simple application of Walker's and Malone's hair growers and scalp conditioners. The beautician slid the hair through the her oiled fingers and then painstakingly combed the hair with a long-toothed, heated metal comb. The hairdresser employed the "pressing" comb to separate the hair strands and to push them flat by pressing the teeth nearly parallel to the hair while pulling the hair against the base of the comb and through its teeth. The beautician began by moving the comb from the scalp to the hair ends and then reversed the process, carefully working her way over the entire head of hair. Section by section the operator flattened the hair against the teeth of the hot comb, a press that straightened the hair with considerable risk of burning the hair and the scalp. The beauty salon appeared in African American neighborhoods in the early twentieth century partly because heated pressing irons and metal hair rollers complicated the use of commercial hair preparations. Salons rather than individuals soon became the major venue for manufacturers in beauty culture with companies' insisting that salons carry only their products. African American demand for the broad array of beauty merchandise had fueled the growth of several large black-owned business houses by the 1920s.

Anthony Overton built the first large black-owned cosmetic firm in the country. Overton, an attorney who had pursued several lines of work, opened the Overton-Hygienic Company in Kansas City in 1898. Starting the Overton company to manufacture baking powder and other food items, Overton's fortunes blossomed after he introduced High Brown Face Powder, a preparation that utilized the technology and equipment that produced his grocery line but targeted African American beauty tastes. As Overton tested the strength of the ethnic market, cosmetics emerged as his main enterprise. After moving Overton Hygienic to Chicago in 1911, Overton's business boomed, and by 1915 his business had matured into the largest black-owned manufacturing enterprise in the nation with annual sales in excess of $250,000. In line with those who built other African American businesses, Overton held fast to principles of racial betterment by employing persons of color exclusively in his operations, and in the process he built a personal fortune in excess of a million dollars. In time Overton diversified into banking, publishing, and life insurance. Among other initiatives he launched the *Chicago Bee,* an African American newspaper. His enterprises centered in Bronzeville, a section of Chicago's South Side that became the major locus of the city's African American commercial and cultural activities. Overton's banking and insurance enterprises failed in the dark times of the 1930s, but the *Bee* and the cosmetics business survived for some time thereafter. When beauty schools emerged after World War I, Overton financed the establishment of the Overton High-Brown Beauty College and named his daughter Mabel Overton to head the school.[15]

Annie Turnbo Malone, Sarah Breedlove Walker, and Sara Spencer Washington, the three giants in the field of hairdressing, amassed large fortunes based on product sales. These profits financed the chains of beauty schools that vied for dominance in the African American market after World War I. These women did not have counterparts in the white cosmetics business although cosmetics also produced millions in revenues for white business owners. Malone, Walker, and Washington built companies that employed hundreds of African Americans, contributed substantial sums for the betterment of their communities, and enlarged the leadership roles of women in African American civic affairs. Annie Turnbo Malone most likely was not only the first African American to become a millionaire but also the first self-made American businesswoman to achieve such wealth.

Although there were several firms founded at the turn of the century, the Poro Company of Annie Turnbo Malone and Sarah Breedlove Walker's Madam Walker line dominated the trade and fought fiercely with each other for market shares. The third major firm of the Jim Crow era, Sara Spencer Washington's Apex beauty company, emerged at the close of World War I.

Washington opened her first beauty shop in Atlantic City, New Jersey, in 1918, and soon thereafter she moved into marketing her own line of manufactures. Before World War II Washington added a chain of beauty schools to her operations, schools that outlived most Madam Walker schools.

Not long before Washington opened her Atlantic City salon, Nobia Franklin (Madame N. A. Franklin) opened her San Antonio beauty parlor, a move that was similarly followed by movement into product manufacturing and sales as well as beauty-culture education. Nobia Franklin differed from the three women who became industrial giants by the modesty of her success, but she also differed by beginning her activities in the South and later moving north. Franklin's history characterizes the early days of the beauty industry when small entrepreneurs carved out a bit of the market and built viable concerns but never achieved the personal fortunes that distinguished the three giants.

The constant battles for market share in which the Walker and other companies engaged demonstrated how easy it was to enter the trade and how difficult it was to rise to the top. Because products were based on commonly known formulas that had developed as home remedies or had been passed from mother to daughter, many hopeful entrepreneurs entered the market. Annie Turnbo Malone claimed to have perfected her Wonderful Hair Grower in her high-school chemistry lab. Giants such as Poro and Overton Hygienic Products fought for market shares in a national arena while small-scale manufacturers worked to capture local customers and upstart businesses appeared daily. Combs, irons, and petroleum-based hair treatments were the stock in which the African American businesses traded. Although each major manufacturer held patents for chemical compounds, hair combs, and irons, the products of one company bore marked similarities to those of its competitors. A beautician "trained" in the Walker System might be equally adept in employing the Poro or other competing product lines. Consequently manufacturers set out both to steal agents from their major competitors and to detect and punish their representatives who attempted to carry rival products. A Walker sales representative in Florida gleefully informed the Indianapolis office that she had won over five beauty operatives from a competing product line and that she was hard at work to induce a sixth to turn in her Poro certificate for the Walker counterpart.[16]

The early history of the Walker enterprise further documents the common roots and ferocious competitiveness of beauty firms. Annie Turnbo Malone's and Sarah Breedlove Walker's rivalry was personal as well as professional, as Walker had worked as a Poro agent and had patterned and named her initial hair product after Malone's Wonderful Hair Grower. Both women claimed that assiduous application of their product would cause a woman's hair to grow faster and stronger than by nature alone. Walker's threat to the Poro enterprises pushed Malone to apply for patents on her products, a practice that Walker followed assiduously.[17] Intraracial competition thus introduced the first elements of regulation into the business as African American entrepreneurs little feared competition from the separately developing businesses that catered to white clients.

After the turn of the century, to complement her meager earnings in domestic work, Sarah Breedlove had begun marketing Annie Turnbo Malone's hair preparations. In 1906 Breedlove married Charles J. Walker, a traveling agent who saw tremendous potential for economic growth in the beauty industry and who encouraged Sarah to devote more of her energies to the Malone enterprise. Initially Sarah concentrated on increasing her Malone sales, but she soon turned to manufacturing her own product under the label Madam Walker's Wonderful Hair Grower.[18] In 1910 the Walkers relocated to Indianapolis, a city of more than twenty thousand African Americans that proved fertile ground for growing the Walker fortune. Another African American who sought success in Indianapolis was the young lawyer F. B. Ransom, whose business acumen carried Sarah Breedlove Walker to singular success. In 1911 Ransom facilitated the incorporation of Walker's enterprise. Sarah Breedlove Walker, C. J. Walker, and Sarah's grown daughter Lelia Robinson held equal shares in the Madam C. J. Walker Company.[19]

Under Ransom's guidance the Walker company moved swiftly and forcefully to broaden its sales and to suppress competition in any way possible. When a former Walker saleswoman in California tried to emulate Walker's behavior and market her own hair products, she received a nasty letter from F. B. Ransom:

> Dear Madam:
>
> I have your ad, before me, and it seems strange that you would make such statements to the public. Do you know that you render yourself amendable to the laws of California when you send such advertisements over the country. You know who and what grew your hair, and who and what grew the hair of your alleged customers, and we would be sorry to see you, in court, trying to produce those thousands whose hair you have grown.
>
> Now if we see any more such adds [sic] and hear of any more such statements we shall inform the proper authorities, both state, and federal, and have you arrested and punished for obtaining money under false pretense.[20]

Where Walker could not cajole the little guy out of the market, the company might buy out potential competitors. In 1924 Walker Manufacturing paid one thousand dollars to Louis B. Cason of Cincinnati for the patent rights to a metal comb that he had perfected for straightening hair.[21]

By the second decade of the twentieth century, Sarah Breedlove Walker had amassed an estate valued at more than one million dollars through the sale of her cosmetics and hair-care preparations. She built a mansion on the Hudson River north of New York City and maintained a Harlem residence where daughter Lelia preferred to stay. Walker opened "Lelia College," a training school for prospective beautician-agents, in Harlem. Naming the school after her daughter, Walker also named Lelia to oversee the school. By the time of her death in 1919, Madam Walker had already ceded practical control of her company to her daughter and to F. B. Ransom and Ransom's assistant Robert Lee Brokenburr.

As historians have documented, Madam C. J. Walker's success rested heavily on an artfully crafted appeal to racial pride. The Walker company avoided the words "bleach" and "straighten" in describing its merchandise, writing instead of the healthfulness of Walker products and their abilities to enhance women's natural beauty. Both Walker and Annie Turnbo Malone alluded as well to the spiritual benefits reaped from a healthy and well-groomed appearance. Although Sarah Breedlove Walker had set the tone of her advertisements, corporate managers Ransom and Brokenburr were largely responsible for carrying out Madam Walker's marketing strategies. After Walker's death Ransom and Brokenburr turned more openly to describing the bleaching or straightening properties of Walker wares while assiduously avoiding those very words.[22]

In the early twentieth century the Madam C. J. Walker Company, Malone's Poro organization, and other cosmetics firms maintained pyramid direct-marketing networks in regions of the country with sizable African American populations. National advertising made the Walker and Poro companies household names in African American households, and manufacturers solicited mail orders, but mail orders were small and costly to service. In addition use of the products required some skill. Thus a network of agents who both demonstrated and sold products was a critical component of cosmetic sales, and this approach emerged as the central marketing strategy in the African American beauty industry. Indeed this agent system was the model adopted by the white-owned Avon Company. Virtually all African American cosmetics manufacturers of the early twentieth century relied upon a network of untrained beauticians to market their products either through direct sales or by creating demand by using their products in grooming their clients' hair.[23]

In addition to marketing her products through advertising in the African American press, Walker traveled the nation to demonstrate her hair and skin preparations. Regular paid announcements in the *Negro Farmer*, billed as the "National Farm Journal for Colored Farmers," targeted rural residents whom Walker failed to reach in her travels. Walker recruited retail sales agents through the mail and during her travels. In the years preceding World War I, Madam Walker signed up agents through the nation, touting the industry as a unique opportunity to combine service to the race with personal advancement. Walker advised agents that "We are anxious to help all humanity, the poor as well as the rich, especially those of our race."[24] Walker enrolled sales agents on the company rolls after their completion of a one- to two-hour product demonstration. For a fee of twenty-five dollars, a price that had emerged as an industry standard by 1915, a prospective beautician received a kit of tools, written instructions on product use, a starter pack of products manufactured by the Walker Company, and authorization to sell the Walker line. Thus the company recouped the costs of recruiting, training, and supplying new agents before a single sale had occurred. Once the demonstration course had been completed and paid for, the agent could set up a Walker salon in her home or take the products to the homes of others to sell her service as well as products. The Walker Company also offered donations of one hundred dollars to African American schools that initiated training in beauty and hair care with the use of Walker products.

The Walker Company, under the management of F. B. Ransom, furnished agents with flyers that described "Madam C. J. Walker's Wonderful Preparation." Under Madam Walker's name, Ransom counseled new agents to master the company version of Madam Walker's biography because the inspiring story of her life and inventions would prove a powerful marketing asset. Advice to Walker agents, whom the company instantly recognized as beauticians, included hints on personal appearance and comportment as well as guidelines for product use. The company offered instructions with the advisory that "Madam Walker is very desirous for all her agents to make good." The company predicated its advice on the expectation that agents might well work in their homes, setting apart a room that should be cleaned daily and aired regularly, regardless of weather, to "drive out the germs." The personal appearance of the beautician herself contributed to the healthful atmosphere of the beauty parlor, but also gave the client as feeling of trust and confidence in the agent. Agents were advised to groom their own hair flawlessly "in order to interest others" and to brush their teeth faithfully and employ mints to cover bad breath. Clean hands and fingernails not only contributed to the illusion of a healthful atmosphere but were also "a mark of refinement." The Walker literature suggested that beauticians should dust themselves with oxide of zinc to ward off offensive body odors and that the enterprising beautician would keep small bags of the powder on hand for sale to customers.[25]

Regarding procedures for conditioning and setting hair, Walker cautioned agents to sterilize combs and sponges after each client and to keep extras on hand for sale. On the employment of heated combs, Walker warned against working two combs simultaneously because of the necessity to watch closely that the combs were not so hot as to burn the hair. Similarly the company discouraged the use of "hair pullers," irons that straightened hair by flattening the strands, because they damaged and ultimately thinned the hair. Carefully attuned to the economic realities of African American communities, the Walker Company concluded its prewar advice in admonishing agents not to be "narrow and selfish to the extent that you would not sell goods to anyone because they do not take the treatment from you."[26]

Walker Company marketing literature touted the ease of earning three to five dollars per day and advised that agents could earn up to one hundred dollars per month. The company promised that highly successful agents would earn a salary in addition to commissions, but only a handful of agents ever advanced to the status of salaried employee. Madam Walker hoped that her agents would develop into hard-nosed, driving businesswomen who would "make every moment count," remembering that a sales call was not a social occasion. Should the agent be troubled by a lack of confidence, the company prompted her to "Keep in mind that you have something that the person standing before you really needs, imagine yourself a missionary and convert him."[27] The company demanded loyalty of its agents and sought testimony of their devotion to the scion of the company as well as to the corporation. Upon prompting from the Indianapolis headquarters, a Pittsburgh Walker agent wrote "I sing her praises as long as I can speak and when I become speechless I will write it down as I can say I never met one like her in all my life, for kindness, generosity, business ability and moral character."[28]

Through the 1920s F. B. Ransom and his assistant Robert Brokenburr managed the Walker Company well as they had done during Walker's lifetime. Ransom and Brokenburr both emerged as Indianapolis community leaders, Ransom heading the nascent NAACP chapter and Brokenburr eventually gaining a seat in the Indiana Senate. While Ransom and Brokenburr adhered strictly to Walker's principle of employing African Americans exclusively, their hiring practices advanced men over women. Although fiercely proud of her accomplishments as female business owner, Walker did not challenge long-standing gender lines that developed in the Walker organization following F. B. Ransom's employment. She had hired F. B. Ransom to run the

Indianapolis operations, and when he employed male agents, he exercised expectations and pay scales that differed from those he applied to women. Ransom and Brokenburr engaged men as wholesalers who sold to drug stores and
to "supply stations," outlets that often included a beauty salon but made their
principal trade in reselling products to smaller beauty shops. Female employees traveled, as had Walker herself, to demonstrate products and to recruit
Walker agents. Male company representatives were salaried employees with
expense accounts who earned commissions on top of their base pay. Despite
the dedication to women's advancement that Madam Walker had demonstrated, Ransom and Brokenburr consistently chose men for the better positions in the firm, and they paid them more than their female employees.[29]

Among the Walker Company representatives who traveled the nation in
the World War I era to supply, advise, or train Walker agents were Marjorie
Stewart Joyner and Alice C. Burnett. Joyner and Burnett organized sales workers into Walker Clubs, called on existing clubs, and recruited new sales agents.
Company representatives earned a small salary and received commissions for
signing and training new agents and for organizing and meeting with Walker
Clubs. John F. Johnson, also a Walker representative, called on large salons
that supplied Walker agents and on drug stores. The Walker Company paid
Johnson's travel expenses, commissions ranging from 25 percent to 50 percent
of sales, and a salary of $150 per month or two to three times what female trav-
elers earned.[30] Johnson did not organize Walker agents nor did he demonstrate
products. Rather he called on existing accounts and relied on brand recognition of the Walker line to gain shelf space in additional stores.

Burnett, who had been a personal secretary to Madam Walker, covered
the country in search of new Walker agents, and, for some years after Madam
Walker's death in 1919, Marjorie Stewart Joyner's travels mirrored those of
Burnett. Burnett arrived in a city and contacted agents whom she already
knew through the company, advised them of new products or procedures, and
relayed agents' concerns back to company headquarters in Indianapolis. Johnson and Burnett both kept a sharp eye for bootleggers and price cutters, some
of whom they learned about from the Walker agents they met in their travels.
A Pittsburgh agent expressed great alarm at the East Coast travels of a vendor
selling an exact copy of the Walker comb "because the secret of the whole art
lies in the comb."[31]

Burnett's primary job was to locate and train women who would agree to
become Walker agents, and it was this task upon which her commissions were
based. Her job was much more difficult than Johnson's in that there was no
outlet such as a drugstore that attracted a walk-in client base. Although Walker
products were well known among black Americans, recruiting new agents was

challenging. The "training fee" of twenty-five dollars, upon which Burnett's pay depended, exceeded the immediate reach of most African American women, and the company did not subscribe new agents on an installment plan. Target audiences, then, were middle-class wives and daughters and women who had already established successful patterns of wage earning. Burnett did most of her recruitment at night and on weekends to reach the working women in a community.

In addition to meeting with Walker Clubs, Burnett contacted prospective agents through local churches and community organizations or by going door-to-door in African American neighborhoods. While working in New Orleans, Burnett contacted members of the Louisiana association of African American teachers who were holding their statewide meeting in the city. After signing up two new agents from among the teachers, Burnett reported to Ransom on several marketing problems the company faced, writing that "I found in New Orleans some were treating heads for $1.00, 75 cts., and 50 cts. Some people buying Walker hair goods from the drug stores and doing work calling themselves Walker agents."[32]

The world of Alice C. Burnett, of other traveling company representatives, and of hairdressers changed as industry regulations came into play at the end of the 1920s. The costs of equipping a beauty salon in the 1920s remained low in comparison with some other retail trades: combs, irons, a small stove, a chair, and a basin or sink were the basic requirements. As states began to regulate salons, however, the costs rose sharply. In 1927 Illinois became the first state to license cosmetologists, and Marjorie Stewart Joyner participated in drawing up the Illinois code. Other states soon followed suit, and by 1940 all forty-eight states had passed laws regulating the training and licensing of beauticians and setting standards for sanitary conditions in shops. Texas required only the barest set of tools for the establishment of a salon, but the Pennsylvania code was considerably more demanding. Under its 1933 regulations, shop owners required a license in addition to the operator's license, and a salon license could be obtained only after the owner had obtained all of the following equipment:

> One Universal Chair
> One Hair Dryer
> One Dresserette with Mirror
> Appointment Desk and Book
> One Manicuring Table
> Manicuring Tools
> One Permanent Wave System (Machine or Machineless)

One Marcel Heater
One Shampoo Tray
Six Combs
Six Brushes
One Dry Sterilizer
One Wet Sterilizer
One Finger Wave Lotion Dispenser
One Absorbent Cotton Container
One Towel Cabinet
One Waste Container (covered)
One Covered Container for Hair Pins
One Neck Strip Dispenser
One Hamper for Soiled Linens (covered)[33]

Manufacturers such as the Walker Company helped finance beauty salons as a way to showcase products, an especially attractive inducement as state regulations inflated the costs of operating salons. The equipment costs of setting up the simplest one-booth salon stood at about one hundred dollars, and such a cash outlay exceeded the resources of the average person of color. Consequently most hairdressers of the 1930s worked out of their homes, as salon employees, or in space rented in others' salons. In time traveling representatives such as Burnett settled into their own salons or took on the task of overseeing salon chains sponsored by manufacturing companies.

In her biography of white hair-salon magnate Martha Matilda Harper, Jane R. Plitt touts Harper as the originator of the business franchise. By 1925 Harper had established more than 450 salons in the United States, Canada, and Europe. Harper compelled each of her salon managers to finance her own equipment and to buy it from the Harper company. Plitt argues that Harper resorted to the practice because she could not finance expansion salons from her own resources. In contrast the Madam C. J. Walker Company established both salons and schools from its considerable earnings, but no chain of salons, African American or white, spread as widely as the Harper salons. Plitt champions Harper as the generous benefactor of thousands of working-class white women who never could have entered the business world without her assistance. The same could be said of Annie Turnbo Malone, Sarah Breedlove Walker, and Sara Spencer Washington for African American beauticians. While generosity may have characterized all of these beauty-industry giants, none could have built her empire without a ready supply of self-supporting, poorly educated women eager to improve their lot and flee the drudgery of unskilled labor. Occasionally a disappointed office clerk or schoolteacher turned to hairdressing as an alternative career, but most beauticians were high-school dropouts bent on escaping field, factory, or domestic work.[34]

Ambitious beauticians such as Alabaman Mrs. M. C. Crutcher sought to expand their income by employing other beauticians under their direction. Until the 1930s salon owners faced nearly insurmountable odds in finding skilled hairdressers. To meet these needs beauty shop operators began to take on apprentices. Some enterprising salon owners such as Nobia Franklin found that beauty instruction itself offered a second revenue stream as market demand allowed them to charge women for their training. Thus beauty schools emerged in numerous towns and cities that supported even a modest salon trade. Franklin, who had groomed hair with her own preparations, followed this pattern in San Antonio, Texas, before World War I. After relocating to Fort Worth, Franklin found teaching a central source of income and thus the Madame N. A. Franklin College of Beauty had its start. Although no agency regulated beauty instruction in the second decade of the century, Franklin tutored women in a basic set of principles for conditioning, straightening, and setting hair that other African American schools of her time also taught. Her ambitions drew her to Houston and ultimately to Chicago, where she enjoyed mid-level business success.

Despite the never-ending succession of new equipment and products to straighten, curl, color, or condition hair, a basic repertoire of techniques in hairdressing persisted. All students in African American beauty schools from the 1920s through the 1950s learned the use of heated combs, irons, and curlers; practiced finger waves and pin curls, and mastered knowledge of a number of compounds applied to the hair and scalp. Advanced classes included hair cutting and less commonly hair weaving, but the first lessons prepared the future beautician to manage and groom hair according to customer preferences. Madam Walker's complete beauty course of the 1930s included a brief introduction to characteristics and common diseases of the skin and hair and the fundamentals of manicure. Beginning in the 1930s cosmetology textbooks stressed the importance of sanitation, and injunctions to sterilize all equipment replaced earlier advice about cleanliness. The fundamentals of hair care in Madam Walker materials — closely paralleled by instructional literature utilized in other African American schools employing trained teachers — covered the subjects of shampoo, hot-oil treatment, hair pressing, marcel wave, croquignole, pin curls, finger waves, permanent waving, and water waving with combs. Training for styling the hair of young girls differed from techniques employed for adults largely on the basis of the age-appropriateness of hairstyles. Instruction in scalp care, skin care and make-up, eyebrow shaping, and hair dyeing or bleaching completed the basic instruction of the beauty-school students. The vast majority of the students' training consisted of practicing the various techniques of hair conditioning and setting.

Black and white beauty culturists shared a number of common practices despite the differing demands of their clientele. In the early decades of the trade, many salons offered facial, scalp, and upper-body massage as part of their beauty regimen. The body massage included only the arms and shoulders, and beauty operatives claimed that massage both relaxed the client and stimulated blood circulation, thereby promoting healthy hair and hair growth. Although upper-body massage became part of Nobia Franklin's operator training, her early courses included only face and scalp massage, both finger massage and treatment with an electric vibrator. Franklin warned that "Sometimes headache may be caused by too vigorous a movement or too rapid a flow of blood to the head. In this case, you should run the applicator up and down the spine between the shoulder blades."[35] Through the 1930s cosmetology textbooks informed students that massage was a scientific method of relieving the symptoms of headaches and of some scalp diseases and that scalp massage stimulated hair growth.[36]

Madame N. A. Franklin's 1921 instructional manual emphasized discretion in dealing with clients:

> An essential to success in this work is the personal neatness of the operator and the careful attention she gives to the little wants and peculiarities of her customers. You should be tactful, diplomatic and patient in handling your customers. The successful Beauty Culturist never gossips about her different patrons and never discusses her competitors and of course never tells any one the many little secrets which her customers confide to her. You should never talk or laugh loud or become too noisy while giving your customer service. You should also avoid discussing your own troubles and private affairs, as this will greatly bore the customer.[37]

Martha Matilda Harper's 1926 guide for white operators in her salon chain offered similar advice that shop owners should "never permit gossip."[38]

While salon managers strove to maintain a dignified environment, the atmosphere in some shops was decidedly unpleasant. As Washington, D.C., beautician Elizabeth Barker explained of the early years, African American women generally sought the services of beauticians who employed heated irons to straighten or "press" hair after they had applied an oil, working to cover each strand of hair. When she opened a new salon in the 1930s, Barker determined to avoid the smoking gas stoves that beauticians employed to heat hair irons:

> Another thing we did very early was to eliminate gas fumes. When we started, most black shops had gas stoves. Every operator had her own gas stove, and you'd put these hot irons, pressing irons, on the gas stove and most black businesses had a very heavy grease. I don't even like the word *grease*. Most of the manufacturers (the famous manufacturers for black hair products) felt that the only way to handle a black customer's hair, was to control it with this very heavy grease which was made out of yellow petroleum and mineral oil, and beeswax. And it sort of laid down the hair. . . . But because they had gas stoves and this, what I call axle grease, the shops were always smoking. . . . So I decided early on that we weren't going to spend our days in a smoke-filled beauty shop, and we converted to electricity."[39]

By the 1950s a variety of chemical relaxers had replaced the straightening comb of the earlier years, but heat remained an essential part of setting hair from the 1920s onward. The marcel iron, also heated, crimped hair by pressing it over a rounded surface as does the contemporary curling iron. After World War II individual metal curlers supplemented with hair dryers largely replaced the marcel iron, allowing the beautician to set the entire head at once. Finger waving consisted of arranging waves in oiled hair with the fingers, allowing the oil to hold the wave in place as drying occurred. While some of these beauty techniques crossed racial boundaries, salon trade and the beauty school remained segregated through the 1950s. Segregated salons and schools followed patterns that both law and custom had earlier set in place.

As Marjorie Stewart Joyner's participation in Illinois's original codification initiative illustrates, cosmetology boards recognized the significance of African American beauty markets from their inception. While Illinois did not segregate beauty instruction by race, the 1927 law established separate examination criteria for African American and white license applicants. As licensing spread to the South, racial segregation of examinations followed. Racial prejudice and discrimination shaped state beauty codes, but racial separation also reflected differing consumer demands by race. African American women's needs for particular products that minimized brittleness and hair breakage — as well as the taste of some women for hair-straightening processes and the relative lack of need for products to add curl to their hair — encouraged beauty operatives to specialize in particular techniques. As young girls experimented on their own hair or that of their sisters and friends, their experiences led them to develop some knowledge about working with particular types of hair. While such a history did not dictate that a hairdresser would work with persons of her own race only, prior experience led in that direction, and beauty codes institutionalized the separation of beauty shops.

Racial discrimination defined the structure of the hair-care industry, but segregation also protected one market sector for African American women. African American beauty-school owners, beauticians, and representatives on state boards of cosmetology conscientiously worked to protect the African American sector at the same time that they welcomed regulation of the industry. Once licensing was in place, beauty-school teachers and boards of cosmetology often resisted efforts to raise entry requirements to beauty college or to increase the hours of training necessary for licensing. Increasing the cost of training or raising the secondary school prerequisites for training would place the trade beyond the reach of the comparatively poor and educationally disadvantaged, among whom a disproportional number of African Americans found themselves.[40]

After regulation of the industry took place in the 1930s, fewer women succeeded in parlaying a salon into a manufacturing operation although many women and men opened independent beauty schools. One salon owner who moved successfully into manufacturing was Rose Meta of Harlem, whose Rose Meta House of Beauty turned to the development of cosmetics "To glorify the woman of color."[41] Morgan combined her experience as a beautician and salon operator with the business acumen of New York University graduate Olivia Clarke to build a successful manufacturing business on top of a $45,000 salon profit. The Rose Meta House of Beauty was the largest African American salon in the nation in 1948, and it claimed Lena Horne, Katherine Dunham, and other cover girls among its clients. A Rose Meta salon opened in Detroit, and Rose Meta Products, Inc., appeared in major cities through the United States and reached Africa and the Carribean. Before the end of the decade Rose Meta succeeded in gaining shelf space in major white-owned five and dime chains such as W. T. Grant.

Like Rose Meta, Detroit inventor-beautician Jesse T. Pope entered the trade after commercial hairdressing and cosmetics had been widely accepted by African American women. Pope's lack of capital and the discriminatory lending policies of the 1940s, however, made it exceedingly difficult for her to manufacture and market the thermostatically controlled electric curling iron that she invented. Pope secured U.S. and Canadian patents for her device after Eleanor Roosevelt took an interest in her invention, but Pope did not succeed in putting together sufficient capital to build a manufacturing facility until the late 1950s. Pope ultimately achieved success party because the decline of early firms such as the Madam C. J. Walker Company opened doors for new players in the beauty-product business.[42]

By the 1950s, when Pope's enterprise finally bore fruit, J. H. Jemison and Marjorie Stewart Joyner had reached their prime years as beauty educators. Joyner and Jemison had entered the field of beauty culture before state and federal regulations controlled the industry, but licensing and inspection had spelled the key to their success. Joyner and Jemison had actively supported governmental oversight because they recognized that licensing of beauticians would raise their own status. Nevertheless Joyner and Jemison could not have risen along the educational paths they pursued had not Anthony Overton, Annie Turnbo Malone, Madam C. J. Walker, Sara Spencer Washington, and Nobia Franklin blazed trails in advance of them. These pioneers set standards in the industry and gave teachers such as Joyner and Jemison their first opportunities to excel in beauty culture. Joyner and Jemison would use their beauty legacies well, employing their skills to style generations of hairdressers and to bring race leadership to bear on politics as well as business. The career of Marjorie Stewart Joyner, whose history follows in the next chapter, began as Walker's personal leadership crested. Joyner's leadership in the beauty industry enriched the lives of countless women whose careers she assisted, just as the Walker Company had opened opportunities for her.

CHAPTER 2

Traveling

The Madam C. J. Walker Company, Sales Agents, and Marjorie Stewart Joyner, 1916–86

In 1986, the ninetieth year of her life, Marjorie Stewart Joyner journeyed to the nation's capital, where she had traveled frequently before to attend cosmetology gatherings, meetings of the National Council of Negro Women, and political functions. On this occasion, her last visit to the capital, the nation honored Joyner. Marjorie Stewart Joyner's early career formed a centerpiece in a Smithsonian Institution exhibit titled "Field to Factory" that saluted the accomplishments of the thousands of African Americans who migrated to northern cities in the early decades of the twentieth century. The Smithsonian's inclusion of a replica of Joyner's 1916 Chicago beauty salon in the "Field to Factory" museum presentation recognized the importance of the beauty industry, but it also acknowledged Joyner's singular contributions to the industry and to her community. Joyner eventually parlayed her knowledge of hair care into a national organization of beauty-school teachers, and she formed friendships with African American leaders in all walks of life. At the height of her leadership in the industry, Joyner supervised the more than two hundred beauty schools that comprised the Madam Walker chain, and she traveled the nation at company expense. In 1945 she founded the United Beauty School Owners and Teachers Association (UBSOTA), over which she presided until her death in 1994. Like the industry giants who preceded her, Marjorie Stewart Joyner rose from humble beginnings. The beauty industry brought her a middling income, influence, and respect, but it did not bring her wealth or lasting financial security. After her retirement from the field of beauty culture Marjorie Stewart Joyner lived simply on her monthly Social Security benefits. Although she died in near poverty, Joyner left a legacy of professional and civic leadership that few have equaled.

Marjorie Stewart Joyner developed a close friendship with Mary McLeod Bethune, was a founding member of the National Council of Negro Women, and was a loyal Democrat. Joyner's life exemplified the critical role that the beauty industry played in supporting legions of women outside the economy controlled by white Americans. For middle-class African Americans of Joyner's time, individual success carried the opportunity as well as the responsibility of race leadership, and Joyner exploited every situation that promised improvement in the economic circumstances and civil rights of her community. Her business and her civic associations echoed the pattern of strong national ties demonstrated by other African Americans of the middle class.

Born in Monterey, Virginia, in 1896, Marjorie Stewart moved to Dayton, Ohio, with her father in 1906, which placed her closer to her mother, who had earlier moved to Chicago. Marjorie thus got to know both her mother and the city. At the age of sixteen she moved in with her mother and took a job at Overton Manufacturing, then the largest African American cosmetics firm in Chicago. Although her father had been a barber as well as a teacher, it was the Overton experience that interested Marjorie in beauty culture. Stewart financed her own way through the formerly all-white A. B. Molar Beauty School in 1916, enduring racist remarks from the Molar teaching staff while she completed the course. She graduated and opened her first salon before her twenty-first birthday and thus began a lifelong dedication to beauty culture. Also in 1916 Stewart married Robert Joyner, a Chicago podiatrist. The newlyweds took up housekeeping in Joyner's house at 5807 South Wabash Street, where Marjorie Stewart Joyner lived until her death. Robert Joyner provided financial backing to help Joyner open her first salon, and he remained a staunch supporter of her undertakings through his life. In time the Joyners raised two daughters, Ann and Barbara.

Soon after the marriage Robert Joyner's mother introduced Marjorie to the products and techniques of Madam C. J. Walker. Having learned to set the straight, limp hair that characterized many white clients, Marjorie failed miserably when dressing tightly curled hair. Joyner's mother-in-law expressed more than mild disappointment after Marjorie's grooming of her hair left it standing out wildly from her head. The elder Joyner had heard about Madam Walker and offered to pay for Marjorie to learn the Walker method. Walker introduced Joyner to methods of pressing hair with the use of heated irons. While pressing dried the hair and made it more brittle, the process inflicted less damage than the system of pulling hair with tongs that Garnett-Abney and others had employed in an effort to stimulate hair growth or straighten locks. Marjorie Stewart Joyner completed additional instruction under Madam Walker and learned from Walker, but Joyner also taught Walker the marcelling method she had mastered at Molar. At Molar, Joyner had learned hair weaving—the braiding of extra strands of hair into a woman's natural hair. Hair weaving of this time added thickness rather than extensions to the hair, making thin hair more luxurious and covering over bald spots. Through Joyner's contributions to the Walker beauty system, hair weaving became a standard part of the curriculum of Madam Walker schools. Impressed with Joyner's skills, Madam Walker offered to bring Marjorie into the business, and soon thereafter Joyner began traveling for the Madam C. J. Walker Company to market products and recruit Walker agents. Together the two women developed products and techniques that combined hair fashion of the day with the grooming needs and styling demands of women of color.[1]

Marjorie Stewart Joyner's fellow Walker representative Alice C. Burnett began traveling in the late teens, covering towns in the South and Midwest. Burnett's extensive correspondence with the home office has preserved the immediacy and the poignancy of the challenges that confronted women of color who traveled and the difficulties of earning well in the Walker employ, hardships that Joyner also endured. Alice C. Burnett of Jackson, Mississippi, a single mother of two, worked southern and midwestern districts to pay her daughters' residential school expenses, but she also boarded her daughters in order to travel. Unlike Joyner, Burnett had no family member at home to provide child care in her absence. Generally able to meet her personal expenses, Burnett seldom earned enough to add to her meager savings. Always at the edge, Burnett attempted to negotiate better terms at each contract renewal. In August, 1917, she wrote to F. B. Ransom, general manager of the Walker enterprise, in an effort to secure a working agreement for the coming fall: "Now Mr. Ransom please write me at your earliest [sic] I want to know what Mme is going to have me do. I have good work offered to me in Chicago, but would rather work for Mme if she can pay me enough salary to take care of my girls."[2] Burnett heard from Ransom in a few days but found the job offer much less than she had hoped. "Now, Mr. Ransom, I cannot get a room and board per day for less than $1.25 and if [Madam Walker] means for me to pay board and lodging you can see how much I will have left out of sixty dollars. I would much rather have a salary and all of my expenses."[3] One week later Burnett wrote again saying that she had no money to begin her travels for Walker and that she would have to borrow money to place her daughters in school. Lacking a quick response she wrote again and had a firm offer by the end of the month for which she thanked Ransom: "Words can't express how much I appreciate you helping me out with my work."[4] Occasionally Burnett asked the company for an advance or a loan. In September, 1917, Burnett asked Ransom to send thirty-eight dollars directly to Fisk University for her daughters' room and board.[5] Summers, when her daughters returned home from school, were difficult as Burnett attempted place the girls in the homes of friends or relatives.

One of the challenges that Marjorie Stewart Joyner and other company representatives faced in the early days was the location of a space in which to demonstrate hair styling. African American churches provided an important marketing venue for beauty culturists partly because church halls or basements offered space that could be used at minimal cost. Churches proved important to the beauty industry in other ways as shown in the activities of Alice Burnett. Churches and the black media provided organizational structures through which several African American businesses as well as civil rights organizations gained access to local communities. Burnett relied on clergy to introduce her to clients and also to locate safe, affordable, and respectable accommodations for a woman traveler in a segregated world.

Simply traveling to one's destination in Jim Crow America could prove difficult and mortifying. Marjorie Stewart Joyner, interviewed frequently in her later life, often recalled that racial discrimination impinged on her freedom and comfort in her travels until the 1960s. She frequently recounted the story of a train trip that sorely tested her determination to continue. When attempting to board a train for Texas, an agent informed her that the train carried no Jim Crow car and that therefore her ticket would not be honored. A Pullman porter who knew Joyner to be a frequent traveler convinced the agent to let her make the trip in a baggage car. In 1939 Joyner successfully sued the Burlington Rock Island Railroad for racial discrimination, claiming not only that she had been denied equal accommodations but also that she had shared the baggage car with a corpse on its way to an out-of-state burial.[6]

Joyner and Burnett attended church services in the towns and cities they covered, and each would announce her commercial intentions when called upon to introduce herself as a visitor to a congregation. Beauty agents and cosmetics firms attended denominational conventions and demonstrated their products for male and female delegates with whom they shared Protestant evangelical traditions. Denominations defrayed some of the costs of holding their meetings by renting convention space to cosmetics vendors who set up booths on the premises. In planning her attendance at a Baptist convention in Muskogee, Oklahoma, in 1917, Burnett asked a local minister to recruit in advance of her arrival a group of women interested in Walker training. Once at the convention Burnett also sought out delegates who were already Walker agents as well as representatives of their congregations at the denominational gathering. Existing agents assisted Burnett in recruiting new agents as there was always room for growth in the burgeoning beauty industry. Convention delegates came from many towns or neighborhoods that agents did not reach and that Burnett was unlikely to visit. Thus church conferences opened new opportunities for Burnett, and her recruitment of agents at these assemblies posed no market threat to women already in business.

Late September, 1918, found Alice Burnett in South Bend, Indiana, where the African American community numbered approximately six hundred. Burnett spent considerable time cultivating relationships with women's church organizations as likely groups in which to recruit for Walker. The inscription of new agents in small towns proved especially difficult because agents of any company feared competition. Burnett first wrote to F. B. Ransom from South Bend to say that she had received the slide projector he had shipped and that she could soon give the illustrated lectures through which she interested women in taking up beauty culture. She had gone "over to the church last night to a big quilting. I think I interested one woman. All the others thought one agent was enough for this town. There are two 'Poro' agents here. I think these women would rather work for white people." Her efforts to subscribe the minister's wife had fallen short, but "Rev Readding said 'his wife could take the work but he wish to be better informed.' I think he wants to know about the salary. Mrs Redding [sic] is an educated young woman has the ability. You had better write him a letter and explain the matter to him." Generally Burnett did not deal through a prospective agent's husband, but ministers were the exception for it was crucial that a recruiter not alienate the one person who gave her access to the likely population of agents. One frustration followed another in the smaller cities of the Midwest, and in a final correspondence with Ransom on the subject Burnett concluded that "I really feel that I am losing agents in these northern cities these people are hard to get. They seem to be content to work in service. . . . I want to go where I can make 8 and 10 agents a week. If I fool around here I will be behind next year at the [Walker] Convention."[7]

Taking to the road first with Walker and then on her own, Joyner followed a prescribed agenda as did Alice Burnett. Madam Walker charged her agents to "introduce, advertise, and create new markets . . . to travel as such agent from place to place teaching the art of hair culture, giving illustrated lectures. . . ."[8] In advance of her efforts in a particular town, Joyner sometimes prepared handbills announcing a demonstration of Walker products. In most towns she had the names of existing Walker agents whom she contacted to ac-

Marjorie Stewart Joyner, ca. 1935, shown with the travel trailer in which she demonstrated the latest products and techniques. Marjorie Stewart Joyner Papers, courtesy Vivian G. Harsh Research Collection of Afro-American History and Literature, Chicago Public Library.

quaint them with new products, to check up on their activities, and to get leads about recruiting additional agents. If she had not done so in advance, Joyner located a church or a meeting hall where she could show Walker cosmetics and make a pitch to engage local women in the trade. These first contact meetings often had no demonstrations but might feature a slide show of elaborate hairstyles that could be fashioned with Walker products. Joyner might also go door to door to call on individuals whom she had met through a local church or to whom she had been referred by existing Walker agents. When she subscribed one or more women, she held a product demonstration as training for the new agents. Where a Walker agent had already opened a beauty salon, Joyner might use the Walker shop to demonstrate the company line. As Walker beauty colleges proliferated in the 1930s, Walker facilities provided the locus for demonstrations that churches and beauty shops had provided in earlier years. During the 1930s Joyner often traveled by car with a small trailer in tow that carried supplies and provided a space for her to show Walker products and the Walker method to one or two women at a time.

Alice Burnett, like Marjorie Stewart Joyner, traveled through the 1920s. Burnett's intense wish to settle permanently in one spot remained frustrated, but her road assignments varied through the 1920s, and the changes brought increased financial well-being and security. During the 1920s, as Walker sales agents increased in number, the company's travelers abandoned the door-to-door canvassing for agents and concentrated on organizing agents into Walker Unions, clubs composed of agents, and coordinating union activities. Alice Burnett, Marjorie Stewart Joyner, and Mrs. P. E. Osborne covered the nation during the decade and brought closer to fruition Madam Walker's dream of a network of Walker Unions.

Walker clubs allowed Burnett, Joyner, and others to concentrate on improving sales by motivating groups of sales agents and introducing them to new products. Meeting in churches, YWCAs, and other central locations that attracted African American women from outside the Walker family, the clubs also offered a venue for recruiting new agents. Once a group of new recruits had been identified, a representative from headquarters, most frequently Burnett or Joyner, offered a training course and certified new Walker agents upon its completion. During the 1920s and 1930s, the company's recruitment campaigns became increasingly elaborate. The company organized public meetings on the heels of visiting with its local clubs, arranged slide shows or films about the Walker Company, and brought in General Manager Ransom to address these gatherings. In 1940 the company produced "From Cabin to Mansion," a film that took many liberties with the history of Sarah Breedlove Walker and the Walker Company in disseminating the story that Madam Walker had been the first African American female millionaire and that her success had helped liberate countless women of color from poverty and from notions of inferiority.

Through the 1950s the several remaining Walker clubs — with memberships ranging from about five to twenty — met, elected officers, collected dues of twenty-five cents per month per member, and sent delegates to annual Walker conventions. Locally Walker Unions undertook charitable activities and aided needy club members. Walker Union affiliation carried a death benefit of fifty dollars for survivors of members who maintained their dues through their lifetimes. Into the late 1960s, when Walker Unions had become more fiction than fact, the heirs of paid-up members wrote to the Walker headquarters in Indianapolis to claim the death benefit. The company continued to pay the benefit, but club members who survived into the 1960s had generally joined their clubs in the 1930s and had paid well in excess of the fifty dollars. Walker had never issued benefits to members who had paid in the fifty dollars over the years, so individual beauticians could ensure some return for their beneficiaries only by continuing to pay the union dues long after they retired from the trade.

Despite the tantalizing promises of the Walker advertising department, neither Alice Burnett nor Marjorie Stewart Joyner achieved personal wealth from her hard work on behalf of the company. The Walker Company, using her employment as leverage over Marjorie Stewart Joyner, induced her to surrender the potential profits from her own beauty inventions. In 1927, in work undertaken at her own Walker school, Joyner improved upon the heated pressing irons that Walker used to wave hair, inventing an electric machine that held several irons suspended from a hood. Using multiple irons simultaneously, Joyner's machine greatly accelerated hair processing. After gaining a patent for the machine in 1928, Joyner sold all rights to the invention to Madam Walker for one dollar.[9] In the same year the Walker company purchased Joyner's formula for a scalp salve for "one dollar and other valuable considerations."[10] Joyner also designed a straightening comb that the Walker Company patented and popularized through its schools and salons. Joyner received no royalties or other forms of compensation on any of her patented inventions, but at no time in her life did she express bitterness or regret that her inventions had failed to enrich her.

Alice Burnett, who had so long wanted a shop of her own, accepted the challenge of helping others open Walker-owned beauty salons and then moving on to other assignments. During the late 1920s the company awarded franchises to individuals in nationwide sales contests. In December, 1928, Alice Burnett was in New York to set up the beauty salon that had been won by Sarah Mottley as second prize in the 1928 contest. During that year Burnett had journeyed to Baltimore and other Atlantic coast locations, worked extensively in New York City, and traveled throughout upstate New York. In June both Burnett and Marjorie Stewart Joyner were on hand for the dedication of the Madam Walker Beauty Shop in the recently completed Lawrence Dunbar Apartments in Harlem. Mayor Jimmy Walker, the architect Andrew J. Thomas, and the philanthropist John D. Rockefeller attended the dedication and toured the facilities of the Walker salon. In 1929 Walker kept three women on the road recruiting new sales agents, coordinating Walker Unions, and organizing new clubs. Burnett again made her way down the East Coast and back to New York; Joyner traveled from the Midwest to Texas; Roberta Ole, like Joyner, covered the Midwest territory; and Erlyne Osborne worked Texas and Oklahoma.

Alice Burnett, with her ongoing contact with Madam Walker's business interests in Manhattan emerged as a major adviser and support for Madam Walker's daughter Lelia, who had been placed in charge of a Walker salon and

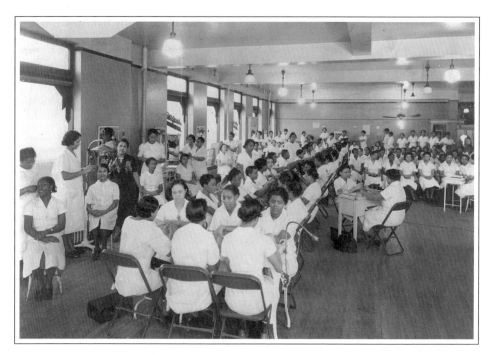

A carefully posed photograph of Marjorie Stewart Joyner with Walker students, ca. 1940. Joyner appears just to the right of the permanent waving machine that she patented in 1928 before selling the rights to her invention to the Walker Company. The practice room shows a lecturer in the background to the far right, students working on practice hair in the center rear, manicure practice at the center front, and hair styling at the left of the photograph. Marjorie Stewart Joyner Papers, courtesy Vivian G. Harsh Research Collection of Afro-American History and Literature, Chicago Public Library.

the Walker school in New York. Although Lelia assumed the title of president of the company after her mother's death, she remained in New York and took no direct role in running the national business. Lelia largely ceded direction of her Manhattan interests to Burnett, who stayed in the city weeks at a time to direct the local staff. In September, 1930, the Walker company named Burnett to head the Madam C. J. Walker school and beauty parlor in New York, clearly indicating that Lelia had completely withdrawn from those operations. When Lelia died in 1931, Burnett finally received long overdue recognition of her contributions to the company through the generosity of A'Lelia Mae Perry, Lelia Walker's daughter and successor.

Unlike Lelia Walker, who had hoped to build her own fame and fortune as a Harlem hostess and tearoom proprietor, A'Lelia Mae Perry did take an active interest in the Walker enterprise, now known as the Madam C. J. Walker Manufacturing Company. Closely following on her mother's death, Perry moved to Indianapolis with her husband and children and participated in company decision-making until her own death. While company manager Ransom had consistently denied meaningful rewards to Burnett, Joyner, and other loyal female employees, Perry insisted on recognizing women's contributions to the company's growth. Perry tapped Alice Burnett as "First Vice President for Life" and assigned her permanently to the oversight of the Walker school in New York and the Walker salon in the Dunbar Apartments. Joyner would continue to travel, but Perry promoted her to "Second Vice President."

Burnett's desire to own her own salon reflected the economic disappointments associated with her travels for Walker, but she also wished the stability that a life at home could provide. Never a single mother and already a salon owner, Marjorie Stewart Joyner enjoyed tremendous advantages over Burnett. When Joyner first took to the road, she had no children, and thus she did not face the double bind that constantly worried Burnett. When at home in Chicago, she oversaw the Madam C. J. Walker school that had grown out of her salon. Joyner and her husband raised two daughters, but motherhood did not necessitate an end to her travels as family and friends provided steady oversight of the girls.

In 1918, while traveling in the company of Madam Walker, Joyner made the acquaintance of Mary McLeod Bethune, who would much later draw Joyner into civic and charitable activities with a nationwide reach. After Sarah Breedlove Walker died in 1919, the company named Joyner to supervise Walker beauty schools throughout the country, a post she would hold through the 1960s. Marjorie Stewart Joyner emerged as the "National Supervisor" of the Walker schools, operating in Dallas, Tulsa, Chicago, Indianapolis, New York, and Baltimore with each enrolling a maximum of thirty students at any one time. Joyner's work first as a traveler for Walker and later as national supervisor of the Walker schools allowed her to develop ties to black communities throughout the country. Working to gain entree into local African American communities, Joyner soon gained recognition for her hair-grooming skills, and she continued to demonstrate Walker products throughout her active career. Joyner's position as national supervisor provided some salary and expenses as well as commissions on sales of Walker products to the schools she oversaw. However, the Madam Walker School of Beauty in Chicago eventually became her main enterprise.

Joyner's life in Chicago reflected the economic and political realities that marked the daily existence of other African Americans of the middle class. Although she had stuck with her career in beauty culture through the 1920s, she questioned her job choices, as did Alice Burnett. Despite family assistance,

home life pulled, and Joyner cast about for alternatives that would both enhance her sales abilities and offer other employment in Chicago. She believed
she had hit on the answer when she enrolled in a course in elocution and public speaking at Chicago Musical College early in 1924. After competing the
course, Joyner attempted to launch a career in entertainment. She engaged
the St. Elizabeth Assembly Hall for the evening of June 30, 1924, and advertised tickets at fifty cents each for her "Dramatic Recital." She failed miserably
in the entertainment business, and the disappointing response to her stage de-
but reinforced the earlier career path she had chosen. Joyner, who had earlier
traveled with Sarah Breedlove Walker on temporary assignments, accepted
full-time employment with the company in 1924.

The 1920s had been the optimal time for an association with the Madam
C. J. Walker Manufacturing Company. F. B. Ransom and his assistant Robert
W. Brokenburr provided dynamic leadership that expanded sales. Both Ransom and Brokenburr followed the national sales circuit after female representatives had laid the groundwork by recruiting agents and organizing Walker
Clubs. On a single Sunday in 1929 Robert Brokenburr spoke at three churches
on behalf of Walker sales agents.[11] Through the leadership of Marjorie Stewart Joyner, the company built a chain of beauty schools that clearly led the nation in training African American beauticians for a changing environment of
operator licensing and parlor inspection. In the area of product sales, the company maintained a series of contests that emphasized race pride and advertised
individual earnings as but one component of Madam Walker's contribution to
community advancement. Among the most innovative of these contests was
the Trip around the World Contest of 1925 and 1926. The Walker Company
announced that it would send four exemplary African American contest winners on a land and sea voyage around the world. Every Walker product included a ballot with which consumers could cast a vote for the nation's most
admired African American. The ballot included a slate of persons who had
been nominated by sales agents. Although the vast majority of Walker agents
were women, the nominees were overwhelmingly male, and the clergy led
in numbers of candidates. A leading contender who was not a church pastor
was C. C. Spaulding of the North Carolina Mutual Life Insurance Company.
North Carolina Mutual Life personnel jumped on the bandwagon immediately and urged their employees and customers to buy Walker products in
support of Spaulding's candidacy. Thus the Walker management worked to
promote customer loyalty to its products and loyalty to the company among
prominent African Americans throughout the nation. In most Walker contests
churches, clubs, or civic groups might also work through an agent or a group
of agents to sell products and retain some of the profits. Other than the travel

contests, Walker promotions generally offered a large reward to winners of sales contests in addition to their earnings from sales commissions. Salon franchises, such as the one won by Sarah Mottley, were one of the most desired rewards, but the top prizes for sales winners of the 1920s were new Ford coupes.[12]

Marjorie Stewart Joyner, like other national representatives of the Walker Company, could not participate in sales contests. Joyner's task remained that of recruiting and training would-be beauticians and overseeing the emerging chain of Walker beauty schools. Through her national travels for Madam C. J. Walker enterprises, Joyner earned a nationwide reputation as an expert beauty culturist, and that distinction stayed with her throughout her life. In 1927 Joyner cooperated with a handful of white beauticians in Illinois in drafting the nation's first cosmetology law, becoming herself one of the first licensed cosmetologists in the United States. In May, 1928, the company announced that Joyner had passed the newly instituted California beautician's exam and would begin training African American women for licensing in California. Walker claimed to be the "only company preparing people for state exams."[13] The company continuously boasted of the high state examination grades earned by candidates whom Joyner had trained. In January, 1931, the firm learned that all of Joyner's students had earned better than 85 percent on the Illinois board examination.[14]

By the end of the 1920s, the Madam Walker School of Beauty in the city had earned Joyner firm membership in Chicago's African American leadership circle. Bronzeville, the bourgeois economic and cultural center of African American life on Chicago's South Side, housed the *Chicago Defender* as well as Anthony Overton's *Chicago Bee*. In 1929 the *Chicago Defender* named Joyner to head up its charity bureau, a post she would hold to the end of her life. In 1929 she helped Robert S. Abbott, *Defender* founder, in organizing the first Bud Billiken parade. Abbott and Joyner named the parade for Bud Billiken, a mythological protector of children of color. Still held today, the Billiken parade provides a demonstration of black commerce and the cultural achievements of Chicago's African American residents. Revenues from the parade augment the treasury of the *Defender* charity bureau. Joyner's work with the *Defender* made her a powerful community figure and kept her name before whites as well as blacks in the city. The Bud Billiken parade also kept the name of the Madam C. J. Walker school before the public and provided a celebratory occasion for Walker students. Each year the students at Joyner's school chose a queen and a court who joined the Billiken parade and rode the Walker float through Bronzeville's streets. The Walker Company also announced that Joyner spent August, 1929, vacation time attending the Jamaica Convention of the Universal Negro Improvement Association.[15]

The year 1929 brought business advancement as Joyner moved her salon and the Walker Beauty School to the South Center Department Store. Located at 47th Street and South Park Boulevard (now Martin Luther King Jr. Boulevard), South Center Department Store catered to the elite members of Chicago's African American community, and the move signaled Joyner's rise to the top of the city's salon trade. The year had also begun well for the Walker Company, and after the first half the management urged its sales workers onward, encouraging them to believe that there were bright earnings prospects if they engaged in unrestricted sales warfare:

> We have played the first half of the game. We know that immediately ahead in the second half if things move forward we must employ more energy, thought and skill if the game is to be ours. This is true whether we did well in the first half or not. Let us enter the last half of the grim battle for honest dollars with such a will to succeed that was never exhibited before by us. . . . Some of us have talked hard times so much that we have believed that Negroes actually have no money and of course do not try to sell to them. . . . People in alleys and courts appreciate our preparations as much as anybody, sometimes more. So let us get up and go after them.[16]

Company officials clearly could not foresee the Great Crash and the devastation it would wreak on the well-being of the nation's African Americans. At the half-year mark in 1929 Walker had encouraged employees to believe that it would end 1929 with its highest sales on record, but such was not the case. Sales slackened in the second half, and by 1930 the signs of disaster were too numerous to overlook. In May, 1930, the company announced that it would "postpone" its annual convention until the following year because "For the past 3 months we have been receiving letters from our agents from all sections with reference to our National Convention scheduled to be held in Washington this year. Nearly all of these agents have stated that because of conditions it would be utterly impossible for them to attend without great sacrifice." In January of the following year, manager Ransom urged Walker agents to embrace a better future because "There is a great deal of optimism in reference to business at this, the beginning of 1931. The paper reports that thousands of men and women return to their former jobs and large numbers of new jobs that have been opened up. . . . When an agent fails, even in depression, it is because she did not go after business rather than because there was no money to be obtained."[17] The very next month, however, the company reported that it would reduce wholesale prices on some products in order to increase agents' profit margins on sales.

The Great Crash took a toll on the fortunes of the Madam C. J. Walker Manufacturing Company and its employees. Through the 1930s and the 1940s, the company restructured its operations and branched out into numerous Indianapolis-based enterprises, but its operations had peaked, and the glory days of the late teens and early 1920s never returned. Walker sales had crested in 1920, the year after Madam Walker's death, at more than $500,000, but in the 1930s sales failed to reach $200,000, and they reached a low of $48,000 in 1933. Alice Burnett, secure in her post in Harlem, stayed the course until retirement and remained a vice president of the company through the 1940s. Marjorie Stewart Joyner remained with Madam Walker also and made a career for herself by capitalizing on her renown as a gifted hair stylist and teacher. What the company failed to do for her, Joyner did for herself despite the disaster of the Depression, and in the process she kept the legacy of Madam Walker alive.

The Walker Company fought the declining fortunes of its agents by continuously reassuring the sales staff that African Americans, although poor, did have money for beauty products and that agents performed a service to the race by tracking down customers. The company carried on an extensive but futile campaign to increase membership in Walker Unions to five hundred, promising to increase its survivor's benefit from $50 to $100 once the goal had been achieved. The death of Sarah Breedlove Walker's only daughter in 1931 precipitated a crisis of confidence among Walker agents who had not realized that Lelia's involvement in company activities had been marginal at best. To some extent the company managers had encouraged misapprehension through their efforts to create and maintain the fiction that one woman and a daughter who carried on her legacy had made and dominated the Madam C. J. Walker Manufacturing Company. Rumors reaching the Indianapolis headquarters prompted Ransom and Brokenburr to declare that

> The Madam C. J. Walker Manufacturing Company is an Indiana corporation. It was founded by Madam C. J. Walker not for her day and her benefit only, but to live and grow throughout the wide expanse of years and be a guiding beacon from generation to generation to a self respecting ambitious, proud, dauntless race. Its business is to reveal to a skeptical world the beauties and charms and graces of one of the world's most ancient and maligned races by using beauty formulas revealed to its founder in the small hours of the night by the grace of God. All through the years its field of operation has been wherever on the face of the earth there was a Negro soul to fire and make conscious of its divine origin and its great destiny with beauty's charms. It laughs

in scorn at its imitators because its products can not be imitated and the intelligent public will find this out. Although it regrets the coming of death among the noble members of its family it has no fears for its existence by reason thereof for in the beginning it was given life everlasting.[18]

Despite the company's emotional propaganda, revenues at the Walker Company continued to decline. When receipts from the sale of beauty products failed to rise substantially, company managers attempted to find new sources of income by diversifying their operations in services and goods within Indianapolis's retail markets. The posh Walker Building, movie theater, café, and drugstore proved only to be money sinks that further diminished the company's strength.

Although the fortunes of the Walker Company dwindled, Marjorie Stewart Joyner thrived personally and professionally during the 1930s. Her preeminence in the field of beauty education redounded well for the school that she then headed in Chicago. In 1931 the school moved yet again to larger quarters to accommodate its enrollment of thirty students. In 1934, as the Depression still endangered enrollments in beauty colleges, Joyner completed a sixteen-page booklet for Madam Walker beauty instruction by correspondence. While Illinois already had a cosmetology licensing law, most states did not, and women could set up practice with only the Joyner guide. The correspondence course targeted women who wished to set up beauty operations within their homes. While licensed beauticians had sought to close down the cheaper and totally unregulated home salons, no state had the means to police the system in the 1930s. Thus, while Joyner traveled to oversee Walker beauty schools, she simultaneously acted to undermine their students and encouraged some women to avoid formal instruction. The Walker Company calculated that correspondence courses would reach women who would not otherwise study beauty care or who lived outside the recruitment reach of a Walker school and that some profits might be gleaned from the sale of the correspondence materials.

Through the Depression, Joyner participated actively in her community, and she marked new milestones in her personal life. In 1934 she helped to found Chicago's Cosmopolitan Community Church, an institution that flourished partly through her lifetime support of it. The Depression years brought new joy to the Joyner household with the arrival of daughter Barbara in 1935. In June, 1935, Joyner earned her high-school diploma from the Chicago Christian High School by completing the courses she lacked when she left public school in 1915.[19] Joyner continued to work with the *Chicago Defender* charities, and these activities kept her keenly aware of the Depression despite her own well-being. Joyner strove to spread the *Defender's* resources as far as possible to relieve the suffering among African Americans in her community. Joyner was still presiding over *Defender* charities through the dislocation of World War II, an event that accelerated migration and put heavy claims on the city's volunteer services. In recognition of her success as a community leader, the Roosevelt administration named Joyner to head Chicago's center for African American servicemen, a duty she discharged from 1940 through 1944.

Marjorie Stewart Joyner had emerged as the Walker Company's premier teacher at a time when beauty instruction lacked standards or regulation. At the end of 1933, the Women's Bureau found that training through apprenticeship was still practiced widely and that privately owned beauty schools often used students as cheap labor that competed with the more highly skilled hairdressers working in shops. Among the four cities that the Women's Bureau surveyed, two offered public instruction. New Orleans offered a course for white girls in a vocational high school. The all African American Vaschon Vocational School in St. Louis had inaugurated its course of study for girls in 1930, and it prepared about forty students annually for the Missouri cosmetology examination. The bureau concluded that the private African American schools that it investigated — six in Philadelphia and two in St. Louis — struggled to survive. Pennsylvania had just passed a law regulating beauty schools, and only four of the Philadelphia schools had applied for licensing. In St. Louis the bureau found that only five or six students had enrolled in each of the two schools and that the students worked as beauty operators at lower than average pay rates in the shops associated with the schools.[20]

Licensed private beauty schools thrived in the first half of the twentieth century because public instruction failed to keep pace with demand and also because private schools tailored their programs more carefully around the realities of poor women's lives. Private beauty schools, whether they recruited black or white students, concentrated wholly on beauty instruction. Students at private institutions did not enroll in academic subjects such as business math or business English that public vocational schools mandated. Private school students could pursue their studies at any time after dropping out of high school, and private programs allowed students to proceed at their own pace, attending classes part-time or full-time as their circumstances dictated. In the early years of beauty culture, students might earn their way through beauty school by performing an array of simple tasks inside the salon schools in which they learned the craft. By the end of the 1940s the Walker chain had grown to its pinnacle of two hundred schools through Joyner's energies, and

the schools' profits far overshadowed the shrinking profits of Walker's manufacturing side and its assorted small Indianapolis enterprises.

,   In the late 1930s Joyner served as president of the National Beauty Culturists League (NBCL). Founded in 1919 by the owners and agents of a rival
beauty company, the Godfrey Manufacturing Company, the NBCL func-
tioned as an information clearinghouse for beauticians of color and sought to
raise standards of beauty care throughout the nation. The NBCL grew gradually to include agents and beauticians who dealt in several product lines.
Joyner helped build the NBCL's financial resources, and in 1947 the organization purchased a building at 25 Logan Circle in Washington that has remained its headquarters to the present.

The NBCL incorporated the race values and needs of its members. It supported civil rights activities and respected African American religious traditions. Like mutual benefit societies of the nineteenth century, the NBCL
provided death benefits to the heirs of its members. NBCL leaders urged
members to hold their meetings in churches, sanctuaries, or meeting halls,
and religious services formed a consistent feature of NBCL conventions. The
NBCL has continuously endorsed and supported the NAACP and the Urban
League.[21]

The NBCL faced significant changes in the industry as government regulation broadened during Marjorie Stewart Joyner's presidency. In 1938 new
federal provisions required labeling to identify the contents of hair products,
which manufacturers had sought to hold confidential. Joyner and the NBCL
struggled but failed to devise a method through which manufacturers could
protect the secrecy of their formulas from public disclosure. As NBCL president, Joyner assisted in the organization of the Atlanta Beauty Culturists
League, a local group affiliated with NBCL. The Atlanta group had come into
being largely in response to a Georgia bill to provide licensing and inspection
of beauty operations.[22] In her capacity as NBCL president, Joyner also traveled
to Washington in 1939 to discuss practices in beauty shops with representatives
of the Women's Bureau. As part of its nationwide study of working conditions
in beauty parlors, the bureau sought information on health standards in salons, on wages and working hours, and on competition from unlicensed operators. Joyner wrote NBCL members, "I am therefore asking you to mail me
immediately any complaint you have of unfair practices that you might consider as evils of the great Beauty Culture Industry."[23] Joyner sought to reach out
to those outside the NBCL through an announcement in the *Negro Beautician*, which had begun publication the previous year under the guidance of
editor Andrew F. Jackson of Montclair, New Jersey. The highlight of a busy
year was the NBCL convention at Chicago's Savoy Ballroom, a gathering that

Joyner organized and over which she presided. At one session Joyner demonstrated the hair-weaving techniques that she had first learned at Molar Beauty School and had perfected through the years.

Marjorie Stewart Joyner's work in the beauty industry merged at many points with her personal and civic life. With space for meetings at a premium in the African American community and the industry having good relations with churches, the Walker School utilized neighborhood sanctuaries for graduation exercises. World War II exacerbated this shortage in Chicago, and Joyner in turn permitted women's groups to meet at Walker from time to time. In 1942 Joyner received a note from Capt. Marva Louis of the Joe Louis Chapter of the Women's National Defense Corps thanking her for "letting your school as a meeting place when, we so badly needed one."[24] Whether loaning or borrowing space, Joyner expected that an exchange of funds, however modest, would occur.

Wartime space shortages may also have been an issue when Joyner used school facilities for personal use. In 1942 Joyner and her husband hosted a wedding reception for their daughter Ann Douglas at Walker College. Ann Douglas Fook, who had received a B.S. in physical education from Northwestern University, completed her beauty training at Walker college in 1944 and entered the business. Ann gave her mother much support and added to the stability of the Chicago school, and Ann continued at the Walker school until 1976, when a hit-and-run driver ended her life in an accident that devastated the Joyner family.

Joyner's World War II direction of the servicemen's center kept her name before black Democrats, and in 1944 the party asked her to head the Negro Women's Committee for the reelection of President Roosevelt. In the fall of 1944 Joyner sent out twelve hundred letters to beauticians and other women urging African Americans to help reelect Roosevelt because "President and Mrs. Roosevelt have always been interested in the Negro and all race problems. We need such a man at the head of our country to guide us safely in these most trying times. Women, as you know, have always exerted a significant influence on the voting trends. I want to request that you cooperate with us as much as possible by contacting the women of your community who are active in city and county affairs. . . ."[25] In a six-week period from late September to early November, Joyner gave twenty campaign speeches and one radio address. In addition to addressing audiences in Chicago, she traveled to nearby Gary and to Tulsa, Kansas City, Detroit, and Baltimore.

World War II drew Joyner more directly into political action at the same time that the conflict complicated day-to-day operations in the beauty business. Wartime shortages of supplies affected the availability of hair preparations, and personnel shortages drew potential beauty students into war industries. Early in the war effort Walker manager F. B. Ransom strived to make the best of the company's difficulties: "I am happy to report that 1942, in many respects has not been a bad year for us. While we have been disappointed over our inability to get many of the ingredients, and over our inability to get any definite promise as to our containers, and many other things concerning the manufacturing process, we are happy over the fact that in 1942, we have been greatly encouraged because of the universal loyalty of the members of the Walker Family, and the ever increasing popularity of Walker products."[26] Soon after sending this consoling letter, Ransom wrote Joyner to notify her of the necessity of deducting the 5 percent Victory Tax from her paychecks and asking her to advise her employees of the same.[27]

During the war, as before, Joyner traveled widely for the Walker schools while the headquarters staff seldom met with Walker employees outside Indianapolis. Joyner stayed in the limelight as Madam Walker's highest-ranking beauty expert. Beauty organizations and civic groups throughout the country valued her counsel and often invited her to address local meetings. The National Beauty Culturists League asked Joyner to speak at their twenty-fifth anniversary convention in Philadelphia in 1944 and also to demonstrate her heatless wave process.[28] In advance of the meeting, the NBCL solicited revenue by offering thirty-two convention booths for rent to manufacturers or organizations at fifty dollars per booth. The NBCL gathering, reflecting both the shared culture of its members and the national emergency, also featured an opening session at Cherry Memorial Church conducted by the church's pastor and a statement by the president of the National Negro Business League, who had spearheaded African American efforts to raise money through the sale of war bonds.

Although the African American beauty market had recovered from the stresses of the Depression, the postwar environment encouraged white cosmetic firms to attempt again to market products to Americans of color. During World War II the demands of black soldiers for particular hair-product lines had caught the attention of government provisioning officers who alerted white cosmetics manufacturers to the potential for new markets.[29] As the war came to an end, Joyner's business and political lives had taken important turns into larger arenas. Joyner organized UBSOTA, an association that absorbed most of her energies for the remainder of her career, and she strengthened her ties to female race leaders including Mary McLeod Bethune and Jeanetta Welch Brown. As she turned her attentions in new directions, the fortunes of her own Walker beauty school began to lag, and Joyner came in for harsh condemnation from the Walker management team in Indianapolis, who ques-

Chicago's Madam C. J. Walker College of Beauty Culture supports the war effort, 1944. Marjorie Stewart Joyner Papers, courtesy Vivian G. Harsh Research Collection of Afro-American History and Literature, Chicago Public Library.

tioned her decisions and refused her requests for additional travel funding or to hire employees at the Chicago school.

In the spring of 1947, the Indianapolis headquarters advised Joyner that she should fire two teachers, plan no more out-of-town travel, increase product sales, and recapture delinquent students because her receipts for the first quarter were five thousand dollars below the first quarter of the previous year. Company secretary Violet Reynolds wrote that "While [Walker general manager] Mr. Ransom did not talk a great deal about the situation, I gathered that he is greatly disturbed over your increasing outside activities."[30] Without doubt Joyner's efforts to juggle so many undertakings undercut her management of her Chicago beauty school. To her mind Ransom's or Brokenburr's questioning of her judgment further complicated her direction of the Chicago school, but her management there persisted, and the facility generally showed a small profit.[31]

In the 1940s Joyner worked to reestablish the connection between African

American beauticians and Mary McLeod Bethune that Sarah Breedlove Walker had initiated. Although the National Beauty Culturists League headquarters at Washington's Logan Circle was only steps from Mary McLeod's base on Vermont Avenue, the NBCL had not worked extensively with Bethune. The absence of a close relationship between Bethune, or the National Council of Negro Women, and the NBCL left the door open for Joyner as she contemplated forming an organization for cosmetology teachers. Joyner's work with the Democratic Party in the 1944 election helped her cement a strong relationship with Bethune. Jeanetta Welch Brown, who then managed many day-to-day activities for the NCNW, also assisted Bethune with the efforts to get out the vote for FDR in 1944. Brown invited Joyner to attend a three-day meeting of the African American women's Democratic National Meeting at the NCNW headquarters in Washington, advising Joyner that "Mrs. Bethune will need us."[32] Bethune later reminded Joyner of the importance of these national connections, writing "Your fine achievements for the women of America is another link in this great chain of mutual endeavor which we must continue to strengthen and support in every possible way that we can. May you continue to increase your contributions to the women of our race and people to help them climb steadily upward with courage and unwavering determination."[33]

Through her employment with the Madam C. J. Walker Company and her ties to the Democratic Party, Joyner developed a warm friendship with Mary McLeod Bethune. Sarah Breedlove Walker had supported Bethune-Cookman College, a cause that Joyner also adopted. Mary McLeod Bethune assisted Joyner in developing the acquaintance of other leading African American women. In 1935, through her association with Bethune, Joyner had participated in the establishment of the NCNW, an umbrella organization that Bethune had envisioned would unite African American women's clubs throughout the nation.[34] From its Washington, D.C., headquarters, the NCNW lobbied the federal government on behalf of African American rights and on behalf of working women of color. Joyner remained active in NCNW until old age restricted her activities, and from 1935 forward Joyner depended heavily on Bethune's support of her activities.

As World War II ended Joyner began to implement her ideas for a national organization to unite cosmetology teachers. Meeting at Mary McLeod Bethune's Washington, D.C., residence and the NCNW headquarters in October, 1945, with thirty-five teaching associates, Bethune, and Illinois congressman William L. Dawson, Joyner drew up charters for a Greek letter "sorority and fraternity" of beauticians and the parallel UBSOTA. In reality there was no distinction between the sorority Alpha Chi Pi Omega and UBSOTA except that beauty operators, who were not eligible for UBSOTA

Marjorie Stewart Joyner, Mary McLeod Bethune, Eleanor Roosevelt, and other program partici-
pants at Bethune-Cookman College dedication ceremonies, ca. 1945. Marjorie Stewart Joyner
Papers, courtesy Vivian G. Harsh Research Collection of Afro-American History and Literature,
Chicago Public Library.

membership, could join the sorority. Because the NBCL already provided an
identity and organizational resource for African American cosmetologists, few
men or women other than cosmetology teachers or beauty-school operators
joined Alpha Chi Pi Omega sorority or fraternity chapters. Joyner's friend
and NCNW executive secretary Jeanetta Welch Brown wrote Marjorie with
an enthusiastic endorsement of the fledgling cosmetology group:

> I expect to be in Chicago in about ten days or more, so I shall call you
> and we can get together for another delightful time as we had in New
> York. I have some ideas for your newly formed organization, and have
> been thinking very strongly on what you propose to do. You know you
> have my support Darling and if there is anything I can do to help you
> do, you have only to ask it. You have a wonderful program in mind and
> it can do wonders for Negro women, with a little help from women
> who are interested in the general welfare of the masses.[35]

UBSOTA identified Mary McLeod Bethune as its founding "national sponsor," and Bethune frequently addressed the group's national meetings. In 1947

UBSOTA held its convention on the Bethune-Cookman campus in Daytona Beach, Florida, and through the years UBSOTA and its members donated hundreds of thousand of dollars for the college's support.[36]

UBSOTA, in deference to industry pioneers, listed Madam C. J. Walker, Annie Turnbo Malone, and Sara Spencer Washington as the founders of African American beauty education. Alpha Chi Pi Omega and UBSOTA adopted goals of raising educational standards in the beauty industry, undertaking "civic work in our communities to keep before the public," supporting African American commerce, behaving in a Christian manner, and supporting Bethune-Cookman College.[37] Marjorie Stewart Joyner was chosen as the national supervisor of UBSOTA, and she held that title at her death in 1994 although daily oversight of the organization passed to the group's president in the 1970s. UBSOTA adopted policies requiring that each local chapter contribute one hundred dollars annually to Bethune-Cookman. Joyner enjoyed early success in recruiting UBSOTA members with the group claiming the affiliation of more than two hundred schools in 1948.[38] Joyner's ties with the *Chicago Defender* facilitated her building of UBSOTA. The *Defender* carried news of UBSOTA meetings, giving Joyner national visibility in the African American community.

Local Alpha Chi Pi Omega chapters varied in the level of activities that they pursued, but all had to meet certain national goals such as paying dues to the national organization and making an annual contribution to Bethune-Cookman. A Christian orientation as well as the humanitarian aims of the sorority (male members were organized into fraternities of the same name, but these groups were few and far between) emerged at the local level. Biblical references pervaded chapter reports to the national organization, and sororal activities bore testimony to the national injunction to do good works. The 1960 report of one Philadelphia chapter opened with affirmation of the principle that "he who would be great among you must serve, humbly." The chapter raised funds for scholarship aid, contributed to a home for the elderly, gave assistance to its own members who fell ill, attended church services together following their annual fellowship breakfast, and viewed a film on the "Negro in the economic world."[39]

UBSOTA sponsored annual meetings; the first at Fisk University in 1946 featured seminars on teaching methods, business practices, and the latest beauty techniques, preparations, and equipment. Bethune-Cookman College hosted the second UBSOTA meeting in February, 1947, and conventions were held annually thereafter. Before the 1947 gathering, Joyner asked each beauty school to contribute one hundred dollars to a common fund. She also canvassed salon owners, asking each to contribute five dollars and encouraging shop owners to solicit a minimum of one dollar each from their beauticians, friends, and customers. In writing to Bethune of her plans for UBSOTA, Joyner promised that a substantial portion of the funds that UBSOTA raised would go to the Bethune-Cookman building fund.[40] Local UBSOTA affiliates were required to send at least one delegate to every convention in order to retain their chapter charter. Locating meetings on a college campus reinforced Joyner's emphasis on continuing education in the industry, but the association moved to commercial venues after the early years. Even when meetings were held at hotels in major cities, the central message remained training in new styles and products and in business methods.

As Joyner traveled about the country, she worked to recruit Alpha Chi Pi Omega members through mass meetings, usually held at prominent churches. While in Los Angeles doing advance work for the 1949 meeting, Joyner broadcast her message through the Los Angeles "Sentinel" program, a regular Sunday feature on station KFOX.[41] Joyner founded Alpha Chi Omega and UBSOTA through her Walker contacts, and the organizations provided a means for her to extend her influence beyond Walker affiliates. Through these organizations Marjorie Stewart Joyner kept contact with beauticians and teachers nationally long after her active work with the Walker company had ended. Into the 1980s Joyner authored articles on business practices and hairstyling methods as part of her continuing association with UBSOTA.

Although the beauty business was the occasion and the reason for the annual convention, Joyner hoped that UBSOTA would support all aspects of the growth and development of its members. Religious activities played a prominent role in the cycle of convention activities as the beauticians' cultural heritage dictated. Each convention during the group's first decade included a church service hosted by a pastor from the local area. UBSOTA members followed instructions for prescribed dress for the service, and the organization made a contribution to the pastor and church. Convention speakers generally included one or more college professors in business, sociology, or psychology in addition to government bureaucrats and representatives of private industry. Conventions featured workshops and classes for "academic" UBSOTA credit toward B.S. (beauty skills), M.S. (master stylist), and P.H.D. (doctor of hair design) certificates issued by UBSOTA.

As the years progressed, conventions became more and more elaborate, occasionally including travel to Europe, the Middle East, or Africa. Texas and California meetings included side trips to Mexico; a Florida meeting ended in a trip to Haiti on which Bethune accompanied the group. The 1954 convention began with a meeting in New York, moved to Paris for sessions in French salons, and terminated in London. UBSOTA held its most elaborate

Marjorie Stewart Joyner led a styling trip to Europe in 1954. The travelers made their way from New York to England and then home from France aboard the SS *United States,* which the United States passenger line touted as "the world's fastest and most modern liner." The ship's captain is right of Joyner, and J. H. Jemison appears standing fourth from the right, rear row. Marjorie Stewart Joyner Papers, courtesy Vivian G. Harsh Research Collection of Afro-American History and Literature, Chicago Public Library.

annual session in 1960, when a host of beauticians, led by Joyner, held a training clinic in Paris and then traveled to Nice, Rome, Beirut, Damascus, and Lausanne before concluding its styling sessions in a London salon.

During the late 1940s Joyner gained the support of Walker executives by using the direct sales approach to schools that Madam Walker herself had exploited through her network of direct sales agents. Satin Tress, a new Walker hair relaxer, was introduced in January, 1949, in a full-page advertisement in *Ebony Magazine.* Joyner wrote all UBSOTA members in advance of the release to explain how she had arranged for them to cash in on Satin Tress sales and also do good for the race:

Dear Co-Worker:
    . . . You know I have your interest at heart. I have talked long and hard to convince my firm that *all* Beauticians should share in this great

product that will unquestionably enhance the beauty of our Brown Women in America. Satin Tress is positively breathless in its beauty.

Because of my persistent letters and long distance calls, my firm has agreed to offer a Franchise to all School Owners who take a Satin Tress Course, and who qualify for a Franchise by purchasing at least $100.00 of its products annually other than Satin Tress products.

Satin Tress is available *only* to those Beauticians who hold our Permit. Satin Tress Clinics will give you a new Course and Method to offer your students. Satin Tress will enable you to make more money, and at the same time, will bring back to your School, many of your former graduates for this advanced work. I know from my own experience as National Supervisor of Mme. C. J. Walker Beauty Colleges, that all Schools can use more revenue at this time.[42]

Joyner concluded her Satin Tress sales appeal by reminding practitioners that "We must think very seriously about how we can retain the So-Called 'Negro Market' for you know how it is being exploited."[43] During the 1940s Joyner also began augmenting her income by writing articles for the black press. Although the vast majority of her efforts appeared in beauty magazines, she contributed a 1948 article of advice on careers for young people to *Negro Digest*. In later years Joyner contributed a regular column to *Beauty Trade*, a periodical that targeted African American beauticians. While Joyner's absorption with UBSOTA undermined the fortunes of the Walker school in Chicago, the Walker company continued to reap sales rewards from the national audience that Joyner retained through UBSOTA. She was the ideal agent to demonstrate Satin Tress because of the long-term respect she had gained for improving the quality of hair care in the African American community. In the late 1940s no other Walker employee carried such authority with beauticians.

The Walker Company vacillated in its support of Joyner's UBSOTA leadership, leadership that proved key in marketing Satin Tress. Before 1949 Walker executives frequently criticized Joyner's travels and expenditures, but they never censured her journalistic efforts. Regular publication of the UBSOTA newsletter and articles that Joyner contributed to beauty magazines cost Walker nothing and always carried a byline noting that Joyner was national supervisor of the Madam Walker Beauty Schools. Robert Lee Brokenburr, who followed F. B. Ransom as general manager of Walker, funded some of Joyner's undertakings, but he watched expenditures carefully. In April, 1948, Brokenburr sent her "a statement of your indebtedness to this company" and chastised her for exorbitant expenditures as she attempted to recruit students and Walker agents:

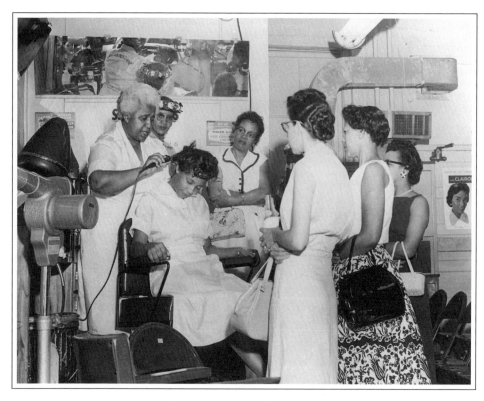

Marjorie Stewart Joyner continued to travel the nation through the 1950s and 1960s to demonstrate the powers of Madam Walker's "Satin Tress," ca. 1965. Marjorie Stewart Joyner Papers,
courtesy Vivian G. Harsh Research Collection of Afro-American History and Literature, Chicago
Public Library.

> When I was in Chicago I thought that we talked about refreshments
> for the meeting of the heads of church clubs and other organizations
> costing no more than four or five dollars for each meeting. We were to
> serve tea and wafers or punch and wafers or something of that sort. We
> said nothing about serving refreshments to [Walker] agents. However
> if the showing of a moving picture on hair styling and hair cutting will
> do the trick and the expense of showing it will not exceed thirty dollars,
> the company will bear the expense and I will send the check there
> from this office.[44]

In the following year Brokenburr supported Joyner's organizational efforts en-
thusiastically, having recognized the marketing potential of UBSOTA, but
Walker did not offer any financial support to the organization. Brokenburr re-

quested that Joyner set aside program space for a training session that would showcase Walker products. When the 1949 UBSOTA convention opened in Los Angeles in 1949, Brokenburr sent Joyner a warm letter of praise and asked her to extend his greeting to the delegates.[45]

Until her death in 1955, Mary McLeod Bethune encouraged Joyner's leadership of UBSOTA, attending the 1952 convention in Florida and Haiti. Bethune canceled her appearance at the 1955 San Antonio meeting because of illness; she died shortly afterward. Bethune had expressed her appreciation for Joyner's and UBSOTA's support of Bethune-Cookman College in ways other than her encouragement of UBSOTA activities. In 1951 Bethune awarded Joyner the Bethune Medallion at the spring Bethune-Cookman commencement exercises. In 1952 Bethune-Cookman College named a dormitory for Marjorie Stewart Joyner. Joyner continued her efforts on behalf of the college after Bethune's death and was named to the Board of Trustees, on which she served until her death in 1994. In recognition of her contributions to Bethune-Cookman, the college awarded her an honorary degree in 1961, and she thereafter used the title Dr. Marjorie Stewart Joyner.

The 1958 UBSOTA convention met in Washington, D.C., and the organization took the opportunity to educate members on citizenship and activities of the federal government. The citizenship activities of the 1958 meeting affirmed the goals of African American clubwomen, including Washington-based *Chicago Defender* columnist Ethel L. Payne, who urged Joyner to use the organization to make African American women more effective voices of civil rights. Writing to Marjorie, Payne argued,

> Women are always the guiding force behind any crusade and Negro women now face a challenge to give leadership in the big drive ahead of us to get Negroes all over the country registered to vote. Congress has passed a civil rights bill — weak, but nevertheless, now a law. Even this won't get off the ground unless somebody pushes it. What we need is real grass roots activity, right down among the plain folk and I can't think of anybody more suited to sound a call to arms, so to speak than yourself with the people behind you.[46]

The group sponsored a reception for Washington diplomats, visited Congress, and received comments from prominent Democrats and women's advocates Katie Loucheim and Marjorie Lawson and Labor Secretary Clarence Mitchell. Workshops were held on voter registration and voting procedures. UBSOTA urged delegates to distribute literature on voter registration through their schools and beauty shops. In advance of the meeting Joyner told members that "Who you vote for and how you vote is your business — that you vote is our business."[47]

Through the 1960s UBSOTA promised many benefits to its members with regard to professional development. Annual conventions delivered hairstyling updates and new product information to beauty instructors, but UBSOTA also promised its members training in business practices and instruction leading to a college degree. UBSOTA did conduct class sessions at its conventions, but the degrees offered through the organization offered no accreditation from any educational agency. UBSOTA gatherings regularly featured speakers with post-graduate educational credentials including political scientists, sociologists, psychologists, and professors of English. Through these addresses UBSOTA worked to raise the cultural knowledge of beauty-school teachers, but the association's courses of instruction included only a few hours of lectures followed by an examination administered at the close of the convention. UBSOTA did provide its members with literature covering principles of office management, record keeping, cosmetology law, student recruitment, and instructional techniques. The most popular of UBSOTA's activities were its several trips abroad, trips that Marjorie Stewart Joyner guided through 1965. Although the group scheduled demonstration sessions at salons in London, Paris, and Rome, travel served more to introduce members to international cultures and the arts. The European salons visited featured white models whose hair differed radically from the tresses of most potential UBSOTA clients or those of their students. Regardless of what they saw and learned, UBSOTA members returned from their foreign travels able to boast that they had up-to-date knowledge of the world and of European fashion. Through regional as well as national meetings UBSOTA members built continuing associations with peers who understood the daily challenges of teaching African American cosmetology students and who could offer advice and support. Although UBSOTA continues to exist, it has shrunk considerably in membership since the 1980s.

Through the 1950s Joyner also continued to head the Walker school in Chicago, and the school brought profits to the company. In 1960 the Chicago Walker branch trained 110 students and generated over $23,000 in tuition. In the same year the Walker company paid Joyner a salary of $425 per month plus occasional expenses for traveling on company business. Although Marjorie Stewart Joyner continued her relationship with the Walker Company after the 1960s, she no longer played a significant role in operating Chicago's Walker School of Beauty, and she did not actively promote Walker products after the inaugural Satin Tress campaign. Joyner had ended her regular tours of Walker schools in the country, but she conducted hairstyling clinics in major cities several times a year. Such clinics attracted both practicing beauticians and beauty-school teachers whose registration fees paid for Joyner's travel and furnished a modest honorarium for her services. During the 1960s Joyner devoted herself to civic leadership and to UBSOTA, which she helped promote through the articles that *Beauty Trade* paid her to write. In 1963 Joyner attended a White House reception that recognized the achievements of African American women and the National Council of Negro Women. On the occasion of the one-hundredth anniversary of the Emancipation Proclamation in 1963, she participated in the White House civil rights conference "To Fulfill these Rights" at the invitation of President John F. Kennedy. At the White House reception that followed the conference, Joyner had her photograph made with the president, an homage to her national leadership eclipsed only in the series of tributes elicited by the 1986 Smithsonian exhibit. Although she continued to contribute an occasional article to beauty magazines into the 1980s, Marjorie Stewart Joyner's world had begun to contract at the end of the 1960s. She traveled less in the 1970s, and she rarely appeared at cosmetology meetings in the 1980s although beauticians regularly invited her presence. She died in humble circumstances in 1994, but she did not die forgotten. Although its activities and size have dwindled, UBSOTA survives, and beauticians of color continue to practice many of the skills that Joyner taught. An inheritor of the Walker legacy, Joyner created a legacy of her own in organizing beauty education nationally and utilizing her place in beauty culture to advance the welfare of African American women. Although she never headed a civil rights organization, Joyner's stature in the trade and her dedication helped the civil rights revolution succeed. The same may be said of Joyner's contemporary and acquaintance J. H. Jemison although his leadership was more localized. While Joyner's history illustrates the national scope of beauty culture, the story of Jemison and of the Franklin School that follows reveals the importance of beauty education in the lives of ordinary women and the significance of local leadership in styling the death of Jim Crow.

CHAPTER 3

Southbound

Jim Crow, the J. H. Jemison Family,
and the Franklin School of Beauty

The history of the Franklin School of Beauty enfolds several stories: a business history, a family history, urban history, African American history, and gender history. It is a history of ordinary people whose aspirations and accomplishments through the Jim Crow era speak both to the injustices of racial discrimination and to the resilience of African Americans' determination to make good in a world that conspired against them. The history of the Franklin School of Beauty carries us into the richness and the complexity of African American communities in the twentieth century, to those junctures at which family, work, church, civic life, and politics all come together. The development of the Franklin enterprises through the century followed a course similar to that of the Poro and Walker companies albeit on a much more modest scale.

Nobia Franklin, like the vast majority of African American beauty culturists of the early twentieth century, had no formal training in skin or hair care and began practicing her craft in her home. Franklin manufactured skin and hair products, sold them to her friends and neighbors, and soon began to teach others the "Franklin way" to style hair through the use of her manufacturers. The initial successes of the Poro and Walker enterprises rested upon a verti-

cally integrated marketing scheme in which the companies trained women to
groom hair with their products and encouraged them to set up their own shops
to generate income by charging for cutting, straightening, or setting hair and
by selling the company's skin and hair preparations. Nobia Franklin sought to
emulate the Walker/Poro model, but she never succeeded fully in building a
network of agents. In the 1940s and 1950s the Franklin School, like hundreds
of other beauty schools in the nation, thrived locally and remained viable not
through product sales but through the instructional fees that it charged.

Nobia Franklin moved to Fort Worth, Texas, from San Antonio in 1916 and
opened her first beauty shop. In 1917 Franklin announced the organization of
the Franklin School of Beauty Culture coincident with the relocation of
her manufacturing, salon, and instructional operations to Houston. In 1922
Franklin left the Houston salon and teaching operation behind and joined the
Great Migration to Chicago, where she also opened a salon and school and
expanded the manufacturing arm of her business. Madame N. A Franklin's
hair and face preparations included

Pom Po Hair Dressing (for men)
Hair Grower
Temple Grower
Pressing Oil
Hot Oil Scalp Treatment
Hair Tonic
Shampoo
Skin Soap
Menthol Salve
Bleaching Cream
Skin Rejuvenator
Massage Cream
Vanishing Cream
Lemon Face Powder
Face Powder
Instant Beautifier
Lay-Rite Hair Dressing (for men and women)
Rouge
Lip Stick
Godfrey's French Lareuse Dye
Pressing Irons
Stoves

Her products, then, mirrored those of scores of other firms that competed for the beauty dollars of African Americans in the 1920s. Although Franklin marketed the basic range of skin and hair products that comprised the consumable goods sold by the major firms, she lacked the patents for straightening combs, irons, and creams or lotions that proved essential to Malone's and Walker's fortune building. Madame Franklin's publications and product labels pictured Nobia Franklin, a woman who looked remarkably similar to Sarah Breedlove Walker, and the company continued to use this image for some time after Franklin's death in 1934.

While Nobia Franklin never achieved the fame or fortune of her better-known predecessors, she provided well for her daughter, Abbie, and she left her property and a business legacy upon which Abbie and her husband built a lasting enterprise. Franklin's success in the beauty trade generated the income to purchase a three-story brick building at 3361 Indiana Street in Chicago; it contained factory, warehouse, and living space. Over the years rental of space in the "Franklin Building" generated some income for the family, but the premises deteriorated in the 1950s. When the property passed on the Franklin's granddaughter Anita in the 1960s, a Chicago realtor estimated its value to be six thousand dollars.

Nobia Franklin's modest success in the beauty industry had allowed Abbie to remain in school, but after school hours Madame Franklin brought her daughter into the shop and taught her hair styling and her product-manufacturing formulas and processes. Abbie entered the Franklin business as vice president and an instructor prior to her high-school graduation in 1926. To encourage the values and practices endorsed by the Franklin Company, Nobia and Abbie organized the N. A. Franklin Association of Beauty Culturists in 1927. Under the motto The Franklin Way Is the Right Way, the Franklin organization sought "To establish the confidence of the public by encouraging standardized, scientific and approved methods of hair and skin treatment as practiced by qualified operators."[1] The association extended full membership to all "persons of good habits" who had completed the N. A. Franklin course of beauty culture and honorary membership to agents selling Franklin products. Association meetings followed an "Order of Services" including song and prayer.

While Franklin and her daughter sought to enlarge their business through the organization, they also envisioned an association that would bolster the spiritual life and welfare of its members. Local chapter meetings also featured song and prayer as well as business discussions and the collection of the annual one-dollar dues. The chapter sick committee accepted the responsibilities of calling upon members who were ill and of recommending financial relief in dire circumstances. Neither Nobia nor Abbie succeeded in building strong association chapters. In Houston, which later became the Franklin headquarters, the first chapter formed in 1931 with eleven full members. In the same year the company had enrolled some twenty-eight sales agents throughout Texas, but the majority of them did not join the Houston chapter of the N. A. Franklin Association. In the late 1930s chapters of Franklin school alumnae replaced the N. A. Franklin agents' circles.

At the end of the 1920s the Franklins hired James H. (J. H.) Jemison, a Hattiesburg, Mississippi, native whose family had moved to Ohio in the early 1920s. Jemison subsequently migrated to Chicago and entered Wendell Phillips High School, from which he graduated in 1927.[2] Like F. B. Ransom, Jemison had good business sense, but, unlike the male managers of the Madam C. J. Walker company, Jemison apprenticed in and practiced hairdressing, a rare vocational pursuit among men of the 1920s. Throughout his long career in the industry J. H. Jemison stood out as the lone man captured in many photographs of NBCL and UBSOTA meetings. Both Abbie Franklin and J. H. Jemison took and passed the newly instituted Illinois cosmetology licensing examination almost immediately after its inception. What had been a skill and a business for Nobia Franklin had become a regulated occupation in the next generation. Nobia Franklin never sat for a licensing examination, and she gradually ceded daily operations to the licensed members of the younger generation. J. H. Jemison's teaching and hairdressing skills matched his business acumen, and his hiring proved a boon in all respects. The business grew, and so did the friendship between J. H. and Abbie, who married not long after Jemison entered the business. The young couple soon had a child whom they named Nobia Anita in honor of her grandmother. Jimmie, as the family called J. H., soon made his authority felt within the operations. With Jemison on board, the manufacturing and instructional sides of the business continued, and the salon prospered. Jemison took charge of the financial side of operations and brought his sister Minnie into the business. Minnie, also a beautician, worked in the Franklin salon, and her husband, Arthur Logan, helped out in the manufacturing end when away from his full-time employment as a printing engraver.

In October, 1934, Nobia Franklin died, leaving Abbie and J. H. Jemison to run the Madame N. A. Franklin enterprises. Abbie's father, who had played no active role in the trade or the family for many years, had joint ownership of the Chicago salon and school, and thus the Jemisons bought out his interest following Nobia's passing. J. H. determined to institute significant changes that he believed would benefit the business. At the time of Nobia Franklin's death, the superior claims of other African American beauty operations in

Chicago remained clear. Overton Manufacturing was still the largest black-owned cosmetics manufacturer in the city. Both Poro and Madam Walker had numerous salons in the Chicago area. Marjorie Stewart Joyner managed a thriving Walker school and salon, and she had already risen to a leadership position in the emerging National Beauty Culturists League. Seeing greater opportunities in a less-competitive environment, the Jemisons looked to open new operations in another location, one where African Americans had already achieved commercial successes but that had few beauty salons. Despite their strong ties to Chicago and the promise of a more open society in the North than in the South, the Jemisons set their sights on Texas and chose Houston as their locus.

Why Texas? The answer lies more in state legislative initiative than in Abbie's or the Franklin School's ties to the Lone Star State. In Austin the state legislature had recently passed the first Texas beauty law, which took effect in 1935, and the Jemisons rightly anticipated that the regulation of the industry would offer an unusual opportunity to get in on the ground floor of professionalization of cosmetology. The 1935 Texas code, similar to the regulatory laws developing in other states, required "beauty operators" to complete one thousand hours of instruction at a licensed beauty school and to submit to a state-administered written and practical examination at the end of the course. The Texas cosmetology law also established health and sanitation standards in the beauty industry and subjected hair salons to periodic examinations by state-appointed inspectors. Throughout the United States, legislative regulation of beauty salons forced major reorganization of the beauty industry, separating beauty care from manufacturing and sales and eventually separating cosmetology training from the beauty salon. The Jemisons continued the Chicago manufacturing arm of the business for several years after opening the Houston beauty school, but manufactures quickly declined as a share of the Franklin earnings. The salon and the school remained virtually one in the same until the state cosmetology board forced the Jemisons to operate each enterprise on separate premises. Because the Texas law, one of the first in the South, and was more stringent than the older Louisiana beauty code, beauticians trained at the Houston-based N. A. Franklin School of Beauty Culture could and did claim a higher level of expertise than beauty operators who had not completed formal training or who had trained elsewhere in the South.

Why choose Houston, a city that historian Merline Pitre identifies as "the most segregated city in the Southwest" in the 1930s?[3] In the 1860s Houston had been a beacon to blacks, and the size of the city's African American population more than tripled from just over 1,000 to 3,700 in this short but turbulent period. In 1900 one in eight African Americans in the Bayou City owned a home.[4] After the turn of the century the African American population growth failed to keep pace with the expansion of the white population of the city, but there were more than 64,000 African Americans in Houston when the Jemisons arrived, making it the largest African American community in Texas and the Southwest.

Strong race leadership and entrepreneurial determination distinguished the African American community of Houston. In 1870 African American voters had outnumbered qualified whites, and these voters had elected Richard Allen to serve as the state's first African American state legislator. In 1912 Houstonians founded a local chapter of the National Association for the Advancement of Colored People, and the NAACP fought the legal measures and intimidation that white Texans utilized to deprive African Americans of an effective voice in politics. Schools and public accommodations had been segregated by practice where not already so by law. While Texas did not disfranchise African Americans, all-white primaries had vitiated African American power at the polls, and the poll tax had further discouraged African Americans from participation in the political process.[5] Although whites had succeeded in eradicating African American political influence by 1930, the city had had a strong tradition of African American participation in the Democratic and the Republican parties.[6]

Both a history of interracial violence and a legacy of African American accomplishments distinguished the Bayou City, so the area simultaneously repulsed and attracted. The *Chicago Defender*, the *Pittsburgh Courier*, and the *Houston Informer*, among other organs, kept African Americans throughout the country abreast of racial issues and the progress of race men in the city. Nationally circulated publications had identified Houston as a center of opportunity although not a trouble-free environment for persons of color. Houston's several African American neighborhoods testified to a tradition of separation, but Houston was not more segregated residentially than many northern cities. Despite challenges Houston's African Americans had proved enterprising, resilient, and determined to educate their children. Tree-lined streets and stately homes bore witness to a stable African American community headed by a substantial middle class. The Great Depression had descended upon Houston as it had on the nation, but economic conditions among African Americans in the Bayou City were less dire than among Chicago's residents of color.

West Dallas Street, where black businesses and professional offices concentrated, pulsed with economic activity. The Negro Chamber of Commerce, founded in the 1930s, exercised little clout inside or outside the black community, but it bound African American businessmen together in ways that fed business to all of its members. The city's Odd Fellows Building and the

Pilgrim Temple, both of which would play important roles in J. H Jemison's rising fortune, contained the offices of black professionals, housed service and retail business, headquartered local fraternal organizations, and provided community meeting facilities. Churches abounded and the African American community boasted a YMCA, a YWCA, a public library, and other civic facilities. Restaurants, bars, barbershops, and cleaning and repair establishments flourished, but beauty shops were few in number, and only one beauty school served the community. Dallas, with a smaller African American population, boasted two beauty colleges, one of which had spacious facilities and strong enrollments, making it a much less attractive market for the Jemisons. Houston's final attraction was its link to earlier Franklin enterprises. Even though all Franklin teaching and salon work in the city had ceased long before Nobia Franklin's death, a skeletal Franklin Association remained in the city, and African American women had some knowledge of Franklin products and the "Franklin Way."

Leaving employees and family members in charge of the Chicago operations, Abbie and J. H. bucked the tide of African American migration and relocated to Houston. Only weeks after their arrival in Houston, J. H. purchased a new Ford coupe for eight hundred dollars. Contracting to pay off the car note at twenty-five dollars per month, Jemison never had any difficulty covering his transportation costs, and he had easy and reliable transportation to the Jemisons' new business. Their first home in the Bayou City was a small apartment at 217 Robin Street in the heart of the city's African American community on the East Side. The Robin Street area included some substantial homes, and on Robin Street itself stood Antioch Baptist Church. Antioch Baptist Church had been pastored by Jack Yates, the leading clergyman in his community in the post-Reconstruction era.[7] Antioch Baptist counted Houston's most affluent and prominent African American families among its members. Later the Jemisons purchased their home on Robin Street, and, after living there for an extended period, they converted it to a student dormitory.

The Jemisons opened their first Houston salon and their school in rented commercial quarters. The salon, largely managed by Abbie, yielded immediate revenue while J. H. concentrated on organizing the Franklin school at the same address. Abbie and J. H. obtained the appropriate licenses for operating a legitimate salon and a recognized school. The requirements for licensing as a beauty instructor in Texas included high-school graduation, a minimum of three years' experience as a licensed beauty operator, and completion of additional training in hair care and styling. Abbie and J. H. qualified easily for their licenses as the state accepted their credentials from Illinois. Abbie paid $5 for a beautician's license to operate the salon, and both Abbie and J. H. received their instructor's permits after paying the $10 fee.[8] As regulated by the 1935 Texas code, cosmetology-school licensing was a fairly simple and straightforward matter. The owner of the proposed educational enterprise demonstrated that the instructors had completed at least three years of beauty practice after receiving their operator's licenses, provided evidence that the school campus met state health and licensing requirements, and filed a $100 licensing fee. In addition to the annual school license, beauty instructors maintained their individual licenses at a cost of $10 annually. In the beginning Abbie and J. H. furnished all of the school's instructional services.

After their years of dressing hair and of teaching beauty culture in Illinois, J. H. and Abbie gained new stature through the Texas beauty law and their entrepreneurial vision. From their 1935 Houston beginning the Jemisons built the largest African American beauty school in the South, one whose graduates eventually found jobs from the Atlantic to the Pacific as African American migration continued through the 1940s and 1950s. As states instituted and revised cosmetology codes through the late 1930s and the 1940s, the Texas code stood as equivalent to or more rigorous than regulations elsewhere in the South but held beauticians to lesser training than that demanded in Illinois, the Pacific Coast, and the Northeast. All states, at the discretion of each school, accepted transfer hours from one institution to another, so an aspiring woman might begin her training anywhere and transfer to another school if she elected to relocate before completing her training. States generally practiced reciprocity in licensing beauticians from other states with equivalent cosmetology codes, and where reciprocity did not operate, a beautician might still transfer hours of training to a school in another state.

The Franklin School location at 502 Louisiana Street offered visibility within Houston's black community and a convenient location for clients. The Odd Fellows Building housed fraternal and civic organizations and catered to members of the African American professional and business classes, some of whom maintained offices in the building. A variety of small retail venues surrounded the Odd Fellows complex. Jemison hoped to draw students and salon clients from the families of the middle-class African Americans who frequented the Odd Fellows Building and patronized nearby businesses. In reality Franklin students would come overwhelmingly from the humblest among the laboring classes, but Jemison's strategic location at the heart of commercial African American Houston helped identify him as an up-and-coming businessman. During the 1930s the school occupied a facility of some 3,500 square feet consisting of a management office, a lecture-demonstration room, a practice room, and cloakroom. The Franklin salon originally doubled as the practice room where aspiring students washed, treated, and styled hair under the supervision of their instructors. The salon was equipped with washbasins for washing hair, electric hair irons, and adjustable salon chairs. The smoking stoves of the 1920s did not have a place in the modern Franklin establishment.

The Madame N. A. Franklin School of Beauty Culture of Houston had opened quietly but not without notice in 1935. In an article accompanied by a photograph of J. H. and Abbie Franklin Jemison, a local newspaper reported "Daughter Pushes Mother's Work in Franklin Beauty School," a Houston enterprise that had been started by "the late Madam N. A. Franklin" and now continued under the direction of her daughter and son-in-law.[9] The Houston Franklin School proffered the opportunity for the young couple to build their own business from the ground up. Other than to a handful of Franklin sales agents familiar with the manufacturer's product line, the "Franklin Way" of hair and skin care was unknown in the Bayou City in the 1930s. During their first decade in Houston, J. H. and Abbie were full partners in the ongoing operation of their beauty enterprises. After the school had been operating for several months, Abbie left the salon, and the Jemisons hired a former student to manage it for them so that Abbie could give her complete attention to teaching.

In forging ahead with their infant enterprise Abbie and J. H. extended the time-honored promise of a speedy and direct path to a steady and reliable independent income in beauty culture to their prospective clients. Despite the Depression the Franklin enterprises, especially the school, did well. Finding a largely local niche within the African American beauty industry, J. H. Jemison organized his operations to capitalize on the paradoxical opportunities of an impoverished African American community in the Jim Crow South. In the late 1930s Jemison listed seventy-five sales agents in or near Texas who marketed Franklin products, although none cleared appreciable profits from her efforts. In Chicago, L. H. Starks, who had managed the plant for some time, continued to oversee manufacturing operations. During the 1930s orders for N. A. Franklin pressing oil and hair grower continued to increase. Starks distributed approximately thirty thousand items a year from the Indiana Avenue plant, but the sales yielded meager profits.

The 1930s presented a unique business environment for the Franklin School and for private schools of beauty culture elsewhere, because the recently adopted cosmetology laws had mandated that aspiring beauticians complete formal instruction before taking the license examination, and virtually no public beauty instruction existed. Although relying largely on salon trade in the early months, the Jemisons set about recruiting students, and the Franklin School quickly generated positive cash flow. Despite the lingering effects of the Great Depression the Jemisons steadily built their enrollments,

The Mme. N. A. Franklin's School of Beauty Culture class photograph, spring, 1937. Franklin Papers, courtesy Houston Metropolitan Research Center, Houston Public Library.

and Franklin routinely matriculated two hundred students annually in the 1940s. Jemison sought new students through advertisements placed in the state's black newspapers and in Texas editions of national African American newspapers, as well as in Houston's telephone yellow pages. The telephone directory listed the Madame N. A. Franklin College of Beauty under "Beauty Salons—Colored" since no category for schools of cosmetology yet existed. Franklin's advertisements assured prospective students of an expedient and sure path to independence. As one announcement proffered, "Dear Friend: Every day we expect to hear from you. Now let us urge you not to lose interest in Beauty Culture. You would certainly be doing yourself a great wrong. Beauty Culture is one of the best paying professions anyone can take up. Think! It only requires 6 months to complete a course and secure a position paying $75.00 to $150.00 a month!"[10]

In the fall of the 1937 Jemison placed a full-page advertisement in the *Houston Informer* that billed Franklin as the largest beauty school in the South. This early foray into advertising promised that students could train to work in white shops or African American establishments, but segregated examinations and the discriminatory practices of employers soon led to the dropping of any claims of cross-racial employment preparation.[11] J. H. and Abbie served as instructors at the school from its opening, and in 1937 a third instructor joined the staff to serve rising enrollments. By 1938 J. H. Jemison had gained sufficient respect for his work as an instructor and for the school that the Texas Board of Cosmetology consented to hold its licensing examination at the Franklin facilities, an arrangement that brought additional revenue to the Jemisons and saved students the cost of traveling to Austin for the test. By the end of 1939, the Jemisons had opened a second beauty salon, and their joint annual gross income had risen to $14,465.

Through the 1950s African American newspapers, eager to showcase the successes of the race, freely featured photographs and short articles on all facets of beauty culture from fashion and style shows to beauty-school dances and commencements. The Franklin School benefited from free press coverage, but J. H. Jemison proved less adept at drawing journalistic coverage than did Marjorie Stewart Joyner. Consequently Jemison relied mainly upon paid advertising. Through advertisements at community events in Houston, Jemison sought to keep the school's name before the public and simultaneously build good will among Houston's African American leaders. When the Texas conference of Bethel and Macedonia ministers met in the city for their 1944 convention, Jemison purchased a full-page announcement on the back cover of the souvenir program. Although Jemison advertised largely in Texas publications, he also took advantage of regional editions of newspapers such as the *Pittsburgh Courier* and the Baltimore *African American* that were widely read in Texas and the adjoining states. The Franklin School drew enrollments largely from Houston and Texas towns within one hundred miles of the Bayou City. Through his advertising campaigns, however, Jemison succeeded in drawing small numbers of students from western Texas, Oklahoma, and Louisiana. In the 1940s and 1950s an occasional student entered the program from as far away as California and Central America.

The reputation of the Franklin School spread partly through commercial outlets, but primarily by word of mouth. As Franklin's former students moved around the country and established themselves in the beauty trade, they heightened awareness of and respect for the school and its program. Franklin graduate Ollie Mae James left Houston for Pittsburgh, where she began practicing her trade before she obtained a Pennsylvania license. James violated

Pennsylvania's beauty code, but the Keystone State, like others, had no effective means of enforcing its hairdressing regulations during the prewar years. James did hope to pass the examination, however, and had written to Franklin for the records she would need to qualify for examination, commenting that "I'm really doing the Franklin way up here and everybody has gone hog wile over my work."[12]

The Franklin School of Beauty proved the most successful of the Jemisons' enterprises. The school offered programs that permitted students to attend school full-time or half-time and to pay for their instruction on a month-to-month basis. In May, 1936, the Jemisons called the members of the Madame N. A. Franklin Association to a convention at school headquarters and a joint meeting with the first graduates of the Franklin School. In the fall of 1936 the school held a memorial service at St. Paul's Methodist Episcopal Church to recognize Nobia Franklin,[13] whose visage graced Franklin product labels and stationery. In their early years in Texas the Jemisons capitalized on the limited but real name recognition that Madame N. A. Franklin evoked in Texas, but in time a photo of J. H. Jemison would head printed items of the Franklin School of Beauty. The second Houston meeting of Franklin agents and Franklin graduates in 1937 drew thirty-seven beauticians. While the majority of attendees came from Houston and Galveston, only fifty miles to the south, delegates came from within one hundred miles of the school. In subsequent years annual conventions expanded as the number of Franklin graduates mounted.

Coming to Houston as young adults, Abbie and J. H. became reacquainted with old Jim Crow, a composite of legalized forms of discrimination that they had escaped when their families had left the South. Houston whites gave no quarter to challengers of segregation, and African American schools remained markedly inferior to facilities for whites. Since the 1920s the Colored Citizens Committee had fought for better appropriations for their children's schools but had enjoyed little success. On the other hand, Houston maintained the only public junior college for blacks in the nation, and the black community supported a number of parochial schools. With a great appreciation of the value of education, the Jemisons would find the city's inferior black schools unacceptable for daughter Anita, who attended a Dallas boarding school for a short time but was schooled largely outside the South.[14]

J. H., despite having been born in the South, had not lived outside Chicago as an adult, but he soon learned to navigate in a new political environment simply by paying his poll tax and casting his ballot. While Abbie demurred from public leadership, J. H. moved early on to establish his claims as an up-and-coming citizen. J. H. Jemison participated in a broad variety of civic and political activities that mark a middle-class, urban lifestyle. He worked tirelessly to build the Franklin School in Houston, but he also worked with local commercial, civic, and political groups to lift the oppressive hold of Jim Crow. Jemison, like most other middle-class Houstonians of color, did not interact daily with the city's white leadership although the races did cooperate on particular civic projects or political campaigns. Rather than looking to white Houston, Jemison and others among the city's leading African Americans focused on the national organizations that supported and assisted their economic development and promoted civil equality. African American commercial and professional leaders typically held membership in a variety of civic, social, and religious organizations that reinforced their business ties with each other. Like their white counterparts, they served on volunteer boards where they saw the same people with whom they conducted business. In 1938 Jemison worked with the NAACP to develop youth activities and to recruit young people into the organization. Consistent with other community-based appeals, the NAACP addressed church congregations to stimulate the interest of Houston's youth in the civil rights association. Although Jemison was frugal, he was hardly stingy. In 1939 he pledged three hundred dollars to the YMCA and immediately paid fifty dollars against his obligation. Through the 1950s he participated actively in YMCA activities, heading a major fund-raising drive later in his life.

Houston boasted the Negro Chamber of Commerce, an organization to which the all-white Houston Chamber of Commerce gave its official endorsement. Nevertheless the Negro Chamber of Commerce strove to convince African Americans to keep their hard-earned dollars within the black community. Dr. C. W. Pemberton, president of the Negro Chamber of Commerce in the 1940s, represented Houston's black insurance companies and local offices at a meeting of the National Insurance Association. Pemberton helped establish the *Journal of Negro Business* and chaired its first editorial board. In later years Pemberton also served the Franklin School as the physician who administered the health examinations required for cosmetology licenses. In 1938 the Houston Negro Chamber of Commerce had invited and hosted the annual convention of the National Negro Business League, an organization that generally met outside the South. J. H. joined the Negro Chamber of Commerce and remained active in the group in years to come. He also joined Phi Beta Sigma, another group that promoted African American business success.[15]

Jemison's involvement with local business and civic groups did not lessen his attention to the beauty trade. He maintained his membership in the National Beauty Culturists League and also kept up-to-date through contact with numerous wholesale agents in the industry who marketed their goods to the Jemisons' school and their salons. Through the National Beauty Culturists League and individual correspondence with other beauticians, Jemison maintained knowledge of problems and opportunities in the industry. Through his association with other school owners, Jemison received valuable information, such as, for example, a warning against the activities of a scam artist working the trade. A Louisiana teacher wrote, "If a man comes to you by the name of Alphodolphus Bell or any other name, saying that he is able to get students for your school through the N.Y.A. there is nothing to it. Call an officer and notify me at once at my expense, I do not know that he is there but you can be on the look out for him."[16]

Investing their energies most heavily in building the Franklin school, the Jemisons continued to profit from the salons that they owned, but their manufacturing operations languished. J. H. kept manufacturing products for use in the school and the Jemisons' salons, but efforts to market products by building a network of agents ceased. Like most beauty salons, Franklin salons also sold products manufactured by other concerns, and in 1940 Jemison decided to add cosmetics to the array of hair products his salons sold. Some of J. H.'s frustrations with the manufacturing arm of the business followed from the lack of efficiency in the Chicago operation, business difficulties exacerbated by personal as well as business problems.

During the 1930s Jemison depended on Minnie and Arthur Logan to manage the Chicago operations, an arrangement that both reinforced and strained family relations. Initially J. H. had left L. H. Starks, a Franklin employee and a tenant, to manage the Chicago operations upon leaving for Houston. Starks performed satisfactorily for a couple of years, but by 1938 he had become disinterested and unreliable. Arthur Logan had to take over the operations, and the Logans asked Starks to leave the premises because he had not paid rent in several months and had made no obvious efforts to find employment after he was terminated at Franklin Manufacturing.

The Logans kept open the beauty salon in Chicago, managed the 3361 Indiana Street building, manufactured products according to Nobia Franklin's formulas, and distributed cosmetics to Franklin agents and to the Houston operations. In the spring of 1938, Minnie wrote to J. H. to bring several business bills to his attention and to request that he pay them as the Chicago manufacturing operations were not self-supporting. Arthur faced problems as well. He was still working independently as a commercial engraver, and balancing two careers taxed his energies. Starks's failures as an employee had complicated Logan's life; he wrote to J. H., "Everything is going along fair here. I am gradually 'ketching' up on the bills and the many things neglected and left undone by Starks. Already I am getting a little exhausted from making so many trips down to 34th Street and back plus doing my art work at home here. So it looks as if we may have to follow your suggestion of moving back there. . . ."[17] J. H. approved the move and offered some assistance in getting the Logans settled. He reminded Arthur that he was soon to be inaugurated "Bronze Mayor" of Houston, and that he would "appreciate a telegram on that night from some of you Chicago folks."[18] As the Logans prepared to move into the 3361 building, Minnie asked J. H. to finance some improvements to the apartment. She had hired a decorator and had put in a new kitchen sink, but she complained that the stove leaked smoke and gas and requested that J. H. replace it. Minnie got her stove, but when she raised an additional wish for a refrigerator, J. H. responded that he had no more money to give them. J. H. wrote that he had already spent $1,000 during his recent Chicago visit and that he had to cover the expenses of the hospitalization of his and Minnie's sister Hattie. Not to be denied, Minnie later wrote that she and Arthur could handle the costs of a new refrigerator as well as their new car.

Jemison had assumed the position of family patriarch, and both Minnie and Arthur turned to J. H. for personal support as well as business guidance. While Abbie had been an only child, J. H.'s family was a large one in which everyone looked to him partly because he had already enjoyed such notable success, a situation that Marjorie Stewart Joyner also confronted during her active work life. Minnie expected J. H. to care for the single women in the family and to maintain connections with far-flung kin. She understood that her participation in the business entitled her to improvements in her living quarters and a company car. Minnie did her part to keep good relations within the family, but she depended emotionally as well as financially on J. H.'s leadership. In the summer of 1938, she had expressed her disappointment that his promised visit had been delayed, writing "I am tired of looking for you. Will you come on to Chicago, or stay in Texas? I have been expecting you every day."[19] She had also asked her brother to return a quilt she had given him because their sister Willie had asked for it, saying "that it is hers and the last thing that Mama had made her."[20]

Jemison's involving Minnie and Arthur in the business had helped him support his sister, but the mix of family and business elevated the importance of strong family ties, and family difficulties could compromise the welfare of the business. Family matters distressed J. H., and in 1939 family problems threatened to disrupt the struggling Chicago operations. Just as the Logans seemed to have been settled in the business and at 3361 Indiana Street, Jemison received a desperate letter from Arthur:

Dear Jimmie,

   It is with regret that the only letter I have time to write you should come with bad news. A most disastrous thing has happened here. Your sister or my wife Minnie [and I] are just about to separate. She is wrapped up in love or infatuated over a roomer here named Maurice Benson. The fellow who occupies the small room next to ours. He made a confession. . . . He simply said, with one hand on his pistol, that he was in love with her and said that she felt the same about him. When I questioned Minnie about this she, of course, broke down and cried claiming she didn't want to leave me. Said she believed she was under some strange influence of his and couldn't get her mind straight.[21]

Arthur went on to say that his rival had quit his job so that he could hang around the building to be close to Minnie and that Arthur had been "struggling to hold down my temper to keep from killing him which I won't do." The letter closed with the news that the apartments had not been on a paying basis since October and that he had had to turn to the Home Owners Loan Corporation for a mortgage that J. H. would have to assume. In concluding, Arthur asked J. H. to respond to "112 W. Madison as Minnie opens the mail." J. H. answered promptly, writing, "I sympathize with you in every respect. . . . Now you know there is no man in my mind that I think more of than you and I am with you 100 percent. I would like to see you all make it if possible for things do come up in peoples lives from time to time."[22] Arthur wrote subsequently to report that he had taken Minnie out of town to stay with his aunt and that she had come to her senses. Arthur informed J. H. that he could again address all correspondence to 3361 Indiana Street.

   Arthur had quit his engraving job in order to devote more attention to Franklin business. J. H. had gained a dependable worker, but he had also gained responsibility for Arthur's and Minnie's livelihood. Soon Jemison heard from Minnie: "We are getting along fine, now that our rumor has moved. I am so sorrow all of that happened to get you and Art so upset. But everything will be O.K. from now on. Things weren't half as bad as they seem. Well, so much for that."[23] On the down side, Minnie had discovered that someone had stolen hair preparations from the factory. As spring arrived, the Logans expressed optimism that the Chicago operations would turn a profit, but federal cosmetic regulations presented a new worry. The Department of Agriculture sent out warnings to black-owned firms reminding them of the necessity of complying before the end of June with federal labeling laws. The Franklin recipes could remain secret, but every product would have to bear a complete list of ingredients. Without patent protections Franklin products, like those of countless other manufacturers, might be copied easily. Labeling regulations did not kill Franklin manufacturing enterprises, but ingredient disclosure was one of several developments that ultimately brought down the smallest commercial cosmetics manufacturers.

While J. H. Jemison did not prove a genius in cosmetics marketing and sales, the Franklin School of Beauty of Beauty grew steadily. Jemison proved more adept at building those branches of the enterprise that he oversaw personally and on a daily basis. Both Abbie and J. H. demonstrated individual concern for their students, and their caring involvement in teaching, when paired with J. H.'s scrupulous attention to financial details, accounted for the Franklin School's viability through the 1940s. As the school prospered, Jemison reinvested a healthy share of the profits back into the business, and he diversified his financial holdings. Shortly before World War II the Jemisons acquired a third salon, and their family fortunes permitted the purchase of a new Buick to replace the family's Ford.[24] J. H. and Abbie bought a home on Live Oak, a well-kept street on the East Side, having earlier purchased the small frame apartment house on Robin Street that had been their first Houston home. The move to Live Oak presaged the conversion of the Robin Street property into a dormitory for female Franklin students.

The dormitory illustrated Jemison's integrated business approach, a strategy that married his relative paucity of capital with the genuine poverty of his clients to the benefit of both. Although the practice has now fallen by the wayside, the provision for student housing was a common feature of beauty schools during the 1930s and 1940s. Rural and small-town African Americans had often sent their children to live with urban relatives in order to take advantage of the superior educational options of the city, much as Abbie and J. H. had sent Anita to family in Chicago in order to avoid Houston's segregated schools. The availability of the dormitory allowed the Jemisons to draw from distant regions students who had no kin living in Houston. Abbie, with the aid of a dormitory matron, managed the housing and supervised the conduct of its residents. One of the Robin Street residents was generally a married or widowed woman who oversaw dormitory operations and supervised the conduct of the younger occupants. The matron lived rent free but received no salary for her services.

At the same time that J. H. Jemison built up the Franklin School of Beauty, he cultivated the community contacts that helped him embark on additional business ventures with other middle-class African Americans in Houston. Multiple investments proved to be the secret of Jemison's success. Finding a place in real estate and other business and civic ventures, Jemison became a pillar of the community. He acquired numerous rental properties in addition to 217 Robin Street. His rapid rise to prominence in the business community paid off in 1938, when his commercial and professional acquaintances selected him as the city's "Bronze Mayor." Through the prewar years the Jemisons' income rose, but their capital holdings rose much more steeply than their liquid assets. Although he engaged in varied professional and business undertakings, J. H. Jemison always kept a watchful eye on the Franklin School. Among his many responsibilities were student recruitment, admissions, tuition payments, and the curriculum.

Schools of beauty culture observed open admissions standards, eager to accept all who could pay their fees. Candidates for admission to the Franklin School filed a one-page application that indicated date of birth, permanent address, level of educational achievement, and schools attended. Each applicant had to secure the signature of a cosigner who accepted financial responsibility for payment of the entire course of instruction. Each new student presented the results of a blood test, and anyone testing positive for tuberculosis or other communicable diseases was denied admission until negative test results had been obtained. Tuition was not the sole expense associated with a Franklin education. Equipment, blood tests, graduation expenses, the state examination fee, and travel expenses to Austin to sit for the examination all summed to expenses equal to the instructional fee. Franklin students purchased tool kits and textbooks from the school that could be returned for partial credit at the end of the course, and students furnished their own notebooks and white uniforms that were to be clean and neatly pressed at the start of each school day. The tool kits generally included combs, curlers, scissors, and manicuring tools. In 1935 the Franklin School charged seventy-five dollars for the complete course leading to the examination for an operator's license. Tuition increased to eighty-five dollars on the eve of World War II. Despite the ease of entry and the youthfulness of most students, the Franklin School enjoyed success in bringing enrollees to graduation.

In order that its students might qualify for the licensing examination, beauty schools maintained complete attendance records on all students who had enrolled in training. Registration and attendance records show that the vast majority of Franklin graduates, approximately 95 percent, were female. Beauty students ranged in age from sixteen to sixty years, but enrollees over the age of forty-five were rare, and the majority of students were women in their late teens or their twenties. Most students were single women, but widows and wives were common among Franklin students. Franklin records also confirm that the majority of women who entered the school in the years before World

War II persisted in their studies to graduation even though most found the relatively low costs of instruction a true financial hardship.

While beauty-school owners designed their courses to meet the demands
of the examinations administered to prospective beauticians, they had a free
hand in conducting their operations and carrying out their instruction. The
state of Texas did not prescribe a specific course of instruction for cosmetology
schools in the 1930s nor did the state regulate fees in any aspect of the beauty
industry. Beauty schools established their own curricula and standards as well
as their own entrance requirements and application procedures. The state demanded only that a candidate for an operator's license have completed the sev-
enth grade, have reached her sixteenth birthday, and be free of tuberculosis
and venereal disease. Beauty teachers had few materials available on which
to base their lectures, and cosmetology texts were almost nonexistent in the
1930s.

The Franklin School utilized a textbook published by Milady Publishing
Company, a firm publishing cosmetology literature exclusively and selling the
same edition to all ethnic markets. Texts existed that had been written specifi-
cally for training students to style and care for the hair of African American
women, but initially these texts were issued by companies such as Walker
Products and Poro that competed with Jemison for students and for customers.
Franklin students enrolled in classes in "theory, permanent waving, finger
waving, facials and [eyebrow] arches, dyes, scalp treatments, iron curling,
shampoos." In the early years the school retained the services of one paid instructor in addition to Abbie and J. H. Jemison as well as secretary Hazel Mc-
Cullough, who remained with the school throughout her working life. The
instructional staff presented lectures on anatomy, health and sanitation, "hair
theory," cosmetics for use on hair and skin, and electrical and heated equipment for treating and styling hair.[25]

The hair-care and styling techniques studied in the 1930s included croquignole, a waving method of applying a chemical setting solution to hair that
had been tightly rolled on small curling rods. The finger wave, as described
earlier, was a styling technique in which the hair was wetted with a setting lotion before waves or curls were arranged by crimping hair between the index
fingers of the hands or curling the hair around the finger. The beautician generally secured the waves or curls with pins or clips, netted the damp hair, and
then dried the hair with an electric dryer. While white salon clients frequently
requested finger waves, the technique did not satisfactorily control very curly
hair, and African American women rarely sought this service. Marcel techniques, which utilized heated irons, held popularity through World War II.
Similar to today's electric curling iron, the marcel iron opened like a pair of

scissors with rounded blades that fit into each other, but the beautician creased the hair between the blades rather than winding it around a heated rod. Marcel waves consisted of a series of cascading waves formed by lateral crimps in wide locks of hair. The operator applied the iron to a lock of hair first from the left, then to the same lock of hair from the right and below the first crimp, back from the left, and so forth from the top of the head downward and then working around the head by repeating the procedure. Franklin students also studied and practiced the application of hair products designed to stimulate hair growth, to color hair, to suppress scalp dryness, and to condition the hair to keep it manageable and discourage breakage.

As states began to implement cosmetology licensing in the 1930s, the requirement of one thousand hours of training was a common standard although the larger northern states moved earlier than the South to demand more extensive training. In Texas this requirement held until 1969, when the cosmetology board raised the period of instruction to fifteen hundred hours. Into the 1960s the Franklin School maintained a scheduled six-month term leading to the licensing examination and divided the term into a junior and a senior session of five hundred hours each. Juniors learned the basic rules of sanitation of facilities and equipment, studied theories of hair and skin care through lectures and textbooks, learned how to prepare scalp and hair conditioners, and practiced various techniques on "dummy hair." Seniors continued to practice what they had learned earlier by working on each other's hair or on volunteers. Seniors also learned hair styling and various ways of setting hair such as pressing, marcelling, and pin curling. Franklin also introduced students to hair coloring at the senior level. Although students learned to trim hair, African American schools did not teach hair styling through cutting as part of the course leading to an operator's license. This training was basic to the programs of white schools as bobbed hair became the norm among European-American women after 1930. Basic instructional techniques changed little from the 1930s through the 1950s. In addition to the beautician's course, the Franklin School offered courses leading to the manicurist's and beauty instructor's licenses. Refresher courses and advanced hairdressing were also offered, but the school's revenues came overwhelmingly from training aspiring candidates for the operator's license.

While hair care did not require highly advanced skills or abilities, students did have to demonstrate determination, attention to detail, and discipline in order to complete their training. At Franklin a student's passage from junior to senior status was measured by accomplishments rather than the mere passage of time. Juniors did not become seniors until they had mastered introductory skills, and not all students attended school on a full-time schedule. Students

Franklin students grooming their "practice hair" with heated irons, ca. 1955. Franklin Papers, courtesy Houston Metropolitan Research Center, Houston Public Library.

had to make up work lost during absences regardless of the reasons they had not attended. Thus the Franklin staff instructed students of varying skill levels simultaneously, yet students who could not maintain a high degree of regularity in attending class could not complete the course.

For the Franklin School student who satisfactorily completed her course work, licensing was almost certain. In many examination sessions no Franklin student failed the test, and a failure rate above one in twenty was rare. Franklin's high pass rate on state examinations followed from the highly individualized character of its instruction, meticulous review based on previous licensing tests, and J. H. Jemison's careful advising of students. Jemison strongly discouraged any candidate from sitting for the examination if she were not thoroughly prepared.

While state employees had difficulty completing their rounds of routine inspections of salons and schools, the cosmetology board more readily oversaw the process of licencing beauticians. Texas scheduled and administered two to four licensing examinations per year, a cycle that allowed beauty schools to en-roll multiple classes of students through the calendar year. Candidates for the beauty operator's license took a written test that covered issues such as sterili-zation of equipment, the operating procedures for equipment, and symptoms of diseases of the scalp. The second, or "practical," phase of the examination required the student to set hair, and in this portion of the examination students worked in pairs with one demonstrating on the hair of the other and then the reverse. No candidate could sit for the test without filing evidence that she was free of particular contagious diseases and that over a period of at least six months she had completed one thousand hours of instruction at a licenced beauty school.

The cosmetology law that Texas adopted in 1935 did not introduce race, but the Board of Cosmetology segregated licensing examinations from the outset and held women to separate standards by race. All African American women took the test together and women of other races sat for an examination held on a different day. African American women demonstrated their skill in straightening hair while examiners tested European-American and Mexican-American women in hair curling. By the 1950s the board also instituted pre-scribed beauty-school curricula that made preparation specific to the race of the patrons whom the beautician would serve. In notifying schools and stu-dents of racially specific expectations, the board did not state that African American beauticians could be licensed only to serve clients of their own race. Rather, it listed requirements that qualified a student to take either the "white" or the "colored" examination. The board's requirements did reflect the reality that beauty schools in Texas and elsewhere trained students to work either with straight hair or with very curly hair but did not really train students fully to do both. Whatever the past practices of schools had been, the end result of prac-tice in the Lone Star State was that the Texas Board imposed racial segrega-tion in the industry not only by administering separate examinations, but also by making the content of the examinations different.

Although the Franklin School initially advertised that its students learned techniques that prepared them for employment in beauty shops that served whites as well as in African American shops, Franklin graduates could not rea-sonably expect to launch successful enterprises based on a white clientele.[26] An occasional Franklin graduate found employment in a white salon, but there is no evidence that these beauty workers had been employed to admin-ister hair cuts or permanent waves. More likely, white employers limited their work to shampooing and other assistance. White schools did not teach exten-sively the use of lotions and other compounds to condition hair and scalp nor the use of heated irons to straighten or set hair, and African American schools gave little attention to the chemical curling of hair and the cutting and wet setting of hair that white patrons routinely demanded. While the Franklin School had initially promised to train its students to work in either African American or white shops, the training largely concentrated on working with curly hair. Because the state made no provisions for testing African Americans in permanent and cold waving, the school eventually abandoned its claims of preparing students for employment in salons catering to whites.

Although Texas held racially segregated licensing examinations, the majority of northern states administered uniform examinations to all applicants. Northern states with large African American populations did test African American beauty students on techniques and processes preferred by beauty patrons of color, but states of the Northwest did not. One Franklin graduate, who sought licensing in Washington, found the limp, straight hair of a white woman baffling. Juanita Martin wrote to the Jemisons from Seattle,

> Just a few lines to let you all hear from me, in regards to every things that you did to help me in school. The examination wasn't bad at all. Question was easy. Due to illness I didn't take Dec. but took Feb. Board. But I failed they said. And every question they asks me I answered. But they failed me in hair styling and white hair, of course. Which I had fix it much better before. But my first class was hot iron work marcel paper curl, croquignole curl, non curl and that hair wouldn't set. Straighten right out as tho nothing was put in. I still have another chance. I expect to take someday.[27]

Among Franklin graduates employment in the white trade came along only rarely. A late 1930s newspaper article on the Franklin School noted that one of the twenty-two recent graduates had gained a "paying position in a Houston white shop."[28] A graduate from Lake Charles, Louisiana, wrote Jemison in 1941 to report that she was preparing to take the Louisiana operator's examination and that, in the meantime, she had secured a job in a white beauty parlor as a masseuse and pedicurist at a salary of twenty-five dollars per week.[29] Five years later another recent graduate wrote from Linden, Texas, to say that she planned on coming to Houston in the near future and hoped that the Franklin staff would help her find a job in a white shop.[30] In 1952 J. H. wrote a graduate in Montgomery, Texas, to inform her of an opening in a white salon there, but the letter provided no specifics about the position.[31]

While beauticians did not necessarily earn the seventy-five to one hundred dollars per month that Franklin's advertising promised, jobs in the beauty industry were readily available in most areas throughout the 1930s and 1940s. The Jemisons hired the best of their graduates to work in their own shops in Houston, and they helped others find jobs in the city after they had passed their licensing exams. Through the 1930s most students from small towns returned home to practice their trade. Franklin students had entered their training with high expectations of establishing themselves in a trade that would earn the respect of the community as well as secure earnings. A 1941 graduate wrote that "I remain as ever a loyal Franklin student, one who is proud of my school, and my profession and as one who is doing some fine work."[32]

Franklin graduates took considerable pride in obtaining their beauty operators' licenses and in practicing the vocation partly because most hairdressers had overcome major obstacles in reaching the licensing examination. Mothers, fathers, and husbands sacrificed to send their wives and daughters to the school, but finding money for training was only one of the barriers to educational success. Despite the relatively brief training required for licensing, students faced a variety of personal and financial obstacles to completing their training. The youngest girls, those ages 16 or 17 years, and women who traveled to the Franklin School from outside of Houston often had difficulty taking responsibility for managing their independence and for maintaining the discipline that the school demanded. Although Lillian Mathis was 28 years old when she attended Franklin, the aunt who had sent her to Houston from Oklahoma believed she still had a lot of growing up to do. Lillian's aunt attached conditions to her financial support of her niece's education. Lillian had to demonstrate respectable personal behavior, to maintain steady work, and to perform well in school, and her aunt made her expectations clear to J. H. Jemison, writing

> Dear Sir:
> Since the weather is pleasant and Lillian has work near home, I'll not interfere at the present with her payts, will let her continue as she is; but if at any time she is out of employment or the weather is very bad and she rest for a while; instead of having her to discontinue school for non payments, please notify me at the above address. and allow her to remain in school please. I only want to help her if she needs help, but if she can get along O.K. her self, I'll let her make it. She hasn't ever had too much responsibility, and I think I should give her a chance to see what she can do for her self. However, if at any time you think I should come in and assist her, let me know.[33]

Virtually all Franklin students surmounted obstacles in following their dreams of a life of economic independence through beauty culture. The stresses of school overwhelmed a few Franklin recruits, and, although such occurrences were rare, some women had their studies cut short by death or disease. The student most likely to fail to graduate was the young girl who boarded in a private home in Houston, away from relatives and away from the oversight of the Jemisons for most of the day and night. A Clarkesville, Texas, father wrote Abbie Franklin Jemison in an effort to untangle the web of developments that had led to the mental illness of his nineteen-year-old daughter.

> Madam,
>
> Am writing this letter concerning my daughter Emma Dell Samuel, who has been a student in your school for the last few months, I presume. However, my daughter came home Sunday, February 2, in a very unusual condition. In fact something very unusual is wrong with her. I've tried every way I could to contact the people where she roomed. I am asking you, her teacher and any one there who came in contact with her if she acted any way like her mind was affected; she doesn't know when she left Houston, nor who carried her to the Bus or where her clothes are, or anything. The attending Dr. says its her nerves, but just what caused her to get that way he can't say. She hasn't slept since she came home.[34]

Abbie Jemison responded promptly and kindly to the father's inquiry, writing that Emma Dell had been a model student who demonstrated no signs of emotional fragility and that her landlady reported that the young woman had been "very obedient and stayed home when she was not at school." She concluded, however, that Samuel had been absent from classes for a number of days. Although a classmate and her landlady informed Jemison that Emma Dell had wanted to return home, the student had not made her wishes known to her teachers.[35] Emma Dell Samuel's parents retained an attorney who sent J. H. Jemison a second letter, correspondence that included a signed note from her physician diagnosing her condition as neurasthenia. The parents wanted a refund on the $85 they had paid for the complete course of instruction at the Franklin School. J. H. replied that Emma Dell had signed up for the full one thousand–hour beauty-culture course and that the school would welcome her back at any time that she was well enough to reenter her classes. When contacted by an attorney for the Samuels, however, J. H. Jemison offered to refund twenty-five dollars to mollify the parents, and they accepted the compromise.[36]

J. H. Jemison's careful management of all aspects of the Franklin business partly accounts for his success over the years. J. H., Abbie, and school secretary Hazel McCullough stressed cleanliness and order in their salons and the school, and their meticulous habits paid off. Beauty schools as well as salons were subject to periodic inspection, but with only one or two inspectors to cover the entire state, enforcement of the Texas code remained lax before World War II. The Jemisons strove to keep a sanitary and orderly facility and met inspection standards without difficulty in the early years. In 1938 a Texas inspector accorded the Jemisons "all a's," noting that Franklin was "a very nice school and so nice and clean."[37] A 1940 inspection similarly resulted in a straight A report. The school's 1945 inspection reported a violation of the beauty code, a beauty salon sharing the premises with the school. Jemison remedied the problem by walling up an opening that had permitted students, instructors, and operators to pass back and forth between the school and the salon.[38]

Because most Franklin students paid their tuition in monthly installments rather than all at once upon matriculation, student retention was important to the everyday operation of the business. Furthermore, referrals from happy graduates brought new recruits through the portals of the Franklin School. J. H. Jemison enjoyed immediate and lasting success in enlisting cosmetology students, but Jemison also attained notable accomplishments in retaining recruits until graduation. The costs of beauty training were not insignificant among the overwhelmingly poor families that sent their daughters to the Franklin School. Although the Franklin course could be completed in six months, students did not necessarily complete the course in that time as some enrolled part-time and others attended sporadically. Financial difficulties, illness, family matters, or lack of discipline proved barriers to regular attendance among Franklin students. Jemison kept careful track of each student, partly to assure that contracted tuition payments were made and partly out of the desire to help students achieve their goals. When a student had been absent from classes without explanation, Abbie or J. H. attempted to track her down. Almost all students who left the school offered an explanation for their departure and indicated their desires to return. Correspondence demonstrates that most Franklin students had already made a serious commitment to becoming beauticians, but for some women the obstacles were too great to overcome. After receiving a letter from the school one student replied, "I didn't have a fair chance of telling you that I had to stop going to school all because of my husband. He come after me so sudden not telling me fore he came. I am truly sorrie, and please let me know at once how much money I owe the school." Jemison penned a curt reply, "You owe $15 for February. The balance on your account is $100. We hope that you will be able to return soon."[39]

Family and financial complications sometimes prevented students from completing their courses. A married New Waverly, Texas, student wrote, "Mr. Jemison, I receive your letter glad to hear from you. Am sorry I can't return to school at present. My mother is still sick." She wanted to return to school when her mother's condition permitted, but poverty remained a barrier. She had hoped that she could get a position as a matron at the Franklin dormitory and obtain a part-time job in addition while she attended classes. Jemison wrote back that Franklin did not permit matrons to accept outside work, and he did not hear from her again.[40]

Because applicants for beauty licenses had to submit proof of their freedom from venereal diseases and tuberculosis, the school maintained a health testing policy, and students who tested positive for these diseases were dropped from the rolls. Jemison wrote a student who had left school after contracting a communicable disease, "Dear Miss Ransom, We have missed you from school for a long time. When will you get your negative blood test report? Let us hear from you."[41] The student replied promptly that she hoped to be certified free of contagion in six weeks, but Jemison never heard from her again, and his follow-up correspondence elicited no response.

While the Franklin School made every effort to recapture students who left before graduation, Jemison accepted the fact that some would never return. Where they had left bills unpaid, which was most often the case, Jemison worked diligently to collect fees, although he had few means to compel payment. In 1939 Jemison retained the services of N. F. Freeman of the United States Credit Bureau in an effort to collect monies owed him, but Freeman's results were disappointing, and Jemison did not subscribe for continued activities. Jemison largely dealt with delinquent accounts through correspondence, and he usually received a reply even though not all of his former clients would or could pay their bills.

During the 1940s Jemison received a letter from former student Gertrude Irving, who had left her account unpaid. Irving had not surrendered her dream although she had no plans of returning to Franklin. Irving outlined her career aspirations:

Dear Sir,

How are you? I am well. I am sure you have wonder about me. But after I had begin back to school I didn't still see much chance for my mother paying all of my schooling and room and board also I wanted to help myself some. So I had a very dear friend here in San Antonio she wrote me asking me to come over here and work and save my money so I could finish without any trouble. So I have apply for a de-fense job here which I think I will get soon. I also after being here for several days I heard that Miss Hick had open a school here. And I got in touch with her she is doing nicely here so I decided I would try to go here I wanted my hours transferred also I think I have in around 365.[42]

J. H. responded,

> Dear Mrs Irving:
>   Your letter of February 27, was received. You enrolled for a com-plete course in Beauty Culture and contracted for the same. We can-not make refunds, as the amount paid was applied on the complete course. It would be better for you to complete your course at this time, if possible. . . . You now owe us a balance of $66.50.[43]

When a student found it necessary to transfer midcourse to a school elsewhere, Jemison provided, at a cost of $5, a record of the hours of study completed at Franklin so that instruction would not have to be duplicated elsewhere. Stu-dents' desires to carry their hours to another school sometimes helped Jemison collect on back bills, but he was not so lucky in Gertrude Irving's case.

Beauty schools worked to establish loyalty because satisfied students en-couraged others to follow their path, and students might return for the nu-merous clinics and refresher courses that schools sponsored. To these ends the Jemisons took a personal interest in their students, encouraging them on a daily basis and striving to maintain a friendly and caring environment within the school. On the whole their philosophy succeeded in instilling student con-fidence and building an affectionate bond between students and the staff. The Jemisons inspired student loyalty through tradition as well as personal con-cern. Over the years individual classes learned school and class songs, partici-pated in student fashion and style shows, gathered for an official class photo-graph, purchased class rings or pins, and exited the school through formal baccalaureate and commencement exercises that featured staff and student addresses. Spring graduation ceremonies coincided with the annual reunion of Franklin graduates, a weekend-long affair that included equipment, styling, and preparation demonstrations and concluded with a banquet and ball. In 1938 J. H. wrote proudly to his sister Minnie and her husband:

> We have just completed our state wide convention and it was the largest in the history of the firm and quite a success. We also had our

graduation exercise at Antioch Baptist Church and there were 24 graduates to march down the aisle and they wore white caps and gowns and
they sure were pretty. Following the graduation we went over to the
largest dance hall and had our graduation party with Milton Larkins
14 piece orchestra playing and we danced to the wee wee hours of the
morning.[44]

Franklin instructors spent some time building up student expectations
about graduation and Franklin alumnae gatherings, and students often expressed their eagerness to attend commencement. Juanita Martin, the married woman from College Station, Texas, who later encountered difficulty
with the state of Washington examination, completed her one-thousand hours
of Franklin training in 1942. While the twenty-seven-year-old Martin eagerly
looked forward to graduation, she remained skeptical about the upcoming
May state examination that she planned to take. Martin wrote Hazel McCullough about her fears that she could not pass the portion of the examination
covering the use of electrical equipment. After consulting with J. H. Jemison,
McCullough wrote back advising Martin to keep studying at home but to wait
until July to take the licensing test. In early July, Martin wrote Abbie Jemison,

> I am feeling fine. Hope this will find every body all OK and ready
> for the finally days. I received my letter to day and that even made me
> nervous (smile) my husband want me to ask you If you felt that I just
> had to come back to school or could I go from here to Austin he feels
> that he has just about all the expense that he can afford. I am studying
> hard. And I do feel up in everything and if you could mail me the rest
> of the things that I need to work with and just what it will cost . . . and
> write and tell me who my pardner will be. . . .
> Ask Mr Jemison if he thinks I will be able to get a dryer, shampoo
> bowl, shampoo chair & 2 revolving chairs from Joyce that we was talk-
> ing on before I left. If not I wont build a shop but if I can I want to know
> what to do please.
>
> Juanita Martin[45]

J. H. Jemison wrote back and advised Martin to come back to Houston several
days prior to the examination in order to review. He promised to help her locate the equipment and supplies she would need to begin work, advising,
"When you are ready to get them, we will go with you to make your selection."
In early August, Jemison received a final and gratifying letter from Martin, "I
received my license on Thursday was I glad. I am working in Bryan with an-

other operator hoping to open a shop on Oct. 1. Will start building it on Monday, will let you know just when I will be down to get the things I mention . . . sure will miss you all."[46]

Returning home after completing their state examinations in Austin, students frequently wrote back to the Jemisons or to school secretary Hazel McCullough of their pride in their accomplishment and their gratitude to their instructors. As one former student wrote, "This is to inform you that, or I am sure you have heard I received my license, and how happy I am. And assure you that your patient instructions were so very much appreciated. I shall always recommend the 'Franklin Way as the right way.' Hoping to forever be in your memory."[47]

Among the Franklin graduates who wrote most glowingly of their affection for the Franklin School and its staff were women who had roomed in the dormitory during their training. The dormitory generated significant revenue for the Jemisons, but it also assisted them in supervising matriculants from out of town. The residential experience also built emotional ties among students and with instructors. While J. H. Jemison managed most aspects of Abbie's and his enterprise, Abbie bore primary responsibility for overseeing the dormitory and its residents, a task that required diligence and continuous patience.

An occasional student proved so disruptive in the dormitory that Abbie forced her to leave. In 1941, shortly before end of the spring term, Abbie wrote to Lillie Mae Oliver's mother about her eighteen-year-old daughter's misdeeds:

> We were both so busy last Sunday that we did not get a chance to talk, which I regret very much, as it would no doubt have prevented my writing this letter. Due to various circumstances that have come up, it makes it necessary for me to ask you to change Lillie Mae's living quarters. She simply will not follow dormitory rules. I have talked and talked with her, but it hasn't done any good. She stayed out Thursday night, and she told me that she had to go home to get money for her dress. You'll know whether she came home or not. That was Thursday May 8.
>
> Friday she bought a dress on Marian Esther's charge account, without Marian's consent. Mrs. Oliver, I don't want to cause you any undue worry, but, you can understand my position. . . . I simply can't have a girl doing things like this in the dormitory.[48]

Dorothy Whitfield similarly proved intractable to dormitory rules, and Abbie moved relatively quickly to send her home because of fear for the girl's welfare as well as out of the interests of other dormitory residents. Abbie first wrote Dorothy Whitfield's mother one month after an alarming series of developments in the teenage girl's life:

> Dear Mrs. Whitfield:
>
> I am writing to you about Dorothy, as long as things go nicely, I don't write, but, when things get out of my control, I have to write the Mother. First, Dorothy had a fight Sunday. She didn't start it, the other girl jumped on her and she had to defend herself. The fight was just two girls fighting, and was minor in a sense, but, the explanation of the fight brought out other things. Dorothy has met a young man since she has been here and I am not sure that she knows just how far to go with him. She has even prepared a meal and taken it to him at his rooming house. To my way of thinking, a girl of 17 should not do things like that. I don't know what you think about it. I do feel, however, that Dorothy is trying to do as she sees the other girls doing. Mrs. Berniece Myers is over the girls, and she said that Dorothy is one of the three girls that goes out the most. Her reasons for going out are always reasonable, as she wants to go to the Drug Store, supper, and such, but, after she gets out, she stays too long. Dorothy asked me to whip her and not to write to you, but, Mrs. Whitfield due to this boy situation, I had to see what you thought. She feels that you will take her out of school. I don't want you to, but, I would rather lose her as a student than for her to lose her good name. She is doing nicely in her school work so far. Please let me hear from you.[49]

Dorothy's mother answered Abbie immediately, agreeing with Abbie's view that her daughter should not be dating an older man or staying out at night and hoping that Dorothy would settle down to dormitory discipline.[50] Abbie, with Mrs. Whitfield's encouragement, set an 8:00 P.M. curfew for Dorothy and received her assurance that she would follow residence rules, but tranquility did not prevail at the dormitory. Less than a week after Dorothy had agreed to restrict her social activities, a fight broke out at the Robin Street house, and Dorothy was at the center of the dispute. As Abbie described her interactions with Dorothy after the unfortunate fray,

> Dear Mrs. Whitfield:
>
> I received your letter and had talked with Dorothy. She said that she liked her work and wanted to continue in school. So I set down

some rigid rules for her and was willing for her to remain in the dormitory and continue her school work. However, her young soldier boyfriend and this young man here that she goes with, had quite a run in last night, and I am sending her home. The young man's name is Sterling. He even threatened to kill her if she didn't come off the porch with the young soldier friend. I had asked this young man to stay away from the dormitory and threatened to place him under a peace bond, but, he won't stay away. To keep Dorothy from getting hurt, it is best that she come home with you until you can find a family for her to live with here, where there is a man in the house. Those kind of things are difficult when only women live in a house.

We are deducting $6 from the room rent that you sent, and giving it to her for her train fare. I am sorry that this had to come up, but, young girls can become involved with young men so quick, as Dorothy has only been here a little over a month.[51]

If Dorothy Whitfield ever achieved her goal of securing a beautician's license, she did it without future help from the Franklin School. Dorothy's expulsion terminated all contact of the Whitfields with the staff.

Parents frequently worried about their daughters' welfare in Houston and relied on the Jemisons to guard their safety. Parents expressed confidence in the Jemisons' oversight of their daughters but were usually reluctant to allow them to rent space outside the dormitory, as one series of correspondence reveals:

Dear Madam,

I received a letter from my daughter (Ernestine Martin) stating that she could not get a room in the dormitory. That she would have to find some thing out in town. If you can't find room in the dormitory for her I'll have to send for her. Because staying out in town and in just any old place just wont suit me as she has never had to do this. Can't you find a little place with some other girl in the building for her. Please try wont you. I do want her to stay and she wants to stay more than you will ever know, she says she is thrilled to death over the work and everything and the location was like a dream. Can you help keep or hold this dream by finding an opening of some kind in the building. I know she will get along better with her work if she is there with the students. I can't see how I can let her stay out in Town all alone if there's no way you can keep her I'll send for her. If she has made the down payment will you refund the amount paid or part of it what every you do will be appreciated (and thanks) maybe she can enroll later. I can get room in the dormitory in Dallas but Ernestine wants to finish from Franklin. Please let me hear from you I am worried about Ernestine as she has never had to stay out like this and with strangers.[52]

J. H. wrote back to Martin to say that they had found her daughter a space in the dormitory.

The dormitory enabled many students to attend the Franklin School, but the school lacked spaces for all who wished to room there. Occasionally Abbie took a young woman into her own home to work for her room and board or to stay with the family until a bed opened in the dormitory. Abbie agreed to take in Christine Moore but later doubted the wisdom of doing so. Christine's behavior prompted her to convey the following message to the girl's mother:

> I have been trying to write to you all week, but have been very busy and a little ill. I had the secretary write to you during the Holidays to see if Christine could stay with her Aunt until there was a vacancy in the Dormitory, as I was expecting company on my return and did not feel that I would have room for her. I was away when your answer came, so Christine and I returned at the same time.
>
> I didn't like it because Christine left for Christmas Holidays when she did, and I told her so. She left her clothes on the line, and her room dirty. Her excuse for going home was that she had a "funny feeling" . . . So I told her to have you keep her home until Friday when I had a vacancy at the Dormitory.
>
> Her school work is good and I have a place for her at the dormitory when she is ready to return to school.[53]

Out of familial concern, parents frequently wrote the staff about their children's problems and desires. In the fall of 1943 Sophia Maxie wrote Abbie a letter granting qualified permission of her daughter's wish to attend social gatherings outside the dormitory,

> I am writing you in the favorite of my daughter Ernestine. She is asking for permission to go to the dances. You may let her go if it is a nice place to go. You know just when she ought to go to the dances. Because she is in your care. I like very much for her to go to some of the

dances, if it's the right place to go. Sence you live in Houston and I live
in Eagle Lake you should know just about where she ought to go.

Maxie's letter received a reassuring response from J. H. that conveyed the
Jemisons' respect for family ties and acknowledged their *in loco parentis* role.
Jemison wrote, "We will permit her to go to some of the dances, that we think
will be all right. We shall be pleased to hear from you at any time."[54] Another
mother, Lillie Jones of Somerville, Texas, asked the Jemisons not to allow her
seventeen-year-old daughter to attend dances because

> I don't want her to go out at night as she is a miner she doesn't no
> the town city I mean I don't want her to get hurt please keep her there.
> And about the dances don't let her go. And where she goes or need to
> go I write you. Doris doesn't have a father only a mother and sister.
> I am trying hard to put her through any help you can give me I will
> appreciate it.[55]

Jones's fears for her daughter's welfare were not without foundation. A short
time later Abbie wrote to Lillie Jones asking her to find Doris another place to
live as

> She has become quite attached to a young man that lives near the
> Dormitory and he is a bit older than she. He is a nice young man, but,
> Doris is not old enough to cope with a man of his age. He took her to
> the movies Thursday night, and kept her out until after 12 o'clock. Both
> of them know the rules of the dormitory. He should not have kept her
> out, and she should not have stayed out.
> Then too, Doris says that she suffers with headaches and has to
> miss school one day a week. She feels that we are picking on her be-
> cause we are all ways calling her in, but, we are just interested in her
> doing right. She is a good student and she is smart in her books. I told
> her you had written for her to move, but, she does not want to move
> now, and I feel that it is because of the young man. Will you please let
> her know that you have made arrangements for her to move so that she
> won't feel that we are making her move, which we might have to do if
> she continues to break the rules by staying out late.[56]

Doris Jones proved a continuous challenge to Abbie. Under pressure from the
girl's mother the Jemisons had relented to her remaining in the dormitory, but

one problem followed another. Only three weeks after Abbie had written Doris's mother about her late-night escapades, she wrote again.

> We thank you for the $11.50 that you sent for the balance on Doris' kit. We have given the kit to her. We never did get an answer from you regarding our letter of March 27, in which we stated that Doris was disobeying the rules of the dormitory. She continues to disobey the rules, and she causes the matron much concern. She stayed out until 11:30 night before last. Often she checks out from school at 4 P.M., and she says that she is ill. We would appreciate hearing from you immediately.[57]

After Lillie Jones replied, expressing concern and promising to write directly to Doris, Abbie reported that "Doris is acting better now, but, if she disobeys the rules again, we will have to send her home." Evidently Doris had reformed her behavior too late because J. H. soon wrote the Somerville mother, "We are asking you to withdraw your daughter, Doris Jones, from our School to-day. Please send her ticket as she must leave the dormitory. Doris is pregnant, and her account is more than past due. We have kept her at a sacrifice and paid bills for her lodging and training, for which we trust that you will acknowledge and *pay*."[58] Despite Doris's difficulties in school and her mother's difficulties in paying for her training, Lillie was determined that Doris should return to school after the birth of her child. Because Jones had made several payments on her daughter's fees during the period that she was at home during her pregnancy, the Jemisons allowed Doris to return to Franklin. Doris applied herself to her studies upon her reentry and soon passed the licensing examination.

Together Abbie and J. H. had worked out interactions with students and with their families that ultimately benefited the school and also served student interests. Through their long lives together Abbie and J. H. Jemison also adjusted their responsibilities within the Franklin business to accommodate their own family and community responsibilities. While Abbie concentrated on supervising the dormitory and on her instructional tasks, J. H. pursued a broader range of activities, professional and civic lives assisted by Abbie's abilities to oversee Franklin business in his absence. Abbie participated in church and social activities, but she left professional and Texas politics to her husband. Never content to work on a single front, J. H. Jemison also worked during the 1930s and the 1940s to elevate the stature of licensed African American beauticians. Jemison's organization of the City-Wide Beauticians Organization combined his business, professional, and civic interests. Jemison assembled a group of beauticians in December, 1938, to prepare a list of additional regulations in the beauty industry that it would ask the State Board of Cosmetology to place before the Texas legislature at its January session.[59] Composed of Franklin graduates, the group originally consisted of nine members, including Jemison, and was open to all beauticians. Jemison presented the group with a draft constitution that they adopted. The City-Wide Beauticians Association declared

> Whereas, A struggle is on in all capacities of our civilized profession, involving all those engaged in the profession of Cosmetology; our Schools, Shop Owners and the Various Operators, a struggle which grows in intensity from year to year, and will work disastrous results to the toiling hundreds engaged therein if they are not combined for mutual protection:
>
> It therefore behooves the officers and loyal members of the Association throughout the state and the nation, to adopt such measures from time to time and disseminate such principles to the Legislature of our local states as will permanently unite them to secure the recognition of rights to which they are justly intitled [sic].
>
> We, therefore, declare ourselves in favor of the formation of a thorough Association embracing every trade in the profession of Cosmetology. This organization shall be known as THE CITY-WIDE BEAUTICIANS ASSOCIATION. The object of this Association shall be the fostering of a constructive movement in the encouragement of higher standards in the profession, and shall seek to elevate those so engaged, to the principles and its operations to an educational standpoint.[60]

Through the City-Wide Beauticians Association, which grew to a membership of fifty in the early 1940s, Jemison rallied beauticians to support measures calculated to improve their earnings and to elevate the status of African Americans generally. The group worked to further professionalize beauty culture by squeezing out untrained practitioners. Members individually sought to identify beauticians who practiced without a license, and they reported violators to the state board of cosmetology. The organization set out to document unclean conditions in some Houston shops that rented out individual booths and allowed unlicensed practitioners to conduct business on their premises. When the City-Wide Beauticians Association notified the state cosmetology board of these dangers in the industry, the board issued a directive to inspectors to pursue these issues as they traveled the state.[61]

The City-Wide Beauticians Association monitored legislative activities relevant to the beauty industry and sent a lobbyist to Austin to oppose a 1939 House of Representatives initiative to abolish the State Board of Cosmetology. Among the first items of business approved by the organization were resolutions that requested from the state more rigorous inspection of beauty shops, the appointment of an African American beauty-shop inspector, and the prohibition of beauty shops within private homes. When the group petitioned the Texas Board of Cosmetology on the latter two issues, the board's president responded that it had insufficient funds to appoint both a "colored and a white inspector for each region" and that it had no authority to ban home beauty shops.[62] At a 1941 meeting the City-Wide Beauticians Association again endorsed a petition requesting inspectors of color, and J. H. Jemison recommended that each member write to the cosmetology board to request an application to become a state beauty inspector.[63] At the end of 1945 Jemison wrote to the cosmetology board in yet another warning of the state's failures to protect customer and beautician welfare:

> Conditions in Houston are becoming somewhat dangerous in the rental of booth space in Beauty Shops. This condition is leading towards a lowering of standards, as set forth and ascribed in our State Laws, and the requirements set up by the State Board of Cosmetology. I am sure that you are familiar with these conditions in other localities. We also have a large number of persons opening home shops, and operating under one man's license in order to escape taxation, thus lowering standards maintained in larger shops. I feel that in a few years, if some of these conditions are not remedied, the standards of our work will become cheaper.[64]

The City-Wide Beauticians Association kept up its pressure for African American inspectors over the years, but the state did not appoint the first African American inspector until 1953. In the early 1940s the association also set standard rates ranging from $.25 to $1.00 for services performed by their members or in shops owned by members.

As J. H. Jemison's successes mounted, Abbie had remained an active business partner, but domestic obligations vied for her time. Daughter Anita, named for her grandmother, had been born before the couple left Chicago. Educating Anita in Houston proved a major challenge for the couple, both of whom had graduated from superior high schools in Chicago and both of whom had business ambitions that demanded full-time attention. At the end of the 1930s, Anita had been sent to school in Dallas. The separation had proved difficult for all, and in the summer of 1940 Abbie again relished the

presence of her only child, who was paradoxically growing up too fast but filling Abbie with pride in her maturation — Anita had returned to attend school
in Houston.[65] Eventually she would again be away at school, sent to live in 1944
with J. H.'s sister Willie while she attended Abbie's racially integrated alma
mater, Hyde Park High School. Meanwhile J. H. was in Chicago tending to
business and family matters in July, as Abbie readied Anita for the new school
year, cared for J. H.'s invalid sister Hattie, and managed the Jemison enterprises in Houston. J. H. traveled at least once a year to trade conventions or to
take care of family or business concerns, but he was rarely gone as long as the
one-month interval he spent in Chicago in the summer of 1940. In his absence, Abbie bore heavily the burdens of day-to-day business oversight and
family matters. July, 1940, proved particularly difficult for Abbie as Houston
suffered an intense heat spell, Anita fell ill, and house maintenance problems
surfaced. Abbie wrote immediately upon learning that her husband had arrived in Chicago.

> Dear Jimmy:
>
> I received your telegram and letter. I was so glad to know that you
> made your trip safely. I'm feeling just fine — but it's awfully hot here.
> The heat takes all my energy. Baby is not well. I'm taking her to the
> Dr. tomorrow. I believe she has a touch of malaria. I'm giving her 666
> every three hours and cough syrup. Her ears, eyes & throat are sore.
> Will write after she improves.
>
> Hattie is doing nicely. Hasn't been sick since you left. (I'm knock-
> ing on wood.) Everything is going along nicely. Business is slow. We've
> only been able to deposit $137.
>
> The state board examination will be Monday and Tuesday July 29
> & 30. . . .
>
> Mrs. Tennis called about some water standing under the
> house. . . .
>
> We all miss you.[66]

On nearly all matters, Abbie deferred to her husband's judgment, a habit that
exacerbated the stress of his absences. Reporting her activities, Abbie wrote,

> I received your letter yesterday. I had planned to answer right away
> but got busy and just didn't get around to it. It's still very hot here. Anita
> is much better today. But she had quite a spell of it. Fever was high for
> a day or so. It was not malaria, just a cold. Dr. Potter treated her. She's
> growing up so fast.

Floyd and I looked under that house on Live Oak St. — was alright Sunday. It had stopped raining for a day — but if it rains as long and as hard as it rained before, Floyd will dig a ditch to drain the water off. You know old man Jones put a new roof on our house.

. . . The bus company said that they would have to leave at 2 AM in order to get [to Austin for the licensing examination] at 8 AM so the girls want to leave Sunday instead.

Your arrangement with Mrs. Powell is rotten. If you pay her $12 a week she should work every day. She only took in $9.50 last week. She's off all day Tuesdays. She's a sop.

Jesse's doing well with her work and of course Mc [school secretary Hazel McCullough] is alright. Downtown shop netted $7.77 last week and Streamline $5.45. Is that good or bad?

Give my love to Art, Minnie, Willie and all the rest.

As ever your wife Abbie.[67]

J. H. wrote back immediately,

Just received your letter to-day and happy to hear from you and to know that Anita is doing well and every thing is well under control.

Now about Mrs. Powell, I know that she is not up to standard and that is why I prolonged there a week longer than I had planned to stay there. That place out there must have a deal of very careful management and she will not be able to handle it. . . . Now you tell Mrs. Powell to report to work each day especially when I am away. You may also make any reasonable changes that you may come about that may harm the business or improve it.[68]

Abbie wrote back a few days later to report that "money has been slow this week, Mc and myself are urging the students every way we can to pay up."[69] Abbie had completed the arrangements for the graduating students to travel to Austin for the state licensing examination.

At the end of July Abbie reported that the business had taken in $168 in the last week of the month, about $5 more than in the previous week and that "we're trying to make more this week." Abbie tried to convince J. H. to change his mind about refusing to allow Anita to take a summer trip to California.

I am sorry you feel that way about Anita making the trip. I wanted her to go some place this summer. You wouldn't take her with you and you could easily have done so. Pansy and myself want to take a trip and

Three immaculately groomed young ladies board the bus for Austin, where they will sit for the licensing examination administered by the Texas State Board of Cosmetology, ca. 1940. Franklin Papers, courtesy Houston Metropolitan Research Center, Houston Public Library.

by the time you get back Anita will have to start school as her school will start September 3. I really don't see any harm in her going. They will only be gone about 10 days, 2 weeks at the most, and I would like her to make the trip. You write me back and let her go. She wants to go.

Why didn't you drop Hattie a card too. Also drop Mrs. S. Arnold 1415 Sandline. I was out there Sunday. Her eyes are much better. She asked about you.

Anita has learned to ride a bike. She certainly is developing fast. Gets on the bus and goes any place she wants to go. (Just like her daddy.)

I'm rather tired — but is not from over work — It's so very hot — day & night. We sit up until it gets cool so we can half way sleep.

Baby and I miss you so much. We haven't had a watermelon since you left. When do you think you'll be coming home . . . ? Hattie seems to be getting stronger every day. She's doing nicely with her work. . . .

Write me back about Anita. Eula wants to leave Sunday or Monday. Ask Minnie what she thinks. It will be educational for her.

It's too hot.

I'm lonesome.

Yours Abbie[70]

In early August, Abbie wrote to thank her husband for remembering her birthday,

Dear Jimmy,

I'm an old lady today. Some old thing. I have read and reread your letter. It's about the nicest letter I've received in all my life. It made me feel badly because I had prepared a telegram to send you yesterday, but that was my evil day and I didn't send it waiting to see if you would remember. I don't believe you've ever forgotten.

. . . business slow.

Did you see about shipping the piano here? I'm rather concerned about Anita's music. I'm getting her ready for school. Mrs. Ross is making up little dresses for her. She's lots of fun. I'm so happy about her going to [private] school here this year. She's spending the day with Sigma and going to confession in the afternoon. I've put her on an a weekly allowance of 50 cents for car fare, shows, etc. You should see how she tries to stretch it.

She doesn't mind not going to California. She didn't know she was included in the plans until you wrote to her. Eve had been talking about it and Anita had wanted to go, but she didn't know Eula could take her. So I wrote you first before I discussed it with her as I did not want her to be disappointed.

P. F. wants me to go to New York with her. She doesn't want to go by herself. . . . So as soon as you return we'll be ready to go. We will have to buy Anita a ticket. P. F.'s taking me.[71]

A few days later Abbie wrote again:

I'm very tired tonight. Today was just one of those days. The students were very noisy, a bottle of 20 cal peroxide exploded, I fell down the steps and to top it all off the second bottle of 20 vol. peroxide exploded in Hazel's face. Cut her eyes and broke her eyeglasses into a hundred pieces. Oh! We were very excited around here for a while. I sent MC to the Dr. There was no glass in her eye, just her face cut. I stayed down tonight and made a batch of cream. . . .

I had Hattie looking for those formula books yesterday. She couldn't find but one. I sent it on. I finally found the second one. Guess it's too late now to fool with sending it. . . .

I'm putting another girl on the school work. The other kids played out. Then to Vonrille — needs the work as her WPA job gave out and she is too good a Franklin girl not to help out. . . .[72]

J. H. was about to leave Chicago for home when he received a final letter from Abbie. "I am rushing this letter to you before you leave. Do hope everything here is in order. I got so lonesome and blue last night I just had to shed a few tears. I was half sick too. I guess that brought it on. What did you do about the piano? That's what I'm writing about. Anita needs it. One here will cost plenty — even a used one. See about it before you leave."[73] With her letter Abbie sent a note from Hazel McCullough informing him that a man had come by the school to inquire about buying a property that he had been told Jemison owned. Jemison's August bills included a $50 invoice for a piano.[74]

Unlike most Americans Abbie and J. H. Jemison had accumulated earning power and wealth during the 1930s. They had faced personal and business difficulties during these years, but they had managed to move ahead. J. H. Jemison had broadened his links with the beauty industry nationally through the National Beauty Culturists League, and he had emerged as a leading citizen of Houston's African American community. By 1940 the Franklin School of Beauty was operating smoothly and producing a dependable revenue stream. In its first five years of operation, the Houston school had already opened new horizons for many young women whose hopes and sacrifices emerged in the letters that they and their parents wrote to the Jemisons. Abbie and J. H. had learned to balance their mutual devotion to family with a growing business. The Jemisons enjoyed a comfortable home and the accoutrements of middle-class life such as a late-model automobile, regular medical care, and a piano for their daughter. The 1940s and the 1950s would prove even more rewarding for the Jemisons with their income and their wealth rising steadily. The coming decades would bring many changes to the lives of Abbie, J. H., and daughter Anita. J. H. would emerge more strongly as a race leader in Houston, the school would continue to grow, and students would become more articulate about their career goals. Although racial segregation remained firmly entrenched in Houston through the 1930s, J. H. Jemison's responsible leadership in his business and his civic life was helping to build the foundation for the attack on Jim Crow in which he would play a part in the decades to come. The Jemisons approached the new decade with high hopes, not yet seeing the war ahead but also not imagining how their world would change in its wake and how business-minded, middle-class blacks such as J. H. Jemison would crack the barriers of segregation.

CHAPTER 4

Beating Jim Crow

J. H. Jemison and the Franklin School
after 1940

The Franklin School of Beauty of Houston had progressed so splendidly during its first six years that J. H. Jemison determined to embark upon a major expansion in operations. The growth that J. H. anticipated in 1941 would require larger facilities. As Jemison prepared to launch a hefty investment of his and Abbie's savings into his business enterprises, war raged across the Eastern Hemisphere. Radio broadcasts and the newspapers carried daily updates on horrors in Europe and Asia, but what Jemison felt most keenly was the hum of industrial and business activity along the coast of the Gulf of Mexico. By 1941 Gulf Coast activity had fueled commerce within Houston's African American neighborhoods to a level surpassing pre-Depression levels. The prewar boost to black earnings could generate tuition payments for prospective Franklin students.

In June, 1941, the Franklin School moved into spacious quarters in the Pilgrim Building, a black-owned civic and commercial center that was both more spacious and more prestigious than the Louisiana Street Odd Fellows Building where the school had begun. The Pilgrim Building also housed Houston's African American YMCA and provided meeting space for Phi Beta Sigma. Partly through his association with his fellow fraternity members, Jemison succeeded in buying into the ownership of the Pilgrim Building. His decision to invest in the building, a four-story office and meeting complex, proved one of

Franklin School of Beauty lecture in the Pilgrim Building Auditorium, Houston, ca. 1942. Franklin Papers, courtesy Houston Metropolitan Research Center, Houston Public Library.

his most important ventures, repaying him handsomely later in life. Built before the Great Crash, the Pilgrim Building stood as one of the most impressive and luxurious structures that had been erected through the efforts of African American capitalists. During 1930 Lorenzo J. Greene traveled the nation in an effort to raise financial backing for the Association for the Study of Negro Life and History. Writing from Houston, Greene recorded his impressions of the Pilgrim Building,

> the most beautiful, colored-owned building that I have ever seen. A fine, golden-colored brick building, triangular in shape, standing at the apex of West Dallas and Bagby Streets. It is four stories in height with a roof garden. Its interior amazed me, for here was a real attempt at beautification, such as few other Negro-owned buildings can boast. The very lifts of the steps were decorated; the walls were inlaid with white marble and granite. The elevators, too, were the roomiest and most elaborate that I had seen in any "race" building. There were stores, of course, on the first floor, one a white-owned pharmacy.[1]

Despite America's impending involvement in World War II, the move proved auspicious for the Franklin School and for J. H. Jemison. The new and finer facilities attracted more students to the Franklin School and allowed its classes to grow. J. H. became more deeply involved with other business and professional leaders of African American Houston through his daily contacts at the Pilgrim Building. Jemison's part interest in the building allowed him to depreciate business costs rather than paying rent, and at the same time he profited from other Pilgrim Building enterprises. In the postwar years Jemison managed the building, handling repairs and overseeing the operations of the Pilgrim Auditorium. Jemison rented out the auditorium, which included a concession stand, for a variety of private affairs and community functions. The owners of the building generally cleared about two thousand dollars annually from the auditorium.

A mere six months after the Franklin School relocated to the Pilgrim Building, the Japanese bombed Pearl Harbor, and the nation went to war. While Marjorie Stewart Joyner oversaw the Negro servicemen's center in Chicago, J. H. Jemison participated in civil-defense activities but kept most of his attentions focused on the same matters that had occupied him in peacetime. As always, J. H. Jemison kept his business head during the war, paying careful attention to his several investments in addition to managing the Franklin School. The 1940s did not pass, however, without vexing concerns on both the business and the personal fronts. Early in the war Jemison wrote his brother-in-law in Chicago regarding two of his concerns:

> Dear Art:
>
> Thanks for your letter and check with itemized statement, which is in good order. I think you were wise in filling the coal bin and getting your business in good order pending the crucial moment ("the draft"). I, too, am laboring under severe hardships, however, I haven't received any recent information regarding my change in status, but, I am not over looking the inevitable eventuality. Business is operating successfully, but, due to labor shortage, our business is slightly curtailed.
>
> I am keeping my fingers crossed for you, boy.
> Jimmie[2]

While management in the beauty business could hardly earn a draft deferment for Logan or Jemison, they had little to worry about. As married men in their mid-thirties, they were far from the top of the draft list, and neither would be called.

During the war Jemison continued his frequent visits to Chicago. The Chicago visits involved extended family responsibilities as well as business oversight. Writing in January, 1942, J. H. asked Arthur to ship an order of hair products and apologized because his business responsibilities in Houston had prevented his planned holiday pilgrimage to the Windy City. In 1944 Minnie wrote in eager anticipation of J. H.'s impending summer visit and to remind him of his extended family responsibilities: "I am so happy to know that you will be here soon. We will have room for you to stay here. I had planned to go over to Dayton soon, but I think I will wait until you come. I am sure you will go over to see Bee and Helen for a few days."[3]

The war years proved to be prosperous times for Jemison despite shortages in metal tools and in the petroleum products on which cosmetic manufacturers and African American hairdressers depended. Wartime shortages were more of an inconvenience than an obstacle as in 1945, when the Balfour Company notified J. H. Jemison that it could not fill his order for pins in time for the graduation ceremonies because the manufacture of army and navy insignia had delayed its civilian production schedule. The delay proved short-lived as Balfour immediately sent another letter assuring Jemison that his order would be completed within ten days. Although the Franklin School suffered a slight decline in enrollments and in retention in 1942, its net earnings exceeded the profits of 1941, the year in which Jemison had made a large cash outlay in moving into the Pilgrim Building. The Jemison salons and the school all turned profits, and J. H. benefited from a slight rise in rental fees that his several residential properties generated.

World War II had failed to distract J. H. Jemison from his ongoing commitments to building his personal fortune through educating women in the field of beauty culture and retaining the loyalty of his graduates. The summer of 1942 brought the members of the Madam N. A. Franklin's Association of Beauty Culturists together for their twenty-sixth anniversary convention. The Franklin program for the 1942 differed little from that of Walker gatherings of the same era. At some points the convention program demonstrated congruity with church gatherings. Song and prayer featured prominently among sessions devoted to lectures, style shows, and product demonstrations. The 1942 Franklin gathering demonstrated the impact of the war on African American beauty industry. As men and women of color entered into military service or civilian employment on military bases, the quartermaster corps scrambled to find supplies of the beauty products that African Americans sought. Major cosmetic firms in the United States responded, supplying the need in part and identifying a market share that they would exploit after the war to the detriment of African American entrepreneurs. At the 1942 Franklin convention the signs of industrial

PROGRAM
Madam N. A. Franklin's Association of Beauty Culturists
26th Anniversary

MONDAY, JUNE 22

Registration
Opening Song
Prayer
Introduction of Factory Demonstrators and Jobbers
Morning Demonstrations
    Facial and Make-Up
    Back Massage and Make-Up
    Manicuring
    Sterilization
    Hair Dyeing—Clairol

Lunch
Afternoon Demonstrations:
    Hair Dyeing
    Scalp Treatments—Wella Heating Cap Demonstration
    Finger Waving
    Marcel Waving
    Croquignole Curls
    Pedicure
    Liquid Hose
Night—Mass Meeting—Good Hope Baptist Church

TUESDAY JUNE 23,

    Devotions
    Roll Call
    Pep Songs
    Lecture, Mr. MacDonald, Tax Supervisor, State Comptroller Department
    Report of Year's Work from Delegates
    Doctor's Lecture
    Treatment for Diseased Scalp, Mrs. Bertha Raab,
    Nationally Known Scalp Authority, Parker Herbex Corporation
    Salesmanship
    Uses of Hair Attachments and Their Care
    Eyebrow and Lash Tinting
    Hair Dyeing . . . Roux

Lunch
Afternoon Demonstrations
Night 9:45
Hair Style Contest and Style Review
Convention Ball—El Dorado Ballroom

change were apparent in featured product presentations by the Wella and Clairol companies, two giants in the white-owned hair products business.

While the routine of the Franklin School of Beauty continued during the war years much as it had in preceding years, the international conflagration altered the business environment outside the school and inevitably touched the lives of its students in lasting ways. In the long run World War II so changed African American society that Jim Crow enterprises would eventually shrink to a mere shadow of their robust prewar presence. Through the 1940s, though, the continuous growth of African American beauty education suggested otherwise. The civil rights revolution was still in the distance. A few beauty-school students enlisted, and some followed their sweethearts or husbands in the military or migrated to civilian wartime employments elsewhere, but most stayed put until graduation. Many Franklin graduates followed the paths of other migrants who left the South during the war. During the 1940s Franklin alumnae occasionally wrote back to the school to convey news of their careers outside Texas and to obtain records of their schooling to submit for licensing elsewhere. In most cases the licensing requirements in northern and western states required additional training and testing before a Texas cosmetologist could begin practicing after relocation. The Franklin School received requests from graduates in California, Washington, Michigan, Illinois, Pennsylvania, New Jersey, and New York as they sought certification to continue their practices after migration.

All beauty companies felt some impact from World War II, effects that lingered after the war as business conditions continued to change. F. B. Ransom's son Willard, who would later manage the Walker enterprises, received training and experience in the army that prepared him to lead the company in later years. Willard was drafted into the army in June, 1941, and spent most of his duty time at Tuskegee Army Air Field, where he rose from the rank of private to captain and served in the office of the judge advocate general. Although J. H. Jemison never served in the military, he supported the war effort and responded sympathetically to the war-related fears of his students. The beauty industry, both white- and minority-owned concerns, emphasized in their wartime product advertisements both the patriotic contributions of female war workers and their desires to remain beautiful, and Jemison participated in the campaign.

Beauticians naturally turned their attentions to the concerns of clients who found their usual products in short supply and who found little time to devote to make-up and hair care. The industry took the needs of defense workers into account by suggesting hairstyles and beauty regimens best suited to the demands of the shop floor and the time constraints of working heads of household. The Franklin School acknowledged temporary changes in the beauty market shortly after Pearl Harbor and urged its students to be sensitive to the needs of their future patrons. As its first wartime graduation neared, the Franklin School asked three students to write essays on "Beauty for Defense" and selected one of the students to read her essay at the commencement ceremony. In the short run the war proved a boon to the beauty industry and to African American beauty schools. The Walker and the Franklin companies prospered during the war and would see even stronger growth after 1945. J. H. Jemison's taxable income dipped slightly in 1941 but recovered in 1942 and grew by one-third between 1940 and 1943. By the end of the war Jemison had more than doubled his taxable personal income, from $3,400 to more than $7,000.

Through their first decade in Houston, J. H. and Abbie were full partners in the business although J. H. made most major decisions. By 1944 the Franklin School had an annual enrollment of two hundred students, making it several times larger than the other two African American beauty schools in Houston and exceeding the enrollments of most similar schools nationwide. While most schools averaged a graduating class of ten to twenty students, the Jemisons strove to ready seventy students for the Texas cosmetology spring examination in 1944. The comparatively large size of the school required the full-time attention of both Jemisons. By the end of the 1940s, Jemison had brought the Franklin School to a reliably high level of performance, and he had built a level of community visibility that led to invitations to serve on political committees and business and community advisory boards. Throughout the 1940s health inspectors routinely awarded the school the highest ratings for cleanliness and order.[4]

In 1949 Jemison incorporated the Franklin School of Beauty, issuing fifty shares of stock to himself and forty-nine to Abbie, with one share going to Hazel McCullough Semedo, their long-time secretary. The distribution of stock at the time of incorporation symbolized formal passage of control of the business from Abbie, who had inherited her position and her interests from her mother, to J. H., who had headed the expansion of the business. From her mother's death in 1934 through 1948, Abbie had carried the title of president of the Franklin School. At the time of incorporation J. H. assumed the office of president, and Abbie became vice president.

J. H. continued to work through the City-Wide Beauticians Association to attempt to influence the state to maintain desired standards and added a campaign to limit state licensing fees, but the association also turned to broader political goals. City-Wide Beauticians Association members were also affiliated with the National Beauty Culturists League and with the Texas State Association of Negro Beauty Culturists (TSANBC), which had been founded in 1942. J. H. Jemison regularly attended state and national beauty culturists meetings, and he had broad contacts in the industry both through his associations and through the large number of alumnae that the school had generated by the 1940s. As Franklin graduates took their skills to a variety of places outside Houston, the prestige of the Franklin School also grew. Beauticians regularly advertised that their shops followed the Franklin Way. The 1947 president of the TSANBC was Jessie Mae Hicks, a Franklin graduate who had established her own beauty school in San Antonio.

During the war years Abbie Jemison maintained a teaching schedule and cared for her own home at the same time that she oversaw the dormitory. She could not meet all her responsibilities without the assistance of a responsible adult who lived in the dormitory. From time to time she also boarded a Franklin student in the family home to help with the housekeeping chores. The employment of a dormitory matron kept the residence running fairly smoothly and also assisted the woman filling this job in completing her beauty studies. Overall, matrons appreciated the financial support that their positions provided and took their responsibilities seriously. Irizella Mitchell, a dormitory matron and a mother, left her post abruptly. From her home in Corpus Christi, Mitchell wrote to explain her temporary absence and to ask for more time away,

> I am so sorry that I didn't get to tell you I was coming home with my son but I called Miss McCullough and told her to tell you that I was gone and I would be back Monday but if it is alright with you I would like to stay until the 11th. I hate not to be with him these few days because I don't know when he will get to come home again and still I don't want to do anything that isn't lawful and right I want to take the Board when the time comes I have finished the final examination but I know I should be at school but in a case of this kind I know you will agree with me that I will be sure and be back on the 12th.[5]

Franklin wives and mothers fretted over their loved ones during World War II, suffering from the separation and worrying over the dangers of military service. Abbie and J. H., as well as the school's other staff, demonstrated considerable patience and compassion with the dilemmas of women on the home front. World War II changed the ways in which the school conducted business, and one of those ways was that students possessed more latitude in behavior and in attendance than was normally the case. The Jemisons indulged Irizella Mitchell's need to be with her son while he was on military leave, and she returned to fulfill her responsibilities at the dormitory and in school. Within months Mitchell had completed her course and was again home in Corpus Christi from which she joyfully reported

I passed and I got my licenses on the 28th of April. I sure was glad to get them. My husband said if that old woman fail I am going to quit her (smile) he was so happy also my mother and friends. The Board was very easy and the Ladies were very nice to us. I almost knew we were all going to pass. I hope they all did pass. I want you to write and tell me what month and date we will march [in graduation ceremonies]. Also the convention, I want to come back to attend the convension and march so I will get my diploma. . . .[6]

One week later Mitchell wrote again about graduation plans, but she had weightier concerns on her mind as well, "Mr. Mitchell is leaving tomorrow for San Antonio for the army. I don't know weather [*sic*] he will pass. Help me to pray that he wont pass. I am doing nicely in my work. Money comes in nicely (smile). Give my love to everyone. . . ."[7]

Although Franklin enrollments rose steadily after 1942, the war drew some students and employees away from Houston as they followed their husbands or pursued higher-wage work in wartime industries. In 1942 the Jemisons hired Carrie Lou Jones, a Franklin graduate, as an operator in one of their beauty shops. At the end of October, Jones left for vacation and never returned. The following month Abbie received a letter from Baltimore,

Dear Mrs. Jemison:
    I am sorry I did not get a chance to call you before I left. I just had a week's notice to get ready. After I came here I could not leave Nelson, knowing that they may send him away any day.
    I was pleased at the shop. I was just beginning to build up my trade just where I wanted it. I hated to leave, but I thought I owe Nelson that much. He ask if I would just spend my vacation with him, but I got here he talks me into staying. I don't think I am going to work here. I am going to try and go to school while I am here. To take up a course in hair styling.
    I hope you will forgive me and understand. Thank you very much for all the nice things you did for me. . . .
    Love, Carrie Lou Jones[8]

An occasional Franklin student gave in to the call of excitement, comparative freedom, and advancement that she gleaned in the wartime economy. Twenty-year-old Gladys Feeney dropped out of her Franklin studies and migrated to the North as the prewar industrial build-up commenced. Feeney wrote to Abbie Jemison from Connecticut: "Tell folks this is the place to make plenty of money and I'm going to do my best to get my portion. Every thing is nice here no prejudice every man created equal except with cash (smiles). . . ."[9] Feeney wrote two years later to report that she had taken a job as a driller in a defense shop. Yvonne Kinnebrew, who had come from Homer, Louisiana, to enter the Franklin school, left Houston for St. Louis before completing her training. She soon had second thoughts and wanted to train for the beauty industry and pursue a defense job simultaneously:

> By me being in defense training I find it necessary to have [a record of] my hours if possible. I told you that I wouldn't need them, but I see different now. . . .
>
> How is your daughter getting along? How did she like Chicago? I bet she likes up there. I haven't got a chance to go there yet. They are wanting to send me to California on a defense job, but I think my adventurous mind should be prohibited until at least I have gained some profession that will be beneficial after the war. I wish I had finished there & then came here but I had never been away from home before & I wanted to come where my sister was.[10]

A letter from a graduate who successfully combined war work with hairdressing was more sanguine:

> Well I am still here in Sunny Cal. And also learning to like it very much but after all, I be back in Texas some day. Wages are so good out here and expences is so high until it is not even funny but I am doing fine work and also dress hair.
>
> Do you have any iron on hand if so let me know right way or save me a good pair pressing iron and write and tell me weather you have some or not and I can send you the money for them.[11]

Through World War II Abbie remained active as an instructor in the Franklin school and as overseer of the dormitory. In the fall of 1944 Abbie took Anita back to Chicago, where she lived with family while attending Hyde Park High School.[12] The family business absorbed Abbie's full-time attentions, but she regretted Anita's absence and looked forward to traveling to Chicago for a reunion over the Christmas holidays.

After World War II Abbie withdrew increasingly from the business to devote more time to her domestic responsibilities and to her social activities. The birth of the couple's two sons after World War II largely precipitated Abbie's retirement from teaching. The family changes greatly altered the rhythm of activity within the Jemison household, but they had less impact on the chain of authority within the Franklin School of Beauty. J. H. Jemison had emerged as a strong leader within the Franklin enterprises even before Nobia Franklin's death. Abbie had generally deferred to J. H.'s judgment in both business and family matters although she expressed her own wishes clearly and unequivocally in most cases.

Both Abbie and J. H. experienced major changes in their lives as the war ended. J. H. Jemison had borne the mantel of patriarchy from a conviction that family and work formed the centerpiece of a meaningful life, but the burdens of heading the family grew more numerous after the war. His obligations amplified as his two sons came along. Ronald (Ronnie) Jemison was born in 1948, and James (Jimmy) H. Jemison, Jr., followed. The birth of the boys marked a significant turning point in Abbie's and J. H.'s management of their personal and professional lives. Daughter Anita, who attended Howard University in 1948, had spent much of her childhood and teen years away at school, but Ronnie and Jimmy completed all of their primary and secondary schooling in Houston. Abbie spent more time at home than she had previously. She had retired from teaching altogether and increasingly left the running of the school to J. H. She largely withdrew from daily interaction with dormitory students, whom she had actively mentored and mothered from the 1930s through the war years. Yet Abbie stepped in to manage affairs in the business each time that J. H. left town to attend a convention or to take stock of the Chicago operations, although it had been clear since 1940 that business had become a burden rather than a joy for Abbie, with one or more young children at home.

The arrival of his sons also changed the daily routine of J. H., Sr., who clearly interacted more regularly and extensively with the boys than he had with Anita. In the 1950s, under their father's watchful eye, Ronnie and Jimmy began spending some of their free hours at the school or at one of the Jemisons' salons. As Ronald Jemison remembers his childhood, J. H. taught the boys to value hard work by seeking their assistance in a variety of tasks from making hair preparations to sweeping out the school after hours.[13] While Anita did not train in cosmetology, both sons eventually earned a Texas beauty license. The boys' involvement may have come from their having a different upbringing from their older sister, rather than from their predilections, for Jimmy did not enter the business despite his training.

The immediate postwar years brought new opportunities for the Jemisons as working women left defense jobs and as both male and female veterans sought vocational training. The Franklin School signed numerous contracts with the federal government for educational payments under the G.I. Bill after the Veterans Administration approved the expenditure of G.I. educational payments for instruction in barbering and hairdressing. The veterans who matriculated were older than the members of earlier classes, and for the first time significant numbers of students were men. Rising postwar enrollments required the hiring of additional staff. Because cosmetology training consists of the closely supervised hairdressing practice of students, beauty instruction is labor intensive despite its brief duration. One instructor might supervise no more than twenty students at a time as they practiced processes to which they had already been introduced. When students employed chemicals or operated heated equipment for the first time, instructors oversaw even fewer students. In 1947 the Franklin School employed three full-time instructors in addition to J. H. and Abbie, with longtime employee Hazel McCullough Semedo, who had recently married, continuing as school secretary.

While Franklin attracted veterans, its traditional outreach to high-school graduates and high-school dropouts did not diminish. When Robert Johnson entered military service at the end of World War II, he and his wife viewed his army tour of duty as the optimal time for Marjie Johnson to fulfill her dream of becoming a hairdresser. Marjie Lee Johnson traveled to Houston from the couple's home in Abilene, a west Texas town some eight hundred miles away, and completed her training while her husband fulfilled his obligations to the U.S. Army. Despite illnesses and economic hardship Private Johnson wrote the Jemisons faithfully to follow Marjie Lee's progress, and he dutifully sent payments to the school, occasionally borrowing to maintain the payment schedule. He regularly inquired about his wife's progress:

Sept 1, 1946 Service Company, 3d Student Training Regiment, TIS Fort Benning, Ga.

Dear Sir or Madam. ·

I'm mailing the school $26.00 to be applied to the account of my wife's schooling. Mrs. Marjie Lee Johnson. You may keep the receipt and give it to her.
Sincerely, Robert Johnson

October 7, 1946

I'm writing you in regards of my wife who is going to school there. First I would like to know just how is she doing in her school work. And next. What is this she has been writing me about being there until April. Which plan did she select 6 or 8 months. never mind to mention it to her that I ask. hope this isn't too much bother to you, in case of any

raise that may come such as room or tuitions or what not. Please feel
free to notify me before the first of each month.

    Robert Johnson[14]

Marjie Lee was a model student, and J. H. Jemison responded to her husband's inquiries. "Your letter was received. We are glad to inform you that your
wife is getting along nicely in her work. She gets along with the Faculty and
student body nicely. . . . She selected the six months course, but it will be April
before she can take the State Board Examination."[15]

    Weeks later Robert Johnson enclosed another letter with his payment to
thank J. H. "for the splendid job you've done, this far in improving her. From
the letters I get from her she has covered a lot of territory since being there."[16]
In the end both partners were pleased with what Marjie had learned, and Private Johnson conveyed the magnitude of the accomplishment in the eyes of
his family and friends.

    Dear Sir,

        I'm sending you $15.00 for my wife's schooling. Mrs. Marjie Lee
Johnson. as she is finishing this month but will be there until April.
how much would it cost for her until she leaves? I will gladly pay the
same. thanking you for all you have did for her. When she was home
for Xmas. every body went wild over her work. she fixed our mothers
hair. every woman that owns a ship [sic] there wants her. but what
makes her talk like a Dr or nurse now. She uses terms as a Dr do. I really wasn't expecting so much of a change in her she's so different, but
still a Christian. but some how something new has been added. but she
likes it. and I am proud of her. we all are.

        Sincerely, P.F.C. Robert Johnson[17]

In the weeks that followed Robert Johnson sent payments for the remainder of
Marjie Lee's fees, for the purchase of her class pin, and the rental of her graduation gown. To the delight of the young couple Marjie Lee passed the state
board examination and soon had her license in hand.

    826 Plum
    Abilene April 29, 1947

    Dear Sir

        I did not get to express my gratitude to you for my stay in the dor-
mitory and the interest that was showed during that time. . . . I received

my license Monday and expect to start work soon. I shall encourage
others to come that way.

    Marjie Lee Johnson

Eager to promote good alumnae relations J. H. responded:

May 1, 1947

Dear Mrs. Johnson:

    It was a pleasure knowing you and we enjoyed having you serve as
Matron of the Dormitory. We shall always think of you as part of our
official family.

    Give our best regards to your husband, and we hope that we will
get a chance to meet him in the future.

    J. H. Jemison.

While Robert Johnson scrimped to pay for his wife's beauty training, some
Franklin students had public assistance in completing their education. Jemison had long benefited from enrollments arranged by the state of Texas.
There, and elsewhere, the government played a significant role in supporting
privately owned beauty schools. In Texas from the 1930s onward, state funds
supported beauty training in individual cases of persons who qualified for public assistance because of a recognized disability. The official correspondence
between the school and the state's vocational rehabilitation services did not
convey the nature of the individual's handicap, but in one case from the 1950s
the prospective student wrote that she had been a victim of polio.[18] In 1956
alone Franklin enrolled nine students with state funding. For state-supported
students the Texas Educational Agency paid all expenses, including dormitory
fees for students who lived outside Houston. In the immediate postwar years,
the state paid $160 for tuition and up to $300 for housing and meals, a higher
payment level than most students paid. Veterans attending Franklin under the
G.I. Bill incurred the same charges as other students, a tuition fee of $100 for
the complete beauty operator's course and $57.27 in other charges including
blood tests, uniforms, tools, books, and supplies. Gross revenues for these students, the vast majority of whom were men, reached $3,500 in one year. Staff
of the Franklin School worked to retain its VA students through their courses,
but, with about half of the G.I.'s graduating, their success rates were markedly
lower than the students who paid their own way.

Both the Veterans Administration and the Texas office of vocational education enforced a level of accountability and standards that individual students paying their own way did not require. With the VA the negotiations for
payment often proved laborious. In 1948, at the request of federal officials,
J. H. Jemison sent the VA a government-requested notarized letter attesting
that the Franklin School was free of liens and wrote the VA office in Temple,
Texas, that the school had placed all of its graduates in cosmetology jobs. The
Franklin School submitted a separate contract for each student and then
billed the administration monthly for each matriculant. The VA, once it had
contracted to pay for a student, nevertheless balked when a bureaucrat found
an overcharge or irregularity, no matter how minor. The VA sent Jemison a letter notifying him that it had deducted one cent from his invoice because he
had submitted a bill that included a half-cent fee. In the future "kindly prepare
your bills in whole cents," the VA office requested. With regard to one
student's bill, the VA deducted $17.73 because "Our records show that this
veteran's training was interrupted August 31, 1946. You have claimed tuition
through October 3, 1946." The VA declined to pay the $5.00 graduation fee
that Franklin assessed of all students, a charge that paid the costs of diplomas
and gown rental, of hiring a space for the ceremony, and of providing an honorarium for the pastor who presided at baccalaureate and delivered the invo-
cation at the graduation ceremony. A few months later the VA notified Jemison that it had denied a request to enroll a student in a refresher course,
informing him that he would have to negotiate a rider to the general contract
terms under which the VA paid the Franklin School in order enroll "post-
graduate" veterans.[19]

The Veterans Administration escalated its expectations in the late 1940s,
complaining of inadequate toilet facilities, overcrowding, and other short-
comings. The VA conditions for student funding rose as the number of veterans applying decreased, and the revenue that the former G.I.s generated
hardly justified the improvements that the administration directed. Among its
1948 demands the VA required that the school publish a catalog detailing all
of its requirements; listing faculty, hours of operation, and course of instruction; and describing its facilities. Jemison did his best to create a catalog although the Franklin School had previously published only a flyer about its
programs. Again the VA required that Jemison swear before a notary public
that all information included in the proposed catalog was "true to the best of
his knowledge."

In time Jemison decided that the VA red tape outweighed its benefits. After Jemison sent copies of the Franklin catalog to the VA regional office in July,
1950, he received a letter from the office head charging sixteen deficiencies in

the school program. The printed and bound catalog that the VA demanded was expensive and did not serve the needs of the larger student population. By the end of the 1940s, the performance of VA students had declined sharply, with few completing the course. In the fall of 1950 the VA complained to Jemison that VA enrollees were not attending their classes regularly and demanded that the delinquent pupils be dropped. In the same year the government issued Jemison a long list of alleged infractions after a VA inspector visited the Franklin School. The criticisms ranged from the poor attendance of students to inadequate facilities and insufficient faculty. Jemison could not meet the conditions for veterans' tuition payments without considerable expenditures, and his experience with federal support did not justify additional efforts to satisfy the Veterans Administration. Veterans had proved less motivated than students who paid their own way, and the numbers of students seeking to enroll in the school through the G.I. Bill had declined precipitously after 1948. At the end of the year the Franklin School withdrew from participation in veterans' education.[20]

J. H. Jemison's detour into veterans' training had disrupted normal operations at the Franklin School. Poorly motivated students and the constant eye of the federal government over every aspect of the program distracted Jemison and his staff from the careful nurturing of the traditional clientele of the school. Termination of all federal contracts allowed the Franklin School to return to business as usual: low-cost instruction that prepared students with the specific knowledge and skills required to pass the Texas cosmetology examinations. Unlike other private African American beauty colleges in Texas and elsewhere, the Franklin School remained vibrant during the 1950s. While the individual schools in the Madam Walker chain graduated beauticians by the dozens in the 1950s, the Franklin School continued to turn out one hundred to two hundred beauticians per year. In the early 1950s beauty training entered the curricula of Prairie View A&M College and of numerous African American high schools in the state. For J. H. Jemison public schools' entry into beauty training presented an opportunity rather than a threat. Neither the high schools nor the college directed sufficient resources into cosmetology training to prepare students fully. Jemison attended occasional events at Prairie View and cultivated professional relationships with high-school principals and counselors during the 1950s. These relationships as well as nominal scholarships distributed to high schools enabled Jemison to recruit new students in the 1950s. Occasionally a high-school student from the farther reaches of Texas would write to ask for information, and Jemison would extend the offer of a scholarship, usually sending the offer through the girl's school principal. Dorothy White entered the Franklin program in 1955 after finishing public school in Cleveland, Texas, and in the same year Irma J. Little came to Franklin from Lufkin, and Neeva Baker entered from Lovelady, also with the inducements of scholarships from Jemison.[21]

The 1950s proved the school's most profitable decade as the Jemisons consolidated their efforts by phasing out the Chicago location. J. H. Jemison closed down the Chicago manufacturing operations, oversaw the preparation of hair products in Houston during the postwar years, and sold or utilized the manufactures in his salons and the school. Ronald Jemison remembers his father's mixing compounds in the family garage and instructing the younger Jemison on the formulas and techniques for manufacturing the oils and creams used in the trade. Through the 1950s student fees collected averaged approximately $40,000 annually with additional revenues of some $10,000 from the sales of textbooks, equipment, and cosmetic products. In 1950 the Franklin School of Beauty had a net worth of $28,590, and that figure had risen to more than $48,000 by 1958. The staff continued to increase, and staff salaries doubled between 1951 and 1958 as did the school's earnings. Executive salaries, the amount that the Franklin School paid out to Abbie and J. H., rose from $5,340 to $15,275 between 1951 and 1958. By the late 1950s approximately 8,000 African American beauticians were at work in Texas, and more than 1,000 of them had trained at the Franklin School.[22]

The Jemisons also continued to operate three beauty salons during these years. The salons generated earnings for the Jemisons, and the Franklin School provided the couple with the opportunity to identify and hire the most talented new cosmetologists. Dormitory income, which entered into the Jemisons' personal accounts and did not appear on the Franklin School's books, swelled the Jemison's earnings. Jemison charged $50 per month for room and board at the beginning of the 1950s, and the fees gradually rose through the decade. The Jemisons had bought a second residence on Robin Street in order to house additional students, but the total facilities remained small, accommodating about a dozen students. Nevertheless, dormitory proceeds added thousands of dollars per year to the Jemisons' gross revenues.

During the 1950s J. H. had begun to invest his business profits in areas other than real estate. He speculated in a small way in the stock market, generally buying into local or regional businesses. Among other investments, he held stock in the Good State Life Insurance Company and participated with a few other men in buying oil leases. As their businesses prospered, J. H. reached for broader community involvement.

In 1952 Jemison chaired the building campaign committee for the Bagby Street (African American) branch of the Houston YMCA, to which he had donated $1,000, and he served on the local United Negro College Fund. The

Graduates of the Franklin School of Beauty receive the blessing and advice of a Houston pastor, ca. 1952. Franklin Papers, courtesy Houston Metropolitan Research Center, Houston Public Library.

YMCA was one of a few organizations in which J. H. participated that led to his extensive interaction with his counterparts in the white community. In the summer of 1952 white community leaders, well acquainted with Jemison's "Y" efforts, invited him to represent African American interests in the countywide United Fund campaign.[23] Jemison's interracial activities did not carry the immediate promise of racial integration. Like most YMCAs and YWCAs elsewhere in the country, Houston's YMCAs remained segregated in the 1950s, but the governing boards of the local branches regularly met jointly, and in the early 1960s they paved the way for the end of segregation in their facilities. Jemison remained active in Y affairs through the 1960s, agreeing to serve as chairman of the Religious Emphasis Committee of the countywide Metro Board of the YMCA of Houston and Harris County in 1969. Jemison's younger son, Jimmy, eager to experience some independence, lived briefly at the South Central Branch of the Y in 1968, a room for which the elder J. H. wrote a check in November, 1968.[24]

Through his work with the YMCA and his support of the Democratic Party, Jemison had emerged as a thoughtful and articulate spokesperson of black business and of African American rights by the 1950s. Local officials invited him to attend a men's luncheon honoring Billy Graham at the time of his 1952 Houston crusade. At the outset of 1952, Judge Frank Williford, Jr., of the Harris County Criminal Court called Jemison to serve as one of three panel members to draw up a slate of potential grand jurors. Under Texas law, county grand jurors are not selected at random from the list of registered voters. Rather a pool of potential jurors are named by a panel selected by the sitting judge. At the end of the year Jemison wrote Judge Williford to thank him for the confidence he had placed in Jemison in naming him to the panel. Among influential African Americans whom Jemison knew through his Houston business contacts was Hobart T. Taylor, a Texas political activist and a graduate of Prairie A&M College. Also in 1952, Taylor brought Judge W. A. Morrison of the State Appeals Court to visit with Jemison regarding the court concerns of African Americans.[25]

Black Houstonians looked to Jemison for leadership in the 1950s. African American sportsmen turned to Jemison in a campaign to abolish racial segregation in city golf courses. In December, 1952, the Fifth Circuit Court of Appeals, pursuant to a lawsuit against the city of Houston, ordered the city to open its municipal golf courses to African Americans but ruled that the city might continue to deny whites and blacks the right to occupy a given course at the same time. The court decision followed from a complaint against the city filed by Houston's Mandell and Wright law firm in 1952 on behalf of a local citizen who had been denied access to a public facility in Houston, although he would have been allowed on the links alongside a white if he were employed as his caddy. Although not an active golfer himself, Jemison had supported the complainant and had initiated the lawsuit on behalf of all African Americans.[26]

Jemison did not neglect cosmetology during the busy civic year of 1952. He invited the presidents of beauticians' organizations throughout Texas to meet in Houston and plan a strategy to secure the appointment of an African American shop inspector. Lotte Bailey, a Dallas beautician who joined with Jemison in the appointment campaign, hoped that they might gain the assistance of the Progressive Voters League and of the Negro Chambers of Commerce in voicing their demand to state officials.[27] Within a year what had been for Jemison a fifteen-year campaign had paid off. The state named Mrs. Vadie Troy of Houston to be the first person of color in Texas to serve as a beauty-salon inspector. J. H. wrote Gov. Allan Shivers to let him know that the appointment "is gratifying not only to the beauty shop owners and operators, but, is a recognition to over one million disfranchised people who enjoy but little of the full citizenship and economic strength of this great state of Texas."[28] Jemison also

J. H. Jemison joins the ranks of Houston's leading African-American citizens as a member of the Business and Professional Men's Club, January 23, 1952. Franklin Papers, courtesy Houston Metropolitan Research Center, Houston Public Library.

wrote to the governor to recommend African American beautician Bill Stafford as a candidate for the State Board of Hairdressers and Cosmetologists. Shivers politely thanked Jemison for the nomination but did not indicate that he was considering Stafford.[29] The beauticians' victory in the inspector campaign did not last long. When Troy's term of appointment expired, the state replaced her with a white inspector, and it would be several years before another black woman served in the position. Cosmetologists' requests for the appointment of a black salon inspector did not challenge the lines of segregation in the industry, a tradition that showed no cracks. Rather, the beauticians had asked that an African American serve as the inspector of salons catering to an African American clientele.

Rather than moving toward integration, Texas reinforced racial lines in beauty training in the 1950s. Beauty-licensing examinations in Texas had been segregated since their inception in the 1930s, and the examiners had long tested African American and white candidates on different styling techniques, but in the 1950s the state initiated separate curricula by race in schools of cosmetology. In 1959 the Texas State Board of Hairdressers and Cosmetologists circulated its revised instructional standards for graduation from African American and white beauty schools. In a letter to Franklin secretary Hazel McCullough Semedo, a board representative set out the state's expectations.

Dear Mrs. Semedo:

We are happy to comply with your request by listing below the number of hours to be completed in each subject by a student enrolled for the Complete Course:

SUBJECT	TOTAL HOURS	
	White	Colored
Theory	240	240
Permanent Waving	152	44
Arch and Facial	46	46
Shampoo & Scalp Treatments	46	100
Iron Curling	0	164
Hair Styling	154	44
Manicuring	66	66
Dyes & Bleaches	74	74
Dispensary	100	100
Reception Desk	66	66
Optional	56	56
Total Hours	1000	1000

The above list should be posted in your school at all times, in order that the students may see it.[30]

The City-Wide Beauticians Association flourished in the postwar era and proved one of Jemison's most enduring legacies. Although Franklin graduates no longer dominate the organization, the group continues to the present to support its members, keep them abreast of new styles, and maintain industry standards. In the 1940s and 1950s the group raised money through teas, style shows, and dances, contributed to the NAACP, and continued to adopt resolutions that it forwarded to the state cosmetology board. In the postwar era the association amended its constitution by requiring that its members had to hold a current poll-tax receipt and by providing fund-raising for the support of political activities.[31] Through the 1950s his involvement in the City-Wide Beauticians Association and his national memberships in NBCL, UBSOTA, and their affiliates drew J. H. Jemison into a nationwide campaign to increase African American voting. Beauticians in Texas united in the Texas Beauty Culturists League, and the league joined forces with barbers' groups in the state to advance the status of African Americans in the hair-care industry and to fight for their political rights. In the 1950s hairdressers' political efforts focused on increasing the numbers of black Texans who paid their poll taxes.

In 1957 Jemison and a Galveston beautician mailed out flyers to officers of barbers' and beauticians' groups that suggested ways in which beauticians might assist in increasing the number of registered African American voters:

Dear Co-Workers:

The political action committee held its first joint Tonsorial and Cosmetologist Meeting, Monday, December 39, 1957, at the Franklin Beauty School. The two political action committees consolidated to give us more voting strength. In unity there is strength. The main objective of this meeting is to urge every barber and beautician to buy your *poll tax*. Secondly to pass on to every person whom you contact of voting age to buy their poll tax.

This committee is asking that you use any means or ideas to get the *"Buy Your Poll Tax"* campaign moving. Here is what we are asking that you do at once, call a special meeting of all barbers and beauticians in your city, inform them of the campaign, ask each one to cooperate. It is most important.

By all means do so at once. January is the only month left to get your poll tax. January 31 is the deadline.

You know how to get quicker and better response than this committee in your locality. Here are a few suggestions that might be helpful. First start in the shops, urge each patron to buy his or her poll tax, you might also send representatives to the various churches, or you may contact some large concern and have them sponsor a *poll tax dance*. Admission poll tax receipt, or a party of the same nature. Try to get substitute poll tax writers. You may have better ideas, use them, get the ball rolling is the important thing.[32]

J. H. Jemison continued his political activities with the strength of the City-Wide Beauticians Association behind him. In the 1960 election Jemison and his cochair of the Texas beauticians' and barbers' political action committee reminded men and women in the trade that "1960 is the biggest election year in Texas history. By having your poll tax receipt our group in Texas will be in a position to strike a blow against bigotry, segregational economic bias and second class citizenship."[33]

Despite the persistence of segregated practices, African American and white beauticians in Texas recognized that they had mutual interests. African American and white beauticians had a vested interest in suppressing the activities of unlicensed hairdressers who undercut prices. After World War II, as the state moved toward fuller enforcement of cosmetology laws and toward in-

creasing the costs of doing business, white beauticians and their teachers in
Texas wished to join forces with their African American counterparts in op-
posing some of the changes that the state attempted. The logic of cooperation
was clear; beauty colleges hardly constituted a powerful lobby, and segregation
further divided their strength. At the time there were approximately forty white
beauty schools and twenty African American schools in the state.[34]

After it had initiated state licensing of beauty schools in the 1930s, Texas
added a requirement that school operators post a bond of five thousand dollars, to be forfeited in the event of code violations or criminal activities. In its
1960–61 session the Texas legislature considered a bill to increase the bond to
twenty thousand dollars. J. H. Jemison sent out letters announcing an Austin
meeting of persons of color at which an African American liaison to the white
association would report on the legislative threat and strategies for defeating
it. At a subsequent meeting the representatives of the State Board of Cosmetology met with a biracial gathering and agreed to withdraw their request
for the bond increase. Beauty-school owners had succeeded in defeating the
bond change by cooperating across racial lines, and the lesson learned did not
evaporate.[35]

The Beauty School Owners Association of Texas, an interracial group
hastily assembled to fight the bond increase, did not immediately disband
thereafter. At one meeting, Jack Warden, president of the all-white Texas
Beauty Schools, Inc., warned that if white and African American groups
merged, the Board of Cosmetology would institute new standards that would
force the African American schools to change and that the costs would be pro-
hibitive, forcing the minority schools to close. Mrs. U. V. Christian, who had
already represented the case of African American schools before white owners, rose in defense of her colleagues, saying that she had never before heard
that white schools were held to higher standards than those applied to African
American operations. When one member of the Texas Beauty Schools asked
if African Americans had their own state organization, Christian, who had
been named vice president of the Beauty School Owners Association of Texas,
responded that the African American business people understood that their
strength lay in joining with white school owners and that African American
owners had committed themselves to the new organization. One white owner
emphasized that "there is no room for two associations" and attempted to
counter fears that individual schools would integrate, claiming that "there are
two types of hair involved and it takes different techniques." Participants in the
meeting agreed to a subsequent session to consider a permanent merging of
the two groups of owners, but the building of a lasting biracial organization did
not occur until segregation ended later in the decade.[36]

J. H. Jemison joins Marjorie Stewart Joyner in leaving a floral tribute at the statue of Toussaint L'Ouverture in Haiti during the 1952 UBSOTA trip. Franklin Papers, courtesy Houston Metropolitan Research Center, Houston Public Library.

Although civic commitments, Texas cosmetology activities, and the Franklin School all competed for Jemison's attention throughout the 1950s, he regularly attended national gatherings of the United Beauty School Owners and Teachers Association. In 1952 Jemison took a break from his many local responsibilities and attended the annual assembly. That year the UBSOTA meetings were held in Miami and in Port-au-Prince, Haiti. Mary McLeod Bethune accompanied the school owners on the Haiti trip, and the group undertook discussions of the comparative impact of segregation on the schooling of blacks in the United States and Haiti.

Jemison also attended the 1954 UBSOTA meeting, the most ambitious undertaking to date of this group that Marjorie Stewart Joyner had founded and dominated. Those who signed on for the full convention assembled in New York for several days of clinics and meetings and then sailed for Paris aboard the SS *United States*. Delegates on the European trip visited beauty shops in London, Paris, and Rome, where they observed demonstrations of the latest styles in hair fashion. Jemison returned to Houston to find a letter from his sister in Hattiesburg, Mississippi, who chastised him for not writing her. She asked him for a small loan to tide the family over until one of them succeeded in landing a job.[37]

While J. H. Jemison's world broadened, Abbie's realm narrowed and she only rarely ventured outside Texas. Abbie continued to focus first on family concerns during the 1950s, deferring to J. H.'s judgment but expressing her views on the personal side of their concerns. When J. H. traveled to the Mayo Clinic for some medical tests in 1958, Abbie stayed behind to care for the business as well as the family. A late night-letter to J. H. from Abbie reflected both the warmth of their family bonds and Abbie's acceptance of dual responsibilities in J. H.'s absence:

Sat-10:15 P.M.
Hi Pop:
I had to start our letter tonight will finish tomorrow. Had the school cleaned today. . . . I wrapped orders and mailed them.

The boys went to the theater this afternoon. Saw a nice play.

Anita is fine. Heard from her today. Jim, Jr. is in a *mood*. Just can't take Ronnie having to go to the hospital. Ronnie? He's all set. Had his throat blessed yesterday — new pajamas & house shoes — he's happy. . . .

Sunday:
Been up since 5 — cooked. It's so hot & no fan. I think not having a fan is better on Ronnie. Mrs. Mimms & her children will have dinner with us. She's so nice to our kids.

I'll get Ronnie in the hospital this afternoon. Mrs. Grant will spend Monday night with him. We're ok Papa — Pray for Ronnie & all of us. I can hold the fort one more week.

8:10AM. Have to wake the kids so they can go to church.

All my love, Abbie[38]

Although the Jemisons attended a Baptist church, Ronnie and Jimmy attended St. Ann's Roman Catholic school across the street from their home as had Anita before them. Before Ronnie had his tonsils removed, Abbie asked the priest at St. Ann's to invoke God's blessing on the young boy. Soon after Ronnie had recovered from his tonsillectomy, Abbie took the boys to California to visit Anita, who had settled in the West after her marriage to dentist George Sheffield. During the family visit, George cleaned and filled the boys' teeth and took them on a fishing trip. The highlight of the visit was a family trip to Disneyland. In writing of the adventure, Abbie asked J. H. to send her $100 so that she would not run out of cash before the return home.[39]

While Abbie devoted herself to family, J. H. Jemison minded economic interests. Flush with the successes of the postwar decade, J. H. prepared to launch a major school expansion at the end of the 1950s. In 1961 the Franklin School moved to new headquarters at 3402 Dowling Street, a building that Jemison purchased and configured especially for the needs of beauty instruction. The Dowling Street facility, 7,500 square feet in size, more than doubled the school's space and featured well-equipped practice rooms. The location on the North Side of Houston had long been a vibrant community, and the Jemisons had operated a salon on Dowling Street from the 1940s onward. In the short run the move boosted the school's fortunes. For the first time Franklin had its own building with commodious facilities, and the new location added visibility to the enterprise. In the early 1960s cosmetology remained an attractive career opportunity for women of color from varying economic backgrounds despite changing fashion, and J. H. Jemison looked optimistically toward continued growth. Business continued to be strong, but Franklin's new venue did not attract the expansion of enrollments that Jemison had anticipated or that would have justified the expenses entailed. Along with the rest of the South, Houston was changing in ways that did not benefit the Franklin School of Beauty.

The demise of Jim Crow was at hand. Cracks in the walls of segregation had already appeared with the *Brown v. Board of Education* school-desegregation court ruling of 1954. Despite his long-time advocacy of civil rights for persons of color, Jemison did not foresee the ways in which progress would transform black America. The integration of public schools and colleges would soon open many more occupations to African American women and present an unprecedented challenge for the Franklin School. Jemison faced other changes as well. Newspapers had been a major source of paid advertising and free publicity for the Franklin enterprises, but in Houston and in the nation, newspaper readership was declining. In search of students J. H. cast about for new advertising venues. He sponsored the broadcasts of an African

Eager students board a bus in front of the Franklin School of Beauty to make the trip to Austin for the licensing examination, ca. 1960. Franklin Papers, courtesy Houston Metropolitan Research Center, Houston Public Library.

American preacher over a black-owned radio station and purchased advertising spots on stations KCOH and KHUL. The greater Houston audience heard from broadcast announcers,

> Ladies if you would like to be a beautician, the place to go now is Franklin Beauty School. We are happy to have established larger and most modern facilities for properly trained beauticians in all phases of the beauty profession and we plan to bring the most outstanding hair stylists to keep our graduates up to date in the latest trends in styling. Tuition can be arranged on easy payment plan. Franklin Beauty School's new location is 3402 Dowling Street. Phone Jackson 61056. And don't forget dormitory accommodations for out of town students.[40]

Jemison took his recruitment campaign to places where he thought prospective students would be. He posted announcements at Continental Bowling Lanes and purchased on-screen announcements at local movie theaters including the Deluxe, the Jensen, the Park, and the Chocolate Bayou

Drive-In.[41] Jemison carried his message to African American high schools throughout the state, a campaign that proved modestly successful. In 1964 he made the 250-mile round-trip drive to the Texas town of Hearne to address students at Blackshear High School at the annual career day assembly, a talk he repeated at the overwhelmingly black high schools in the greater Houston area. School classes were invited to make a field trip to the Franklin Beauty School. He wrote to school principals asking them to select one or two students to receive $25 scholarships to Franklin toward payment of the $136.40 tuition then charged for the six-week course. Through the 1960s J. H. regularly visited Houston area high schools partly to recruit students, but also to offer career counseling and encouragement. Active recruiting in high schools failed to generate high numbers of new beauty students.[42]

In 1965 The Franklin School celebrated its fiftieth anniversary, having dated its origin from Nobia Franklin's first instructional activities. A letter from J. H.'s sister Willie, who had come to Houston for the festivities, notes the national attention that the anniversary received and also witnesses J. H.'s ongoing attention to family matters:

Hi Brother dear,
    I should have written earlier to thank you for making it so pleasant for me while I was there. Abbie and Ronnie too.
    I received the thank you note and pictures, they were very good. Ronnie looked handsome so did you.
    I was happy and proud of the fact that I could come to the Golden Anniversary of Franklin Beauty School and it was great being with the family.
    Robert was overjoyed to hear that you would like for Jimmy to spend some time with him this summer. He said by all means and be sure to have him come. All of us are expecting him and making plans for his comfort.
    I know you will enjoy the graduations try to stop by here on your return trip. The weekend of May 22 your picture and a write up of the week long celebration was in the Chicago Defender. Good looking picture of you and nice write up.
    Let me hear from you soon.
    Lovingly your sister,
    Willie[43]

The Franklin's golden jubilee trumpeted lifetime achievements in the Franklin and Jemison families, but it also marked the end of the beauty

J. H. Jemison congratulates the queen, the king, and their court of attendants at a Franklin alumni ball, ca. 1965. Franklin Papers, courtesy Houston Metropolitan Research Center, Houston Public Library.

school's best years. J. H. Jemison's vigorous recruitment and advertising efforts of the 1960s succeeded in sustaining but not increasing enrollments. The school continued to operate in the black, but nationwide the fortunes of beauty schools had faded. The African American market for beauty services continued to thrive, but stricter beauty education standards were on the horizon. For the poorest of African Americans, the unlicensed practice of hairdressing had never been fully eradicated, and rising standards, and the costs and time in preparing to meet them, added new incentive for women to practice without certification. Changing hairstyles and the replacement of heated irons and straightening combs with easier-to-use hair-relaxing lotions in the 1950s had encouraged the untutored to strike out on their own. Simpler to manage styles such as the Afro also made home hair styling again attractive, after it had declined in the 1930s and 1940s.[44] The newer hair-care products boosted the fortunes of unlicensed beauticians whom the City-Wide Beauticians Association and state inspectors had never totally suppressed. In addition to changes within the beauty industry, the civil rights movement delivered new opportunities to African Americans. Rates of high-school completion had risen gradually throughout the first six decades of the twentieth century. Community colleges emerged, burgeoning at the end of the 1960s and presenting all Americans with a broad array of vocational-training opportunities in which African American women might now compete with white women.

Although it was not the Jemisons' main source of income in the 1960s, the Franklin School continued to make money, and the Jemisons remained proud of the institution they had built. J. H. regularly carried between ten thousand and fourteen thousand dollars in the Franklin checking account and never had to seek loans or mortgages on his property to keep the school operating. Despite the fine facilities of the Dowling Street facility, Jemison had erred in moving there. The neighborhood suffered precipitous serious decline at the end of the decade, with the school's location becoming a disadvantage in recruiting students. Jemison's Dowling Street properties lost value, and J. H.'s son later moved the Franklin School to Houston's South Side. Enrollments dwindled in the 1970s as African American women's career options diversified, but the Franklin School held on and remained viable. Years later cosmetology moved out of both the university and high-school settings and into community colleges. These changes put many beauty schools out of business, but the Franklin School persisted through a strong reputation established by J. H. Jemison's leadership and through Jemison's persistent attention to detail.

Houston had changed in many ways during the 1950s and the 1960s. While this did not bode well for the Franklin School at the end of the 1960s, the Jemisons did benefit financially from the city's growth. During the 1950s the city of Houston and the Texas Department of Transportation initiated major road-improvement and road-building projects in Houston. One of these projects eradicated large portions of the Fourth Ward business district and necessitated the demolition of J. H. Jemison's two houses on Robin Street, where generations of Franklin students had resided. When the city moved to purchase the Robin Street properties, J. H. retained an attorney to obtain top dollar for the properties. The city made a final offer of $26,554.50 for the parcel, which had appraised at $20,500 in 1958. Thinking there might still be room for negotiation, Jemison did not sign the purchase agreement but sent his attorney to condemnation proceedings, a decision that cost him both attorney's fees and court costs and resulted in a final settlement of $26,658.84 paid in November, 1961. While J. H. had to locate other space for the Franklin dormitory, sale of the Robin Street houses had netted a considerable sum from capital gains. In the early 1960s J. H. and Abbie Jemison's gross income from all sources increased dramatically. By the close of the 1950s the Jemisons' income had risen to $195,000. In 1962 the Pilgrim Building was sold, and total revenues coming into Jemison's several accounts reached $418,000, including the $151,000 that represented Jemison's share of the Pilgrim proceeds. By the end of the 1960s Jemison owned or had owned thirteen pieces of property in Houston. Over the years Jemison had collected about $8,000 annually on the rental of some of his residential properties apart from the dormitory fees. In January, 1970, Jemison deposited a check for $109,154.04 to Texas National Bank of Commerce, the proceeds from a matured certificate of deposit.[45]

The 1960s were years of important transition for Abbie and J. H. as their lives and those of their children entered new stages. The senior Jemisons had begun to feel the effects of aging, and both had brief hospitalizations in these years. In 1960, as a gift to their adult daughter and a sign that a new generation would enter the business, J. H. transferred ownership of the 3361 Indiana Avenue building to Anita. After her three children had entered school, Anita returned to college in an effort to earn her baccalaureate. The young mother juggled schoolwork with the many tasks of homemaking, child rearing, and occasional assistance at her husband's dental office. As she neared the end of a college term in the summer of 1966, Anita wrote to her parents of ongoing family activities and concerns.

> Hi,
>
> [I] am busy studying for finals on Wednesday and writing a term paper I present on the cultural development of the U.S. from 1776 to 1830 and all that Jazz. I hope Jimmie & Ronnie will not be called to this great imperialist war for the people — Vietnam (Smiles).
>
> [Bud] is waiting to post this for me — he is now an enthusiast over his insect collection. There are jars everywhere with plastic & alcohol all over the place. I had to get him a chess table, chessmen, and an aquarium to keep him from bugging me.
>
> Gayle is fine and very mature for her age. Tommie is taking swimming for one month. . . — great fun for all of us — we're going to slow down soon and rest — I hope — I'm so tired but will take a 4 week course beginning Aug 8 at San Jose — I will complete 2 courses on Aug. 4.
>
> Love, Anita[46]

Ronald went off to Fisk University in Nashville, returning to the University of Houston to complete his college studies. J. H felt that his younger son, who was eager to get out of the house, might also benefit from a change of scenery, and he considered sending Jimmy to stay with his sister and her husband in Chicago. In the end father and son settled for Jimmy's enrollment in

Texas Southern University, where J. H., Sr., served as a trustee, and a brief period of residence at the Y.M.C.A.

Jemison's public roles in the 1960s contrasted with his gradual withdrawal from the daily concerns of the Franklin school. Through the 1960s, as he groomed Ronald to assume leadership of the Franklin School, Jemison continued to support political and civic causes of interest to African Americans. In the late sixties he sat on the Board of Directors of the Houston Urban League, which he also supported financially. He maintained a working relationship with Mayor Louie Welch and did not hesitate to offer advice to the mayor when he had a cause or candidate to support. In 1967 Mayor Welch named Jemison an election judge in the city. In the same year Jemison attended a luncheon at the private and formerly segregated Houston Club in honor of George Champion, then chairman of the Board of Directors of Chase Manhattan Bank. When a member of the Houston city council resigned in 1968, Jemison drafted a telegram to the mayor advising him to appoint Judson W. Robinson, Jr., a partner in an African American realty firm and an individual who "would meet a minimum resistance because of his background in political and civic arena. . . . In view of the racial and political tension in our city and nation, this could be a rewarding step to keep Houston well out in front." The biggest change that visited Houston in the 1960s, as Jemison's letter to Welch suggests, was integration in business as well as in public schools and accommodations. Perhaps because of his moderation but also because of his strong history of civic leadership and his sizable economic holdings, white Houstonians frequently called on J. H. Jemison to be an agent of racial change. In March, 1970, J. H. received a reminder of the regular monthly meeting of the Board of Directors of Standard Savings Association and was advised to "be present and on time." Jemison wrote back resigning his place on the board, explaining that he needed to "reduce my activity to further safeguard my health." The time had come to withdraw from his remaining business and civic commitments.[47]

As Ronald and Jimmy had passed through their adolescence and rocketed toward adulthood, their youthful adventures sometimes taxed parental patience. In March, 1969, J. H. paid for auto repairs after a couple signed an affidavit releasing Ronnie and Jimmy from any further responsibility for damages resulting from a February accident.[48] This minor action was one of the senior Jemison's last financial actions as family patriarch. The time had come for his sons to be responsible for themselves and for the elder son, Ronald, to relieve his father of what were becoming burdensome business responsibilities. Although Jimmy did not work in the business, Ronald had begun teaching alongside his father. Both Ronald and Jimmy had completed the operator's course at the Franklin School, and Ronald completed instructor's training as well. Ronald earned a business degree from the University of Houston after returning from Fisk. Also in 1969 Ronald married Franklin beautician Glenda Perkins, and the couple took ownership of the house at 1405 Live Oak Street, where their two children would be born. After his college graduation Ronald worked first for the First National Bank of Houston and then for the Texas Research Institute of Mental Science before taking on the presidency of the Franklin Schools in the 1970s. Glenda would oversee the operations of a second Franklin School location after she completed her instructor's certification in 1971, and Ronald would manage the Dowling Street facility.

Beauty education had begun to move into community colleges, which expanded nationally in the 1960s, but as with earlier public-school forays into beauty training, complete preparation for licensing examinations did not generally develop. Ronald and Glenda found ways to cooperate with the Houston community-college system, teaching courses on public campuses, an arrangement that helps keep the Franklin School in operation in the twenty-first century. The federal government again entered the industry through federally funded beauty training as the Veterans' Administration had done at the end of World War II. The Comprehensive Employment and Training Act (CETA) made new and less-restrictive funding available in the 1970s and the Franklin School again accepted payments from federal sources. CETA students numbered far fewer than the World War II veterans, but the paperwork was simpler, and CETA authorities did not try to change the way in which Ronald Jemison managed the family business. The Franklin School also received federal funding under the Work Incentive Program, which paid eight hundred dollars for each full course of cosmetology instruction.[49]

Ronald Jemison had learned well the lessons his father sought to instill in his son regarding family and community responsibility. Ronald Jemison joined the National Beauty Culturists League, the National Association of Cosmetology Schools, the Texas Association of Accredited Beauty Schools, the Houston Business and Professional Men's Club, and the Houston Rotary. Glenda Jemison, also an industry leader, served as president of the Teacher Education Council of the National Association of Cosmetology Schools in the 1980s. Glenda and Ronald Jemison continue today to manage and operate the business that Nobia Franklin began, and they have brought their own son, Ronald, Jr., into the management of the Franklin School. Ronald, Sr., continues to stress the importance of beauty training not only in preparing for employment, but also in fostering persistence and accomplishment among young people who previously have encountered educational frustrations. Some who now come to the Franklin School of Beauty in hopes of a cosmetology career are white, although African Americans remain in the majority in Franklin classes. Reflecting on his career at the close of the twentieth century, Ronald, Sr., concluded that the discipline acquired in completing a beauty course and the pride of achieving a graduation certificate are more important than the actual pursuit of hairdressing for today's student. For Ronald Jemison, Sr., and for his father before him, beauty education provided an affirmation of self that many women had failed to find elsewhere.

In the early 1960s the African American beauty industry stood on the brink of major changes. The successes of the civil rights and the black liberation movements posed significant challenges to hairdressers and to beauty educators as political values redefined hair fashions and as new employment opportunities undercut the appeal of a career in cosmetology. As historian Noliwe Rooks has written, the politics of liberation often pitted the beauty guidelines of an older generation against those of a younger one. African American hairdressers responded readily in efforts to capture new markets while not losing their traditional clientele. Beauticians learned how to comb and tease "natural" hair and subsequently added hair braiding and hair weaving, which had fallen out of fashion in the 1930s. The civil rights movement also led beauticians to challenge racial barriers in licensing examinations and in salon employment, but Texas lagged behind northern states in embracing integration. Texas cosmetologists did not move as quickly as their northern counterparts to challenge the practices of the past, but J. H. Jemison had had a long history of working across racial lines, and his leadership worked to the betterment of white as well as African American hairdressers in the Lone Star State.

In Texas and other states in the South the legalized segregation of the beauty industry had reinforced the separation of beauticians into professional organizations composed exclusively of African American or non–African American members. Jim Crow laws did not entirely cause the problem, however, as the practice of hairdressing divided along racial lines outside the South as well as within. Even after legalized segregation ended in the 1960s, beauticians nationwide continued to cater largely to women of one race. African American women again began to practice in shops that attracted white women, but racial crossover in salon employment and in customer base remains very small today. Partly because women of color spend disproportionally more on beauty care than do white women, the African American hair trade continues to be more attractive to black beauticians than does employment with white clients. Indeed one of the few institutions as segregated as the church is the beauty parlor. Nevertheless the civil rights movement improved the status of beauticians of color, many of whom had fought long and hard for equal rights. In Texas one sign of this change was the 1972 appointment of Augustine Williams, an African American, as the director of licensing examinations for the Texas Cosmetology Commission.[50]

The decline of the Franklin School at the end of the 1960s postdated that of many other African American schools and other race-centered businesses, but it did fit into a larger trend. Jim Crow in the South and de facto segregation in the North had sheltered and nurtured black enterprises in the early twentieth century, but integration alone did not destroy them. Rather, the decline of the nation's inner cities beginning in the 1950s and accelerating in the 1960s made a wasteland of Chicago's Bronzetown and Atlanta's Sweet Auburn as well as Houston's more scattered but equally vibrant African American commercial and residential communities. In the 1960s school desegregation and the 1964 Civil Rights Act began to open new career opportunities for African American women whose mothers and grandmothers might well have sought independence and mobility in the beauty industry. The demand for hair care remained strong, and preferences for particular services continued to differ by race, but the brightest and best-educated women now had other options, and they exercised them. At the Franklin School completion rates dropped, and instructors faced increased challenges in readying students for the cosmetology examinations.

During a thirty-five–year business career J. H. Jemison quietly helped build the economic and social viability of Houston's African American community through his business, with his work with the YMCA and the Urban League, and in his participation in the Democratic Party. Working as a beauty educator, J. H. promoted the success of the Franklin School through his affiliations with and leadership in local, state, and national beauty-culture organizations.

First through the National Beauty Culturists League and later through the United Beauty School Owners and Teachers Association, J. H. Jemison kept abreast of the latest hair-care techniques and school-management issues. He cultivated professional relationships with Marjorie Stewart Joyner and with Dr. Katie E. Whickam, who served as NBCL president in the 1960s. These contacts supported the business of the Franklin School and similar businesses, but they also served the interests of African Americans in broadening the economic and political rights of the race. Other African American beauticians and cosmetology teachers similarly participated in these groups, and like J. H. Jemison they rarely interacted with white beauty instructors. Not only did the demands of clients differ by race, but the white hair-care industry involved itself in politics only in so far as states and the federal government interfered with their conduct of business. It was this latter circumstance that caused white barbers and beauticians in Texas to reach out for the support of their

African American colleagues in the 1960s. In contrast the African American industry was consciously and continuously political as all cosmetologists recognized their mutual civil disabilities and the utility of their banding together. As community gathering places and as centers of female enterprise, beauty shops nationwide often provided a staging point for civil rights activity,[51] but beauty-school teachers and hair stylists also worked to advance their occupational and their political interests through trade associations. Although his impact was within the state of Texas rather than in a larger arena, J. H. Jemison had a more direct impact than did Marjorie Stewart Joyner in breaking down Jim Crow practices. In his business as well as civic life, J. H. Jemison shared common interests with national figures such as Joyner, but he pursued a local horizon that brought economic security to his family.

Unlike Marjorie Stewart Joyner, J. H. Jemison worked persistently to build his beauty school, and he paid continuous attention to its welfare until his son was able to join him in that responsibility. J. H. Jemison brought good judgment and considerable business acumen to the enterprise. The Franklin School languished as Jim Crow drew his dying breaths, but Jemison had invested his profits widely and wisely. He enjoyed a comfortable retirement and provided a leg up for the next generation just as Nobia Franklin had given J. H. and Abbie Jemison a strong start. J. H. Jemison also held his family closely and dearly. At the end of the century the Jemison homesteads at 1405 and 1409 Live Oak Street remained in the hands of the family as did the Franklin School. Anita Franklin Sheffield eventually left California and moved into one of the two houses while her brother Jimmy lived in the other. Ronald Jemison and family had left Live Oak for larger quarters. J. H. Jemison died on April 24, 1983, only weeks after five hundred Houstonians attended a dinner in honor of his life of achievement in business and civic leadership that helped lead blacks and whites in Texas beyond Jim Crow. Among the many citizens paying homage to Jemison's legacy at the funeral were the congregants of Good Hope Baptist Church, where J. H. had been a long-time member and a trustee.[52]

Because of their wisdom and continuous patterns of thrift and careful investment, Abbie and J. H. Jemison left an inspiring personal legacy and a sizable inheritance for their children. More difficult to measure but as palpable in nature was the Jemisons' legacy of nurturing the hopes and dreams of countless disadvantaged African American women and girls. The correspondence that passed back and forth between Abbie or J. H. Jemison and prospective beauticians and their families documents the ways in which J. H. Jemison's careful and persistent business management turned the generous mentorship of both senior Jemisons to personal profit while they assisted others in making their way in Jim Crow America. From 1935 through the 1970s the Franklin

School of Beauty had prepared twenty-five thousand aspiring cosmetologists with the skills of the trade.[53] Few of these hairdressers in the Jim Crow era collected fees for their services that placed them very far above domestic servants or farm laborers economically, but many Franklin graduates reported their satisfaction and sense of accomplishment and independence in the mobility they had achieved. Franklin graduates corresponded with the Jemisons or with school secretary Hazel McCullough Semedo and expressed pride of craft. While Franklin alumnae described their success, none described their rise up the income ladder. Many Franklin graduates in the greater Houston area succeeded well enough in the beauty business that they attended Franklin conventions and reunions or maintained membership in the City-Wide Beauticians Association that J. H. Jemison founded.

Conclusion

Begone, Jim Crow

In worlds that continually changed around them Marjorie Stewart Joyner and J. H. Jemison provided leadership that raised the economic and civil status of African Americans. Joyner and Jemison were but two players in a sector of the African American economy that supported thousands of men and women through the Jim Crow era, but Joyner and Jemison embarked on their careers in beauty education at an opportune time, and they rode their instincts to the height of the American beauty school's utility in black communities. At the outset of the twentieth century African American migrants to towns and cities throughout the United States supported a panoply of small businesses. Residential segregation in the North and in the South encouraged the development of compact black neighborhoods that spawned retail shops and service establishments. Having little or no access to credit, African American businesses began with small private investments and expanded only as their agents consummated sales based on purchases measured in dollars and cents rather than in hundreds or thousands of dollars. While relying on a population with scarce resources, the beauty industry also sought to pass on its economic successes to the communities it served by employing only African Americans and by buying as much as possible from African American suppliers.

Ronald W. Bailey has written of a historical tension between integrationist and separatist impulses in African American society as posing a dilemma among business people of color.[1] The history of the African American beauty industry suggests a different relationship between ideology and enterprise in the African American past. Both entrepreneur and employee in the beauty industry fully embraced capitalism, and, as they did so, self-help was a constant thread in their outlook on life and on commerce. Yet all African Americans in business, particularly in this era of bank redlining and Jim Crow laws, keenly felt the disabilities of racial discrimination under which they worked to establish and grow their businesses. Consequently race pride and racial solidarity never faded from the daily operations of business. Racial discrimination on the one hand necessitated the creation of enterprises born of the scarce capital resources of black communities and designed to serve African American clients. On the other hand, African American enterprises helped define African American culture and aided in building the institutional frameworks that African Americans employed in their fight for equality. At the outset of the twentieth century African American enterprises sheltered African Americans from some of the worst ravages of racial prejudice. The beauty industry, among others, employed thousands of women and men in jobs within black America. Although Jim Crow was a daily reminder of discrimination, buying and selling within the African American community built mutual respect and self-esteem. In the decades from the turn of the century through the 1950s African American businesses played a central role in setting the stage for the civil rights movement of the 1960s. Entrepreneurs not only built community-based trade groups, they established national organizations and worked alongside African American churches and political organizations to press for an end to racial injustices. Separatism and integration were not then in tension with each other, but linked in a paradoxical symbiotic relationship. Separatism and self-help were perquisites to business success in a racist society, but they were also the parents of protest, raising up the financial resources, organizations, the leadership, and the will to achieve civil equality.

In the beauty industry, gender added another and a central verse in the riddle of separatism and racial advancement. The vast majority of beauticians and sales agents and a notable majority of business owners in the industry were and are women. Working for women within the African American community provided an analogous zone of comfort and self-respect for women in a patriarchal society as it did for black men working inside black communities.

Feminist critics of the beauty industry have foundered on the perceived irony of female entrepreneurs and saleswomen building wealth and influence through the exploitation of femininity, an image and behavior rooted in oppression. As African American women currently spend a larger share of their earnings on beauty products and services than do other American women, the issue is particularly relevant to a discussion of African American commerce. Admittedly thousands of African American women profited from acquainting their sisters with imagined inadequacies and convincing them that particular products would bring them closer to the feminine ideal. Yet appeals to personal vanity are at the very heart of consumer marketing in capitalist economies and in no way limited to persons of one gender or race. In the early days of the industry some cosmetic manufacturers crossed over the line of racial separatism and urged their sisters to believe that they could not only become more white but that this would be a good thing, but such appeals were not universal. As Kathy Peiss has shown, the industry overall embraced the richness of skin and hair variation among African Americans, praising dark as well as fair.[2] An industry that promised to make all women the same color contradicted the complexity of black America and could not succeed in the long run. The industry's marketing of a rainbow of blackness, rather, helped to build racial solidarity among African American women.

A long view of women in the beauty industry helps us to see through the paradox of femininity and understand its importance as a tool. Femininity enabled women of color in establishing a gendered space in a racist society where they could establish a modicum of sisterhood with white women. In the early twentieth century femininity suggested weakness on the one hand, but it also carried the cultural baggage of middle-class respectability and Christian virtue. Femininity helped American women, regardless of race, claim moral leadership within the home. Femininity helped African American women reach out to middle-class white women in the Young Women's Christian Association and similar women's organizations through which they protested against the inequalities imposed upon them. The African American beauty industry helped prepare the modern woman to walk the long road toward equality as did Mary Church Terrell in Deborah Gray White's *Too Heavy a Load*, a vignette with which this analysis of beauty-culture education began. In Mary Church Terrell's time, entry into the hair-styling trade was blocked only by lack of individual skills.

In the fledgling beauty industry of the early twentieth century, capital requirements were very low, no formal training existed, and patent restrictions were few. All of the major black-owned hair-product businesses of the early twentieth century maintained headquarters in a city with a sizable African American population, but each of these operations started in the owner's home. Initial success depended upon the wishful entrepreneur's ability to canvass the compact community in which she lived, carrying her products door-to-door. African American cosmetic and hair-care products made their commercial debuts in urban centers as women such as Annie Turnbo Malone, Sarah Breedlove Walker, and Nobia Franklin manufactured preparations at home and sold their wares door-to-door. From these inauspicious beginnings the African American beauty industry grew into a multimillion-dollar industry. Originating in the kitchens of private homes and in church basements, the three-pronged industry of African American beauty products, cosmetology courses, and hair salons served race needs and calculated prospects and goals in view of the realities of Jim Crow practices. Through the Jim Crow era the beauty industry played a unique role in the black economy, sheltering thousands of women of color from the daily indignities of a white majority and undergirding the financial well-being and civic life of minority communities.

By the 1920s host of major African American beauty-product manufacturers advertised their wares in newspapers nationwide alongside a handful of white companies that vied for a share of the race market.[3] The most successful beauty entrepreneurs of color constructed pyramid organizations of sales agents who worked territories throughout the nation and beyond. Agents searched for new customers in the places where African American women came together, among which churches were the most ubiquitous and the most prominent. Church pastors often welcomed the Poro, Walker, or other agents, who made an initial contribution to the church treasury or paid rent for the use of church meeting space. The Madam Walker Company also sponsored church sales contests that paid commissions directly to church organizations.

During the second decade of the century free-standing beauty parlors debuted in a few African American communities. By the end of the 1920s beauty salons were well established and had begun to cut into the sales territories of manufacturers' agents, a reality that had encouraged the Madam Walker Company among others to establish its own chain of salons. By the 1930s nearly all black commercial districts, even in smaller towns, hosted at least one beauty shop. Indeed the beauty salon was so pervasive in white and in black neighborhoods by 1930 that state legislators began to call for their regulation and an inspection process that would safeguard clients' health.

The adoption of state beauty codes necessitated the creation of licensed schools to prepare beauty operators for their trade, and these certified schools were virtually, if not legally, racially segregated from the beginning. The formal training required to become a licensed beautician in the 1930s was brief, generally one thousand hours of instruction. The cost of cosmetology instruction was low; the Franklin School charged seventy-five dollars for the complete course in 1935. The comparatively low fees nonetheless posed a real and substantial obstacle to the daughters of impoverished communities still in the throes of the Great Depression. Because a cosmetology student likely could not be a full-time wage earner while in school and because of the cash outlay required to compete the course, women entering beauty schools needed support from friends or family members. The decision to become a beautician, then, was not a wholly individual one. Women who had shown some talent and initiative in hair care by grooming the hair of friends or family might be encouraged by a spouse or parent to pursue formal training. As the Franklin School records confirm, the vast majority of African American women who entered into the work before World War II did so at some initial sacrifice, usually on the part of their families as well as themselves.

J. H. Jemison and Marjorie Stewart Joyner well understood the obstacles that women faced in completing their training in beauty culture. Joyner and Jemison worked to build training facilities that allowed women to pursue their operators licenses with almost certain success if they applied themselves to their studies and followed the course to its completion. Through UBSOTA and the City-Wide Beauticians Association, Joyner and Jemison strove to give beauticians the support they needed to practice successfully and to keep up to date on styles, products, and state requirements. While the profit motive drove Jemison's commitment to the Franklin enterprise, Marjorie Stewart Joyner acted more from an ambition to build a network of African American beauty teachers that would catapult her to a unique national stature. Both Joyner and Jemison largely accomplished what they set out to do.

In looking back on their long careers, the formative influence of their early experiences in the beauty business emerges clearly. While they shared a commitment to teaching, their careers differed markedly, and they set their courses early on in their careers.

Floundering somewhat in finding her place in a salon catering to African Americans when she had trained to style the straight hair that was more common among white women, Marjorie Stewart latched on to the promise held out by the Walker beauty system and never let go. Accepting Madam Walker's invitation to travel on behalf of Walker products, Joyner was never thereafter content to stay put in Chicago long despite the pull of her family and her responsibility for the Walker salon or the Walker school that she managed. Marjorie Stewart Joyner craved the limelight, and traveling for Walker or for the United Beauty School Owners and Teachers Association fed that appetite. UBSOTA benefited its members by meeting their needs as teachers and as business people whose interests differed from those of beauticians generally. Through its annual meetings and travels, UBSOTA offered beauty instructors opportunities for the kind of education they could not find elsewhere. Like all other aspects of her legacy to beauty culture, however, UBSOTA did not financially enrich Marjorie Stewart Joyner. Dying in virtual poverty, with clear title to her home but no income other than Social Security, Joyner had not held the almighty dollar closely. From her modest earnings over the years Joyner had given generously to her church, to her extended family, and to other causes. On the anniversary of her birth Joyner religiously solicited financial tribute from UBSOTA members, but these receipts went to Bethune College rather than to Joyner herself.

In contrast with Joyner, Jemison saw his future in financial security through careful investment of his resources. Once hired by Nobia Franklin, Jemison inspired her confidence and the faith of her daughter that he could manage their business affairs well, and he did not disappoint. Jemison understood the business of beauty instruction to require a broad set of administrative skills as well as teaching knowledge. While he hardly built a business empire, he did succeed well enough at all facets of the Franklin operations. He learned to manufacture hair products, he inspired confidence among the students whom he instructed, and he supervised employees well. He was relentless in recruiting new students, at keeping them focused on their lessons and their practice, and in collecting fees from them or their families.

In old age both Joyner and Jemison could and did look back with pride on lives that allowed them to help others as they climbed ladders of success. Both Marjorie Stewart Joyner and James H. Jemison worked steadfastly through their lives to secure broader civil rights for African Americans as did thousands of other business leaders of their generation. Each played a significant role in this regard, but their larger contributions came in fashioning legions of women into financially independent businesspersons who would themselves become conscientious citizens. Beauticians and the organizations to which they belonged provided a means for mobilizing African Americans to achieve a variety of goals, including winning full civil rights and an end to Jim and Jane Crow once and for all.

Comparison of the beauty-school industry with the cosmetics industry reveals that the former provided a steady income to African Americans, but that profits of schools did not approach the level of wealth that the cosmetics trade yielded. While beauty schools, like the Madame Walker schools, might be franchised or built into a national chain, cosmetology instruction is far too labor intensive to yield economies of scale. The potential clientele of beauty colleges, regardless of race, turn to cosmetology partly because their limited educational and financial resources close off other occupational opportunities. The relative poverty of beauty school students, as revealed in the accounts and correspondence of the Franklin School, held down tuition costs and limited the income that school owners could realize. State and federal assistance for individual students provided guaranteed payment of some student accounts, but these resources were few and far between. As J. H. Jemison's difficulties in meeting the requirements of the Veterans Administration illustrate, public agencies set standards and required a level of record keeping that small businesses met only with difficulty. The Walker schools did generate profits for the company, but earnings did not approach the sales and profits from skin- and hair-care products. The costs associated with producing and marketing cosmetics relative to the prices of goods sold were far less a drain on potential earnings than was the case with the instructional side of the beauty industry, and business growth could occur with less oversight from the company as individual sales agents expanded their sales and their customer base. For the Walker, Poro, and Apex schools, beauty instruction followed in the wake of state-level cosmetology regulation. Schools trained their students to use company products exclusively and thus the instructional side of cosmetic companies served to establish a loyal network of consumers and sales agents. Long after Marjorie Stewart Joyner had made the United Beauty School Owners and Teachers Association her primary business activity, the Walker Company continued to employ her and support her undertakings because of her nationwide reputation as an outstanding expert.

The numbers of women in hairdressing grew rapidly from the beginning of the century through the 1960s. Beauty schools advertised that their graduates could find jobs easily and earn high wages. Relative to other occupations in which women have predominated, beauticians have enjoyed low unemployment, but earnings overall have not been high. The U.S. Women's Bureau concluded that, although the Depression had lowered earnings in the beauty industry, unemployment had affected hairdressers less than other African American female workers.[4] While cosmetology continued through the 1950s to hold good prospects for full employment, the growth of the occupation had slowed during the 1950s as African American women found their occupational prospects to be more diverse. Overall the employment of women of color increased by 31 percent during the 1950s, but the number of hairdressers employed grew by only 20 percent. White-collar employment, in contrast, increased by 67 percent as opportunities in nursing, school teaching, and office work grew rapidly, thus allowing for the employment of large numbers of women. White-collar occupations demanded a level of educational achievement not required to enter the beauty trade, but the increasing rewards attached to education encouraged women of color to remain in school rather than drop out to go to beauty school. The median number of years of schooling that women of color completed rose steadily through the twentieth century, improving from 7.2 years to 8.5 years between 1950 and 1960 and then increasing more sharply in the next decade as educated women's employment opportunities broadened. At the end of 1939, after the worst of the Depression had lifted, African American women regularly practicing hairdressing numbered nearly 16,000, of whom 6 percent were unemployed. At the time of the 1960 census, 4.7 percent of white women and 7.9 percent of nonwhite women reported themselves as unemployed, but among hairdressers unemployment was 1.6 percent for whites and 2.4 percent for nonwhites. In that year 32,500 Negro women and 237,000 white women worked as cosmetologists.[5]

The reports of hours and earnings among beauticians were not bright, however. According to a 1933–34 Women's Bureau survey, the average weekly earnings of African American women who worked in the cities of Philadelphia, St. Louis, Columbus, Ohio, and New Orleans was $8, about 60 percent of the wages earned by white beauticians. Only one in sixteen of the African American women earned as much as $15 per week, and the standard work week exceeded 48 hours. From 1972, when the Bureau of Labor Statistics first began reporting on earnings in cosmetology, through 1984 average weekly earnings in beauty shops rose from $86.56 to $156.99, and most employees worked about thirty hours per week. Beauty schools have also consistently advertised that cosmetology presents strong prospects of self-employment and business ownership. In comparison with other occupations, beauticians had higher prospects of self-employment than in all other areas except household service. As late as 1980 40 percent of beauticians were self-employed in contrast to less than 10 percent of all other American workers. Self-employment does not imply that the beautician operates her own business, however. Beauty salons frequently rent out booth space to cosmetologists who establish their own hours but accept the rates set in the shop and have no employer-paid social security or benefits by virtue of their being self-employed.[6]

If remuneration in the beauty trade did not measure up to practitioners expectations, black cosmetologists did enjoy other occupational benefits. Self-employment or work in an African American salon meant not answering to white men or white women. Capital costs of entering the beauty business were so low that hairdressers could start operations without approaching a white-owned financial institution to secure credit. While working hours were long and often irregular, the self-employed hairdresser did have more control over her time than did domestic workers. While earnings were low, beauticians' income compared favorably with the wages of domestic servants, who might also have entered the labor market without a high-school diploma. Rose Morgan, who built the largest and best-known salon in Harlem, encouraged young women of the 1960s to enter the beauty business because "I was a high school drop-out and it gave me an opportunity to prove that I could go as far as those who had been to college."[7]

Many of the benefits of dressing hair within black communities had little to do with hours, wages, or working conditions and everything to do with psychological well-being, a sense of purpose, and pride of accomplishment. African American beauty education from the 1920s through the 1970s emphasized racial advancement through distinctive standards of beauty that encouraged African American women to embrace their many differences of skin color and hair texture. African American beauty fashions changed as rapidly as clothing styles and white beauty standards. While fashions in hairstyles and make-up among both black and white women ghosted the politics of their communities, African American beauty standards consistently held that careful grooming demonstrated self-respect and earned both men and women the respect if not the admiration of others. Madam C. J. Walker, Marjorie Stewart Joyner, and J. H. Jemison all taught women that the lessons of beauty care were as much a component of the client's self-improvement as was advancement in literacy or occupational skills. Beauty educators understood their roles to be teachers of teachers as beauticians carried the lessons of self-improvement into their communities. When Marjorie Joyner was asked late in life what her principal accomplishments had been she answered that "I set up black beauty schools to give girls a chance. I'm a living witness of what can be done."[8] In the same article Katie Whickam, then president of the NBCL, claimed that one-quarter of African American beauticians in 1970 held employment in white-owned salons or served white patrons. While the job market had changed, Whickam concluded that ". . . when it comes to making a living, [cosmetology] is the only real thing the Negro woman has had that she could count on."

The ability of an African American beautician to pursue wage earning free from dependence on the good will of whites compensated cosmetologists in ways that ledger books and tax returns cannot measure. Numerous beauticians of the post–World War II era have testified to the importance of their independence from the white community and the status that they commanded in the community. Bernice Robinson, who founded a literacy-action and voter-registration program in South Carolina in the 1950s, had not completed high school, but her prominence as a beauty-salon owner permitted her to pass the word about literacy and civil rights at her salon and earned her the respect that encouraged others to place their trust in her.[9]

From the 1930s through the 1960s Margaret Holmes worked in a Washington beauty salon that she operated in partnership with two of her sisters. Cardozo Sisters salon employed a corps of beauticians in whom the sisters took personal as well as professional interest, shaping their employment around the women's family responsibilities. Holmes believed that the shop provided a good living for its employees, remembering that "It turned out to be a business for women who somehow managed to do the best possible job at work and in their homes. Through the years, with my sister's understanding of their problems, they had their children, were successful, bought homes; most owned cars, and many of the older operators are still in good health and productively with the shop."[10] All three of the Cardozo sisters who participated in the business recalled the supportive and congenial environment of the shop. The salon included a lounge with a kitchen where beauticians could rest and prepare their midday meals or eat dinner when working evening hours.

As the environment of the Cardozo sisters' salon suggests, African American beauticians understood that their occupational responsibilities included community activism. Through the early 1960s beauticians led prominently in social and political activities in their neighborhoods, and their leadership frequently carried over to state or national organizations. Like barbers, clergymen, and undertakers of color, black hairdressers of the Jim Crow era could take a lead in challenging racial discrimination because, unlike public-school teachers, tenant farmers, or domestic workers, their livelihoods did not depend upon the approval of white employers. Marjorie Stewart Joyner played an exceptionally broad role through her visibility in the Walker organization, the founding of UBSOTA, and her participation in the National Council of Negro Women and the Democratic Party, but other beauticians played important roles even if they kept a lower profile. J. H. Jemison lacked Joyner's national stature, but his relentless efforts on behalf of African Americans led to the broadening of civil rights in the Bayou City and beyond. While not all beauticians marched out front on political issues, most shared Madam Walker's early conviction that well-groomed hair contributed to the self-esteem of their clients and that the self-confidence thus inspired promoted racial advancement.

After 1930, the ubiquity of the hair salon heavily curtailed the role of the manufacturer's agent in the direct marketing of beauty products, and state beauty regulations established the centrality of the beauty school in launching women into careers in hair styling. These changes severed the direct tie between churches and the hair products industry that characterized the earliest days of Madam C. J. Walker's activities. As the beauty industry grew, churches proved too small to house beauticians' conventions, and organizations turned instead to halls rented out by black social or civic organizations. As the twentieth century proceeded, commercial traveling women depended less and less upon church contacts to find suitable lodgings; the African American hotel industry had grown after the Depression. At the outset of efforts to develop regional and national acceptance of commercial beauty products, representatives of Walker, Poro, and other beauty systems set out to win clerical endorsements of the place of grooming in self-improvement and racial advancement. Church congregations provided an assembled target audience, and church buildings offered sales venues when other meeting halls were closed to African Americans. As Walker secretary Violet Reynolds remembered, "To go to a meeting at a church was something to do, so when this woman who was selling hair products and hair *culture* was in town, everybody went."[11] As the African American civic and commercial infrastructures grew, marketing necessarily changed. The proliferation of women's clubs and the expansion of commercial entertainments lessened the hold of churches over social interaction among women, and churches no longer comprised captive audiences. Beauty-system agents faced competition from drugstores and variety stores in towns of all sizes by the 1930s, and the door-to-door agent eventually lost out in selling most cosmetic products to African Americans. Changes in the techniques and processes of hair care also eroded the viability of company agents and encouraged the rise of licensed cosmetologists whom marketers reached through trade shows, occupational organizations, and trade journals.

As beauty schools emerged, churches and Christian beliefs continued to play a significant role in the business lives of hairdressers. United by a broadly shared body of religious values, beauticians regularly turned to African American Christian principles in setting guidelines for ethical behavior and in invoking a spiritual as well as an occupational bond within their trade organizations. Beauticians continued to look to the church, as did Annie Turnbo Malone and Sarah Breedlove Walker, for confirmation of their contribution to racial uplift through beautification, but they no longer relied on direct appeals to church congregations in order to obtain customers. Yet the influence of Christian beliefs and practices persisted in beauty culture. The church was an abiding presence in the lives of Marjorie Stewart Joyner, J. H. Jemison, and the students whom they served. For Joyner and for the Jemisons the church was there at times of personal crisis. Religion attended the organizations in which they participated, and clergymen played roles in school graduations, alumnae gatherings, and beauty conventions.

As access to commercial credit began to expand for African Americans after World War II, the business context of the beauty industry changed. Still, African American businesses failed to achieve equity with other entities in the financial world. While the overall income gap between African Americans and nonblacks also narrowed in the last half of the twentieth century, parity remains illusive. Partly for these reasons but also because of historical allegiances, beauticians continue to support distinctive racial economic and political agendas. In the postwar era the National Beauty Culturists' League embraced nonracialized public goals such as the defeat of polio, but it also continued to remind its membership of the importance of supporting business growth within black communities. This concept was emphasized by the management of Johnson Products Company, the leading black-owned producer of African American beauty products in the 1970s: "For no Black man, in business or not, ever truly makes it on his own. We either hang in there *together* . . . or we simply hang."[12]

In the 1930s and the 1940s beauty culture attracted some women with college degrees as well as those who had dropped out of school with little or no high-school training. Expanding employment options for African American women after World War II lessened the attraction of beauty work as an occupation. During the 1960s significant changes affected the fortunes of the African American beauty industry. Desegregation in the larger society that began in the 1960s had begun to open employment opportunities for African American women in white-owned businesses by the end of the decade. Both desegregation and ever-widening civil rights campaigns eventually had an impact on cosmetology licensing as well. Racially segregated licensing examinations fell by the wayside and in states such as Illinois, where segregation had not been practiced, examiners abandoned their habits of requiring demonstrations of hair-relaxing techniques of African American but not of white candidates. California established a requirement that all beauty students, including whites, be trained to straighten as well as curl hair in order to be licensed. Smaller cosmetic firms could no longer compete with the larger African American producers and white-owned companies had gained considerable market share within the African American market. The popularity of wigs in the early 1960s created a broader manufacturing market but temporarily reduced demand for beauticians' services.[13]

The ongoing tide of corporate mergers and buyouts has eliminated all but a handful of African American cosmetic firms, and the number of students enrolled in privately owned African American beauty colleges has declined. African American beauty colleges continue to operate in larger cities throughout the country, but they persist under the set of challenges that currently confront the Franklin School. Community colleges have emerged to compete more successfully with the private schools than did vocational high schools from the 1920s through the 1950s. Rising educational demands for beauty instructors' licenses have required fully trained instructors such as Glenda Jemison to return to school in order to obtain baccalaureate degrees and state teacher certifications. The continuous fight against segregation has opened the way for African American women to practice their trade in salons that cater to white patrons, but beauty schools must now prepare students in a complete range of hairdressing skills in order to receive their operators' licenses.

The general decline in the fortunes of the private beauty college did not derive from a decrease in the hair trade. Demand for the trained African American beautician has not diminished. The African American beauty salon and individual beauticians continue to flourish. In Texas, although not in all states, girls who drop out of high school before graduation can still aspire to a long-term career with stable earnings through hair care, and the distinctive role of cosmetology training persists. On the other hand, the place of the beautician in the African American economy and in African American communities has changed. Improved school-completion rates and the rapid expansion of higher education for African American women in the years following World War II opened the gates. As barriers to African American occupational mobility began to crumble after passage of the Civil Rights Act of 1964, women of color entered white-collar jobs en masse, rising above the earnings levels and public influence that beauticians achieved under Jim Crow and de facto segregation.

Beauticians continue to command respect and influence, but, like African American barbers, their relative economic and community status has changed. Like clergymen and undertakers, they continue to lead in their communities, but they are no longer *the* leaders. The successes that community leaders of the Jim Crow era achieved opened the doors for people from all occupations to take a public stand on political issues. Between 1940 and 1960 the share of African American working women employed in professional positions such as teaching and social work increased from 4 percent to 7 percent, and by 1990 the percentage had increased to 14 percent. A more dramatic change occurred in the share of women who occupy executive and managerial positions. African American female executives and managers constituted an insignificant statistical group in 1940, but by 1990 they numbered one-half million and accounted for 7 percent of all female workers.

The demise of Jim Crow changed the sources of African American wealth. Black consumers continue to be a central source of wealth for African American business people, but they are no longer the only source, and small business itself is no longer the single path to affluence that it was during the darkest days of segregation. Beauty education, by raising the economic prospects of thousands of black women in the segregation era, helped build the resources to fight Jim Crow, and the independent lifestyles of African American beauticians provided one role model from which female ideas of success rose as racial barriers fell. Marjorie Stewart Joyner and J. H. Jemison contributed to the death of Jim Crow as exemplars and through their leadership. While social change compromised the fortunes of African American beauty schools, race pride and the exercise of free choice have preserved the prosperity of black salons. The need to style hairdressers to beat Jim Crow is gone, and African American beauticians may now pursue their craft in shops that attract women of all races or in salons that cater mostly to women of color. While few hairstylists today know the names of J. H. Jemison or Marjorie Stewart Joyner, all are the inheritors of the industrial and political changes for which they worked.

Notes

Introduction

1. Kathy Peiss explores the politics of African American beauty in *Hope in a Jar: The Making of America's Beauty Culture* (New York: Henry Holt, 1998), pp. 7, 89–95, 203–10, and 227. See also Julie A. Willett, *Permanent Waves: The Making of the American Beauty Shop* (New York: New York University Press, 2000), pp. 22–24. The emergence of Chicago's ethnic market is explored in Robert L. Boyd, "The Great Migration and the Rise of Ethnic Niches for African American Women in Beauty Culture and Hairdressing, 1919–1920," *Sociological Focus* 29 (Feb., 1996), 34–41.

2. Deborah Gray White, *Too Heavy a Load: Black Women in Defense of Themselves, 1894–1994* (New York: W. W. Norton, 1999), p. 21.

3. Ingrid Banks, *Hair Matters: Beauty, Power, and Black Women's Consciousness* (New York: New York University Press, 2000), p. 38.

4. Ruth S. Jones, *Practical Preparation for Beauty Culture: A Curriculum for Schools, Manual for Teachers, Handbook for Operators, and Textbook for Students* (New York: Prentice-Hall, 1939), p. 2.

5. Ibid.

6. A 1946 Atlanta University Study found that 96.7 percent of salons its surveyors located were owned by women. Papers of Project to Study Business and Education among Negroes. Robert W. Woodruff Library, Atlanta University Center, box 2, folder 26, Service Establishments.

7. Carole Marks, *Farewell—We're Good and Gone: The Great Black Migration* (Bloomington: Indiana University Press, 1989), pp. 1–2, 19–48; James R. Grossman, *Land of Hope: Chicago, Black Southerners and the Great Migration* (Chicago: University of Chicago Press, 1989), appendices A, B.

8. John H. Burrows, *The Necessity of Myth: A History of the National Negro Business League, 1900–1945* (Auburn, Ala.: Hickory Hill Press, 1988), pp. 1–19; Carl R. Osthaus, *Freedmen, Philanthropy, and Fraud: A History of the Freeman's Savings Bank* (Urbana: University of Illinois Press, 1976).

9. Papers of Project to Study Business and Education among Negroes, box 2, folder 26, Service Establishments.

10. Copy of interview in the Marjorie Stewart Joyner Papers, box 28, Vivian G. Harsh Research Collection of Afro-American History and Literature, Chicago Public Library. Hereafter cited as MSJP. While Garnett-Abney claimed to have invented the method of

straightening, Annie Malone, the founder of the Poro Company, also promoted a technique of straightening hair with the use of metal pulling tongs. Willett, *Permanent Waves*, p. 18.

11. Interview with Elizabeth Barker by Marcia Greenlee, Dec. 8, 1976. Ruth Edmonds Hill, ed., *Black Women Oral History Project*. Vol. 2. Arthur and Elizabeth Schlesinger Library on the History of Women in America, Radcliffe College (Westport, Conn.: Meckler, 1991), pp. 92–96.

12. Robert C. Kenzer, *Enterprising Southerners: Black Economic Success in North Carolina, 1865–1915*, Carter G. Woodson Series in Black Studies (Charlottesville: University Press of Virginia, 1997), p. 62.

13. Boyd, "The Great Migration," pp. 40.

14. According to Julie A. Willett the National Beauty Culturists League reported that beauty salons employed 150,000 African American women in the 1930s. These claims seem greatly inflated although some of the discrepancy between the industry estimation and the census count reflects the reality that a sizable share of African American beauticians still practiced hair care as a second line of employment in the 1930s. *Permanent Waves*, p. 19.

15. Osceola Blanchet, "The Investigation of Negro Business in New Orleans (1930–1940)," M.A. thesis, Xavier University, New Orleans, 1941, pp. 40–43 and table V.I.

16. Annie Turnbo Malone opened the first African American beauty college, in St. Louis, after the turn of the century. Sarah Breedlove Walker, Nobia Franklin, and Sara Spencer Washington followed, but the potential for growth in beauty culture instruction did not blossom fully until the enactment of license laws.

Chapter 1. The Legacy of Beauty Culture

1. Juliet E. K. Walker, *The History of Black Business in America: Capitalism, Race, Entrepreneurship* (New York: Twayne, 1998), pp. 208–11.

2. Kathy Peiss notes that a white-owned firm first began marketing its hair pomade to persons of color when an African American consumer volunteered testimony about the product's efficacy in beautifying her hair; *Hope in a Jar*, p. 52.

3. Peiss, *Hope in a Jar*, pp. 67–70; Walker, *The History of Black Business*, pp. 206–12.

4. Walker, *The History of Black Business*, p. 182.

5. Peiss, *Hope in a Jar*, pp. 52–53.

6. Ibid., p. 41; Julie A. Willett, *Permanent Waves*, pp. 14–18.

7. Deborah Gray White, *Ain't I a Woman?* pp. 143–44.

8. Letter from L. H. Holsey to J. O. Clark, 1879, quoted in Glenn T. Eskew, "Black Elitism and the Failure of Paternalism in Postbellum Georgia: The Case of Bishop Lucius Henry Holsey," *Journal of Southern History* 58 (Nov., 1992): 648.

9. A'Lelia Perry Bundles, *On Her Own Ground: The Life and Times of Madam C. J. Walker* (New York: Scribner, 2001), p. 66; Peiss, *Hope in a Jar*, p. 67.

10. Elizabeth Barker interviewed by Marcia Greenlee, Dec. 8, 1976, Ruth Edmonds Hill, ed., *Black Women Oral History Project*, vol. 2, p. 93.

11. Margaret Holmes interviewed by Marcia Greenlee, Nov. 9, 1977, Ruth Edmonds Hill, ed., *Black Women Oral History Project*, vol. 6, p. 61.

12. *Pittsburgh Courier*, Apr. 18, 1925.

13. Vishnu V. Oak, *The Negro Newspaper* (Yellow Springs, Ohio: Antioch Press, 1948), pp. 68–70.

14. *Pittsburgh Courier*, Apr. 11, Apr. 18, May 2, 1925.

15. Gwendolyn Robinson, "Class, Race, and Gender: A Transcultural Theoretical and Sociohistorical Analysis of Cosmetic Institutions and Practices to 1920," Ph.D. diss., University of Illinois at Chicago, 1984, pp. 326–29.

16. Alice C. Burnett to F. B. Ransom, Mar. 30, 1918, Madam C. J. Walker Collection, Indiana Historical Society. Hereafter cited as MCJWC. Box 7, folder 19.

17. Peiss, *Hope in a Jar*, pp. 69–70.

18. Sarah Breedlove "Madam C. J." Walker grew into a legend in her own time and, after her death in 1919 the company that she had founded magnified Walker's legend. Through newspaper advertising and cosmetics road shows, companies have mythologized their founders or owners, but none more than the Madam Walker Company. In the case of Madam Walker, partly because of her personal wealth and partly through company propaganda, the legend grew after her passing. The crescendo of interest in African American women's history since the 1960s has rekindled lore about African American leadership in the beauty industry. A recent children's book on Sarah Breedlove Walker claims that Walker developed a formula with fantastic properties, the efficacy of which she proved through applications to her own head: "Soon her hair started growing in faster than it had ever fallen out. Though the ingredients used were strong, they did not burn her hair; and when they were mixed in the right combination, they healed the scalp and made hair healthy." Kathryn Lasky, *Vision of Beauty: The Story of Sarah Breedlove Walker* (Cambridge, Mass.: Candlewick Press, 2000), n.p. Lasky claims that Walker was headquartered in Pittsburgh from 1908 to 1911 and that she and Lelia opened Lelia College there.

19. Incorporation dated Sept. 11, 1911. MCJWC, box 7, folder 1. Company advertising variously referred to Sarah Breedlove Walker as "Madam C. J. Walker" or "Madame C. J. Walker;" Bundles, *On Her Own Ground*, pp. 56–57, 79–91.

20. F. B. Ransom to Mrs. J. Tisem, MCJWC, box 9, folder 9.

21. Copy of contract, MCJWC, box 7, folder 20.

22. Bundles, *On Her Own Ground*, pp. 67–68; Peiss, *Hope in a Jar*, pp. 210–220; Noliwe Rooks, *Hair Raising: Beauty, Culture, and African American Women* (New Brunswick: Rutgers University Press, 1996), pp. 63–64; Willett, *Permanent Waves*, pp. 22–44.

23. Peiss, *Hope in a Jar*, pp. 71–77.

24. "Hints to Agents," typescript, ca. 1915, MCJWC, box 7, folder 4.

25. Ibid.; if a customer's breath were offensive, Madam Walker suggested that the beautician offer her a mint.

26. Ibid.

27. Printed document, ca. 1915, MCJWC, box 7, folder 5.

28. Letter from Mrs. Maggie Wilson, Dec. 21, 1912, MCJWC, box 9, folder 19.

29. Although the vast majority of Walker sales occurred within the United States, agents also represented the Madam Walker Company in Latin America. After World War I, F. B. Ransom engaged the services of Indianapolis resident Francisco P. D'Avila as a manufacturer's representative at a salary of $150 per month, plus $10 per day travel allowance and commissions calculated at 25 percent. D'Avila's territory included Panama, Trinidad,

British Guiana, and Barbados. Ransom also drew up a six-month contract for D'Avila's wife, who was employed for $100 per month with no commission and "actual expenses" for room and board to begin at the time of embarkation for a foreign port. The disparity in compensation between husband and wife reflects a broader pattern of gender discrimination within the Walker company. MCJWC, box 7, folder 19.

30. Copies of contracts, MCJWC, box 7, folder 19.

31. Margaret Thompson to F. B. Ransom, Oct. 19, 1916, MCJWC, box 9, folder 1.

32. A. C. Burnett to F. B. Ransom, Aug. 2, 1917, MCJWC, box 9, folder 19.

33. Ruth S. Jones, *Practical Preparation for Beauty Culture*, p. 199.

34. Matilda Harper purportedly learned her first lessons in hair care from a physician who taught the importance of Castile soap shampoos, vigorous brushing, and an herb-based hairdressing; Jane R. Plitt, *Martha Matilda Harper and the American Dream* (Syracuse: Syracuse University Press, 2000), pp. 19–21.

35. *Madame N. A. Franklin's Improved System of Hair Culture*, 4th ed. (Houston: Webster Printing, 1921), p. 9.

36. Ruth S. Jones, *Practical Preparation for Beauty Culture*, pp. 69–71.

37. *Madame N. A. Franklin's Improved System of Hair Culture*, pp. 4–5.

38. Quoted in Plitt, *Martha Matilda Harper and the American Dream*, p. 70.

39. Elizabeth Barker interviewed by Marcia Greenlee, Dec. 8, 1976, Ruth Edmonds Hill, ed., *Black Women Oral History Project*, vol. 2, pp. 94–95.

40. In the 1960s the president of a predominantly white Chicago association of hairdressers maintained that a black member of the Illinois board of cosmetology had blocked efforts to increase the level of secondary schooling required for licensing in the state because it would have barred the vast majority of African American women who sought entry to beauty schools. David Schroder, *Engagement in the Mirror: Hairdressers and Their Work* (San Francisco: R. & E. Research, 1978), p. 26.

41. Gilbert Osofsky, *Harlem: The Making of a Ghetto, Negro New York, 1890–1930* (New York: Harper & Row, 1966), p. 96.

42. Autumn Stanley, *Mothers and Daughters of Invention: Notes for a Revised History of Technology* (New Brunswick: Rutgers University Press, 1995), p. 382.

Chapter 2. Traveling

1. Toni Castone, "The History of Dr. Marjorie Stewart Joyner," undated typescript, MSJP, box 24, ca. 1983. Joyner provided testimony about hair weaving for a civil court proceeding, transcript of deposition of Marjorie Stewart Joyner in the case of *Christina M. Jenkins and Hair-Weave, Inc., v. Adams Elligan and Lydia Adams Beauty College*, MSJP, box 40.

2. A. C. Burnett to F. B. Ransom, Aug. 2, 1917, MCJWC, box 9, folder 19.

3. A. C. Burnett to F. B. Ransom, Aug. 7, 1917, MCJWC, box 9, folder 19.

4. A. C. Burnett to F. B. Ransom, Aug. 29, 1917, MCJWC, box 9, folder 19.

5. A. C. Burnett to F. B. Ransom, Sept. 24, 1917, MCJWC, box 9, folder 19.

6. "Witness to Chicago's Black History," *Chicago Tribune*, Feb. 4, 1987; Toni Castone, "The History of Dr. Marjorie Stewart Joyner."

7. A. C. Burnett to F. B. Ransom, Sept. 24, 27, 29, 1918; MCJWC, box 9, folder 20.

8. Copy of agent's contract, MCJWC, box 7, folder 11.

9. Copy of patent, MSJP, box 37.

10. Document notarized in Cook County, Illinois, Nov. 19, 1928, that reads in part "Marjorie S. Joyner of Chicago, inventor of certain new and useful improvements in Scalp Protector, for which I am about to make application for Letters Patent of the United States . . . sold, assigned and transferred . . . its rights to The Madam C. J. Walkers Mfg Co, . . . my entire right, title, and interest in said invention. Sold for one dollar and other valuable considerations." MCJWC, box 7, folder 7.

11. *Walker News*, 2 (Mar., 1929).

12. Form letter from J. M. Avery, vice president and secretary of North Carolina Mutual Life Insurance Co., asks "Dear Friend" to buy products and vote for "our President. Please join us in this effort. Dr. Roscoe C. Brown of this office has been asked to manage this campaign and you will also be hearing from him." The men selected for the trip included A. W. Lloyd, grand chancellor of the Knights of Pythias; Dr. William P. Harris, director of the Improved Order of Samaritans; B. G. Collier, grand chancellor of the Knights of Pythias, and Mr. C. C. Spaulding. MCJWC, box 12, folder 22. Spaulding's career is discussed in detail in Walter B. Weare, *Black Business in the New South: A Social History of the North Carolina Mutual Life Insurance Company* (Urbana: University of Illinois Press, 1973).

13. *Walker News*, 1 (May, 1928).

14. *Walker News*, 4 (Jan., 1931).

15. *Chicago Tribune*, Feb. 4, 1987; St. Clair Drake and Horace R. Clayton, *Black Metropolis: A Study of Negro Life in a Northern City*, vol. 1, revised and enlarged ed. (New York: Harper, 1962), pp. 58–64; *Walker News*, 2 (Aug., 1929).

16. *Walker News*, 2 (July, 1929).

17. *Walker News*, 3 (May, 1930); 4 (Jan., 1931).

18. *Walker News*, 4 (Oct., 1931).

19. Diploma dated June 14, 1934; MSJP, box 17.

20. Ethel Erickson, U.S. Department of Labor, Women's Bureau, Bulletin No. 133, *Employment Conditions in Beauty Shops: A Study of Four Cities* (Washington, D.C.: GPO, 1935), pp. 26–30, 44–46.

21. Vernice Mark, *History of the National Beauty Culturists' League, Inc., 1919–1994*, 2d ed. (Detroit: Harlo Press, 1994), pp. 1–38.

22. *Atlanta Daily World*, Jan. 24, 1939.

23. Form letter from Marjorie Stewart Joyner, Feb. 17, 1939, Franklin School of Beauty Papers, Metropolitan Archives, Houston Public Library, box 6. Hereafter cited as FSBP.

24. Marva Louis to Marjorie Joyner, Sept. 16, 1942, MSJP, box 8, folder Walker Co., 1942.

25. Draft letter from Marjorie Stewart Joyner, Oct., 1944, MSJP, box 8, folder Walker Co., 1944.

26. F. B. Ransom to Marjorie Stewart Joyner, Dec. 23, 1942, MSJP, box 8, folder Walker Co., 1942.

27. F. B. Ransom to Marjorie Stewart Joyner, Jan. 4, 1943., MSJP, box 8, folder Walker Co., 1943.

28. Serena B. Davis to Marjorie Stewart Joyner, June 28, 1944; MSJP, box 8, folder Walker Co., 1944.

29. Ibid. Juliet E. K. Walker, *The History of Black Business in America*, pp. 303–7.

30. Violet Davis Reynolds to Mrs. Marjorie S. Joyner, Apr. 23, 1947, MSJP, box 8, folder 1947.

31. Joyner's failure to secure all that she requested from the Walker Company may have vexed her more because of her knowledge that Ransom lived comfortably in Indianapolis on his Walker earnings while he also committed substantial energies to civic leadership. As head of the city's largest employer of persons of color, Ransom enjoyed broad community respect. He worked on behalf of the YMCA and the NAACP, assisted in establishing an orphanage, and served as the first African American member of the Indianapolis City Council. In recognition of his accomplishment the *Indianapolis Star* named Ransom the "Number One Citizen of Indianapolis" in 1946. *Indianapolis Star*, Dec. 3–4, 1946.

32. Jeanetta Welch Brown to Marjorie Stewart Joyner, Oct. 3, 1944, MSJP, box 8, folder Walker Co., 1944.

33. Mary McLeod Bethune to Marjorie Stewart Joyner, Apr. 16, 1946, MSJP, box 27.

34. White, *Too Heavy a Load*, pp. 147–75.

35. Jeanetta Welch Brown to Marjorie Stewart Joyner, Nov. 27, 1945, MSJP, box 27.

36. *UBSOTA Newsletter*, June–July, 1951, box 10, MSJP, box 10; Marjorie Stewart Joyner obituary, *Chicago Sun-Times*, Dec. 29, 1994.

37. "History of United Beauty School Owners and Teachers Association, Alpha Chi Pi Omega Sorority and Fraternity, Greek Letter Beauticians, International, National Local Chapters, and Their Activities," 3d ed., n.d., MSJP, box 3.

38. Mississippi Independent Beauticians Association, *Beautician's Guide and Yearbook, 1948* (Greenville, Miss., 1948). The July 11–13 convention cited Joyner as "the most outstanding Race Beautician in America." MCJWC, box 12, folder 5.

39. 1959–60 Annual Report, Gamma Delta Chapter of Philadelphia, MSJP, box 5.

40. Marjorie Stewart Joyner to Mary McLeod Bethune, Dec. 9, 1946, MSJP, box 27.

41. Copy of radio broadcast script for Oct. 3, 1948; MSJP, box 27.

42. Marjorie Stewart Joyner, copy of form letter, Dec. 30, 1948, MSJP, box 27.

43. J. Unis Pressley to Marjorie Stewart Joyner, Feb. 13, 1948, MSJP, box 8, folder Walker Co., 1948.

44. Robert Lee Brokenburr to Marjorie Stewart Joyner, Apr. 12, 1948, MSJP, box 27.

45. Robert Lee Brokenburr to Marjorie Joyner Stewart, Jan. 24, 1949, MSJP, box 27.

46. Ethel L. Payne to Marjorie Stewart Joyner, Jan. 11, 1958, MSJP, box 5.

47. Press Release, Jan. 25, 1958, MSJP, box 5.

Chapter 3. Southbound

1. Rules and Regulation of the N. A. Franklin Association of Beauty Culturists, FSBP, unnumbered Hollinger box, folder 6.

2. Materials prepared for Franklin Beauty School catalog, FSBP, box 28, folder State Approval Agency Catalog.

3. Merline Pitre, *In Struggle against Jim Crow: Lula B White and the NAACP, 1900–1957* (College Station: Texas A&M University Press, 1999), p. 18.

4. Howard Beeth and Cary D. Wintz, *Black Dixie: Afro-Texan History and Culture in Houston* (College Station: Texas A&M Press, 1992), p. 22.

5. Darlene Clark Hine, *Black Victory: The Rise and Fall of the White Primary in Texas* (Millwood, N.Y.: KTO Press, 1979), pp. 55–60.

6. Beeth and Wintz, *Black Dixie*, pp. 22–27.

7. Beeth and Wintz, *Black Dixie*, p. 27.

8. Public (vocational) schools having a beauty culture department were not required to pay the license fee of $100.00 but were supposed to meet all requirements, use licensed instructors, and register with the cosmetology board. Mimeographed copy of Texas attorney general's rulings covering beauty law #5–22–35. The state also required that license applicants be able to read and write in English. FSBP, box 45, folder 1.

9. Unidentified newspaper clipping, FSBP, box 45, folder 1.

10. Undated advertising copy, FSBP, box 25.

11. FSBP, box 29, folder clippings, 1937.

12. Ollie Mae James to J. H. Jemison, Jan. 7, 1945; FSBP, box 2, folder Jan., 1945.

13. Notice in *Houston Informer*, Oct. 10, 1936.

14. J. H. Jemison to Arthur and Minnie Logan, May 23, 1938, FSBP, box 15, folder 19.

15. Beeth and Wintz, Introduction, Part 3, *Black Dixie*, p. 93; James M. SoRelle, "The Emergence of Black Business in Houston, Texas: A Study of Race and Ideology, 1919–45," Beeth and Wintz, *Black Dixie*, pp. 103–15.

16. Letter to J. H. Jemison from Henri Anna Carroll, Monroe, Louisiana, Oct. 14, 1940, FSBP, box 25, folder 1940.

17. Arthur Logan to J. H. Jemison, Apr. 11, 1938, FSBP, box 15, folder 17.

18. J. H. Jemison to Arthur Logan, Apr. 12, 1938, FSBP, box 15, folder 17.

19. Minnie Logan to J. H. Jemison, June 26, 1938, FSBP, box 15, folder 17.

20. Minnie Logan to J. H. Jemison, Apr. 23, 1938, FSBP, box 15, folder 17.

21. Arthur Logan to J. H. Jemison, Jan. 27, 1939, FSBP, box 15, folder 17.

22. J. H. Jemison to Arthur Logan, Jan. 30, 1939, FSBP, box 15, folder 17.

23. Minnie Logan to J. H. Jemison, Feb. 9, 1939, FSBP, box 15, folder 17.

24. License renewal letter for J. H. Jemison lists four beauty shops and the Franklin School of Beauty, Sept. 21, 1943. Inspection certificates dated May 11, 1943, and Apr. 5, 1944. FSBP, box 25, folder 1944.

25. Printed form, ca. 1941, FSBP, box 25, folder 1941.

26. Anna Dupree, an African American beautician in Houston in the 1920s, maintained a white clientele as did several of her coworkers. The beauticians called at the homes of their clients and performed their services there. In the 1930s, possibly with the assistance of the new licensing regulations, Dupree and others of her race were driven from their white patrons through pressure from white beauticians. Ruthe Winegarten, *Black Texas Women: One Hundred and Fifty Years of Trial and Triumph* (Austin: University of Texas Press, 1995), p. 168.

27. Juanita Martin to Abbie Franklin Jemison and J. H. Jemison, Mar. 9, 1948, FSBP, box 34, folder M.

28. Unidentified clipping, FSBP, box 45.

29. Miss A[nnie] M. Williams to J. H. Jemison, June 9, 1941, FSBP, box 35, folder 14.

30. Matilda Naskins to J. H. Jemison, May 6, 1946, FSBP, box 35, folder H-45–49.

31. J. H. Jemison to Alberta Easley, May 23, 1952, FSBP, box 36, folder E.

32. A[nnie] M. Williams to J. H. Jemison, June 9, 1941, FSBP, box 35, folder 14.

33. Mrs. Coulter Daniels to James H. Jemison, undated, FSBP, box 33, folder M.

34. Ben Samuel to Abbie Jemison, Feb. 5, 1941, FSBP, box 34, folder S.

35. Abbie Jemison to Ben Samuel, Feb. 6, 1941, FSBP, box 34, folder S.

36. Correspondence dated Feb. 2, 1941, and Mar. 10, 1941, FSBP, box 34, folder S.

37. Report of Catherine Marsh, Dec. 6, 1938; FSBP, box 25, folder 2.

38. Notarized affidavit, Dec. 3, 1945, FSBP, box 25, folder 2.

39. Sarah S. Sullivan to J. H. Jemison, May 24, 1946, J. H. Jemison, to Sarah S. Sullivan, May 29, 1946, FSBP, box 9, folder S.

40. Roxie Lee Flowers to J. H. Jemison, Nov. 13, 1945, J. H. Jemison to Roxie Lee Flowers, Nov. 20, 1945, FSBP, box 9, folder F.

41. J. H. Jemison to Ollie Mae Ransom, Dec. 3, 1945, FSBP, box 9, folder R.

42. Gertrude Irving to J. H. Jemison, Feb. 27, 1942, FSBP, box 9, folder 1942. The Miss Hicks to whom Irving referred was Jessie Mae Hicks, founder and owner of the Hicks School of Beauty in San Antonio. Hicks began her teaching career at the Franklin School, and in 1947 she served as president of the Texas Association of Beauty Culturists.

43. J. H. Jemison to Gertrude Irving, Mar. 4, 1942, FSBP, box 9, folder 1942.

44. J. H. Jemison to Arthur and Minnie Logan, May 23, 1938, FSBP, box 15, folder 20.

45. Juanita Martin to Hazel McCullough, May 1, 1942, Hazel McCullough to Juanita Martin, Juanita Martin to Mrs. J. H. Jemison, July 8, 1942, FSBP, box 9, folder 1942.

46. J. H. Jemison to Juanita Martin, July 30, 1942, FSBP, box 9, folder 1942.

47. Juanita Martin to J. H. Jemison, Aug. 8, 1942; FSBP, box 34, folder M; Ernestine McGruder to Abbie Franklin Jemison, FSBP, box 9, folder 1941.

48. Abbie Franklin Jemison to Mrs. Oliver, May 10, 1941, FSBP, box 34, folder O.

49. Abbie Franklin Jemison to Fannie Whitfield, Feb. 17, 1944, FSBP, box 35, folder W.

50. Fannie Whitfield to Abbie Franklin Jemison, Feb. 19, 1944, FSBP, box 35, folder W.

51. Abbie Franklin Jemison to Fannie Whitfield, Feb. 21, 1944, and Feb. 23, 1944, FSBP, box 35, folder W.

52. Mrs. M. E. Martin to Abbie Franklin Jemison, [Oct., 1942], FSBP, box 34, folder M.

53. Abbie Franklin Jemison to Mrs. Ira Moore, Jan. 21, 1944, FSBP, box 34, folder M.

54. Sophia Maxie to Abbie Franklin Jemison, Oct. 1, 1943; J. H. Jemison to Mrs. Sophia Maxie, Oct. 5, 1943, FSBP, box 34, folder M.

55. Lillie B. Jones to Abbie Franklin Jemison, Mar. 1, 1943, FSBP, box 34, folder J.

56. Abbie Franklin Jemison to Lillie B. Jones, Apr. 9, 1943, FSBP, box 34, folder J.

57. Lillie B. Jones to Abbie Franklin Jemison, Apr. 12, 1943; Abbie Franklin Jemison to Lillie B. Jones, Apr. 16, 1943, FSBP, box 34, folder J.

58. J. H. Jemison to Lillie B Jones, Apr. 26, 1943, June 28, 1943, and Sept. 3, 1943; Abbie Franklin Jemison to Lillie B. Jones, Mar. 24, 1944; Lillie B. Jones to Abbie Franklin Jemison, May 23, 1943, FSBP, box 34, folder J.

59. Typed notes dated Dec. [1938], FSBP, box 6, folder1.

60. Typed draft, n.d., FSBP, box 6, folder 3.

61. Correspondence dated Dec. 24, 1945, Jan. 4, 1946, and Jan. 14, 1946, FSBP, box 6, folder 3.

62. Faye Stewart to J. H. Jemison, Jan. 7, 1939, FSBP, box 6, folder 1.

63. Minutes of the meeting of Aug. 18, 1941, FSBP, box 6, folder 1.

64. J. H. Jemison to Members of State Board of Hairdressers, Dec. 24, 1945, FSBP, box 6, folder 3.

65. Abbie Franklin Jemison to J. H. Jemison, July 31, 1940, and Aug. 2, 1940, FSBP, box 33, folder 2.

66. Abbie Franklin Jemison to J. H. Jemison, July 20, 1940, FSBP, box 33, folder 2.

67. Abbie Franklin Jemison to J. H. Jemison, July 23, 1940, FSBP, box 33, folder 2.

68. J. H. Jemison to Abbie Franklin Jemison, July 23 [sic], 1940, FSBP, box 33, folder 2.

69. Abbie Franklin Jemison to J. H. Jemison, July 26, 1940, FSBP, box 33, folder 2.

70. Abbie Franklin Jemison to J. H. Jemison, July 31, 1940, FSBP, box 33, folder 2.

71. Abbie Franklin Jemison to J, H, Jemison, Aug. 2, 1940, FSBP, box 33, folder 2.

72. Abbie Franklin Jemison to J. H. Jemison, Aug. 8, 1940, FSBP, box 33, folder 2.

73. Abbie Franklin by J. H. Jemison, Aug. 13, 1940, FSBP, box 33, folder 2.

74. Invoice, Aug., 1940, FSBP, box 22, folder 41.

Chapter 4. Beating Jim Crow

1. Excerpt from the diary of Lorenzo J. Greene, reprinted in Beeth and Wintz, *Black Dixie*, p. 141.

2. J. H. Jemison to Arthur Logan, Nov. 24, 1942, FSBP, box 15, folder 17.

3. Minnie Logan to J. H. Jemison, July 3, 1944, FSBP, box 15, folder 17.

4. Inspection notice, Dec. 16, 1941, FSBP, box 25, folder 3.

5. Irizella Mitchell to Abbie Franklin Jemison, Sept. 21, 1942, FSBP, box 34, folder Mc.

6. Irizella Mitchell to Hazel McCullough, May 3, 1943, FSBP, box 34, folder Mc.

7. Irizella Mitchell to Hazel McCullough, June 1, 1943, FSBP, box 34, folder Mc.

8. Carrie Lou Jones to Abbie Franklin Jemison, Nov. 2, 1942, FSBP, box 34, folder J.

9. Gladys Feeney to Abbie Franklin Jemison, Apr. 7, 1940, FSBP, box 34, folder O.

10. Yvonne Kinnebrew to Abbie Franklin Jemison, July 5, 1943, FSBP, box 34, folder K.

11. Jessie Lee Matthew to Hazel McCullough, Feb. 29, 1944; FSBP, box 34, folder M.

12. Abbie Franklin Jemison to Johnice Bell, Oct. 9, 1944, FSBP, starred box, folder 4.

13. Author interview with Ronald Jemison, Sr., June 23, 1999, Houston, Texas.

14. Robert Johnson to J. H. Jemison, FSBP, box 2, folder J.

15. J. H. Jemison to Robert Johnson, Oct. 10, 1946, FSBP, box 2, folder J.

16. Robert Johnson to J. H. Jemison, Dec 3, 1946, FSBP, box 2, folder J.

17. Robert Johnson to J. H. Jemison, FSBP, Feb. 1, 1947, box 2, folder J.

18. Tommie D. Ferguson to J. H. Jemison, Sept. 5, 1956; FSBP, box 1, folder 1956.

19. J. M. Wilson to J. H. Jemison, Nov. 6, 1946; J. R. McClain to J. H. Jemison, Jan. 29, 1947, and Feb. 27, 1947; R. L. Temple to J. H. Jemison, June 26, 1947, FSBP, unnumbered Hollinger box, folder 4.

20. Oliver E. Meadows to Franklin School of Beauty Culture, June 6, 1950, Aug. 9, 1950; R. B. Parson to J. H. Jemison, Nov. 24, 1950, FSBP, box 28, folder Veterans

21. Registration records, FSBP, box 36, folder 1955 registration.

22. Data on Beauty Industry in Texas, mimeographed copy, FSBP, box 6, folder 7.

23. Frank A. Watts to J. H. Jemison, Aug. 1, 1952, FSBP, box 7, folder 4.

24. Canceled check in FSBP, box 14, folder Nov., 1968.

25. Frank J. Williford, Jr. to J. H. Jemison, Jan. 2, 1952, J. H. Jemison to Frank J. Williford, Jr., Dec. 23, 1952, W. A. Morrison to J. H. Jemison, May 10, 1952, FSBP, box 7, folder 4.

26. Ben N. Ramey to J. H. Jemison, Mar. 15, 1952, and unidentified newspaper clipping, FSBP, box 5, folder 8; J. H. Jemison's obituary, *Houston Informer*, Apr. 30, 1983.

27. Lottie Bailey to J. H. Jemison, Mar. 1, 1952; FSBP, box 6, folder 2.

28. J. H. Jemison to Allan Shivers, June 10, 1953; FSBP, box 6, folder 7.

29. Allan Shivers to J. H. Jemison, June 24, 1953, FSBP, box 7, folder 6.

30. Bess Blackwell to Hazel B. Semedo, Feb. 19, 1957, FSBP, box 41, folder 5.

31. Constitution and By-Laws of City-Wide Beauticians Association, FSBP, box 26, folder 5.

32. FSBP, starred box, folder 2, and City-Wide Beauticians, box 26, folder 4.

33. H. M. Morgan to J. H. Jemison, Jan. 8, 1958, and Political Action Committee — Barbers and Beauticians, J. H. Jemison, and H. M. Morgan cochairs, n.d., FSBP, box 25, folder Texas Beauticians.

34. Data on the Beauty Industry in Texas, mimeographed copy, FSBP, box 6, folder 7.

35. FSBP, box 4, folder 6.

36. Minutes of the Meeting of the Beauty School Owners Association of Texas, Mar. 26, 1961, FSBP, box 25, folder Beauty School Owners Association of Texas.

37. Lora Lee Jackson to J. H. Jemison, FSBP, July 28, 1954, box 7, folder 6.

38. Abbie Franklin Jemison to J. H. Jemison, May, 1958. FSBP, box 28, folder J. H. Jemison, travel, Mayo Clinic.

39. Abbie Franklin Jemison to J. H. Jemison, June 28, 1958; FSBP, box 28, folder June, 1958.

40. Advertising copy and contract, May 30, 1962, FSBP, box 33, folder May, 1962.

41. FSBP, box 33, folder Jan., 1964, and folder May, 1964.

42. Mrs. A. A. Allen to J. H. Jemison, Apr. 28, 1964, FSBP, box 33, folder Apr., 1964; Gus T. Harris to J. H. Jemison, n.d., box 33, folder May, 1964; J. H. Jemison to Motion Picture Alexander Corporation, Jan. 8, 1964, and invoices, box 33, folders Jan., 1964, May, 1964, and June, 1964.

43. Willie Skinner to J. H. Jemison, May 31, 1965, FSBP, box 19, folder June, 1965.

44. Willett, *Permanent Waves*, p. 178.

45. Summary of Land or Right of Way Purchase Agreements, Jan. 12, 1960; W. P. Hamblen, Jr., to J. H. Jemison, Feb. 9, 1961, and Mar. 3, 1961; FSBP, box 4, folder 1.

46. Anita Sheffield to J. H. and Abbie Jemison, Aug. 1, 1966, FSBP, box 19, folder 1966.

47. Melva J. Washington to J. H. Jemison, Mar. 31, 1969, FSBP, box 14, folder Mar., 1969; Louie Welch to J. H. Jemison, Sept. 19, 1967, FSBP, box 20, folder Sept., 1967; copy of telegram to Louie Welch and members of the City Council, box 14, folder Nov., 1968; J. H. Jemison to Mark Hanna, Jr., Mar. 11, 1970, box 14, folder Mar., 1970.

48. Release form signed by Imogene Lee and William Lee, Feb. 7, 1969, FSBP, box 14, folder Feb., 1969; invoice dated Mar. 28, 1969, box 14, folder Mar., 1969.

49. FSBP, box 18, folder 5.

50. Ruthe Winegarten, *Black Texas Women*, p. 269; "'I Had My Own Business . . . So I Didn't Have to Worry': Beauty Salons, Beauty Culturists, and the Politics of African American Female Entrepreneurship," Philip Scranton, ed., *Beauty and Business: Commerce, Gender, and Culture in Modern America* (New York: Routledge, 2001), pp. 161–94.

51. Willett, *Permanent Waves*, pp. 132–35.

52. Obituary, *Houston Informer*, Apr. 30, 1983, p. 1.

53. Ibid.

Conclusion

1. Ronald W. Bailey, "Introduction: Black Business Enterprise; Reflections on Its History and Future Development," Ronald W. Bailey, ed., *Black Business Enterprise: Historical and Contemporary Perspectives* (New York: Basic Books, 1971), p. 3.

2. Kathy Peiss, *Hope in a Jar*, pp. 203–33.

3. Ibid., pp. 52–53, 110–12, 210–13, 223.

4. Ethel Erickson, United States Department of Labor, Women's Bureau, Bulletin No. 133, *Employment Conditions in Beauty Shops, A Study of Four Cities* (Washington: G.P.O., 1935), p. 44.

5. United States Department of Commerce, Bureau of the Census, *Historical Statistics of the United States Colonial Times to the Present*, Bicentennial Edition, Part 1 (Washington: G.P.O., 1975), Table H: 602–17. Overall the number of hairdressers in the United States increased form 190,000 in 1950 to more than 400,000 by 1970.

6. Erickson, *Employment Conditions in Beauty Shops*. The 1970s and 1980s Bureau of Labor Statistics earnings reports include all beauty-shop employees, counting manicurists, and beautician's helpers along with licensed cosmetologists. The 1980–81 *Occupational Outlook Handbook* reported that the weekly earnings of experienced cosmetologists in 1978 ranged from $330 to $390 per week and that beauticians with ten years' experience might earn more than $500 per week. Beginning beauticians, on the other hand, generally earned $145 per week or less. U.S. Department of Labor, Bureau of Labor Statistics, *Occupational Outlook Handbook*, 1980–81 ed. (Washington: G.P.O., 1980).

7. Quoted in "Integration Comes to the Beauty Trade," unidentified clipping, ca. 1970, MSJP, box 73.

8. Interview of Marjorie Stewart Joyner by Adam Langer, unidentified newspaper article, Sept. 11, 1992, MSJP, box 3.

9. Myles Horton and Paulo Freire, *We Make the Road by Walking: Conversations on Education and Social Change* (Philadelphia: Temple University Press, 1990), pp. 70–75. Julia A. Willett discusses Robinson's activities and the place of beauty shops in civil rights drives in *Permanent Waves*, pp. 133–35.

10. Margaret Holmes interviewed by Marcia Greenlee, Nov. 9, 1977, Ruth Edmonds Hill, ed., *The Black Women Oral History Project*, vol. 6, p. 57.

11. Quoted in Jill Nelson, "The Fortune That Madame Built," *Essence*, June, 1983, p. 154.

12. Vernice Mark, *History of the National Beauty Culturists' League, Inc., 1919–1994*, p. 89.

13. "Integration Comes to the Beauty Business," *Beauty Trade*, May, 1974, pp. 18f.

Bibliography

Archival Sources

Styling Jim Crow is based on three documentary collections: the Franklin School of Beauty Papers, the Madam C. W. Walker Collection, and the Marjorie Stewart Joyner Papers. The Franklin Papers are held by the Houston Metropolitan Research Center of the Houston Public Library. The Madam C. J. Walker Collection is housed at the Indiana Historical Society, and the Joyner Papers are part of the Vivian Harsh Collection at the Woodson Regional Library of the Chicago Public Library. Of these three collections only the Walker Collection has been processed and cataloged. The Mary McLeod Bethune Museum and Archives provided leads to sources on African American beauty care.

Covering the years from 1910 to 1980, the Madam C. J. Walker Collection documents the history of the Walker Company and include considerable information on Walker's life. Although the Walker collection is massive, it is not complete as a large share of the company records passed into the hands of the Randolph family when they purchased the remnants of the Walker firm. Although much of the Walker Collection was formerly closed to researchers, virtually all of the collection is now available.

The Marjorie Stewart Joyner Papers cover the years from 1922 to 1986 and document the history of the United Beauty School Owners and Teachers Association as well as Joyner's other professional activities and some aspects of her civic life. The collection includes little family correspondence or other papers of a wholly personal nature but does include a sizable collection of African American beauty magazines of the 1950s through the 1970s. The papers contain a record of Joyner's participation in and support of Metropolitan Community Church in Chicago and her work with the charitable activities supported by the *Chicago Defender*. The collection also includes some documentation of federally funded antipoverty programs in Chicago during the 1960s and the 1970s. The Joyner Papers have been placed in boxes, but no folders have been established, and much of the collection consists of duplicate materials.

The Franklin Papers cover the years from 1922 to 1986, but the bulk of the collection covers the years from 1935 through 1965. The records document numerous aspects of cosmetology and cosmetology regulation in Texas and include virtually complete lists of students who attended the Franklin School from the late 1930s through the 1950s as well as financial records of the Jemisons' beauty salons, of the school, and of the Jemisons' other investments.

All three collections include abundant photographic evidence. The Joyner Papers include several photographs of Chicago street scenes from the 1930s through the 1950s and numerous photographs of leading African American leaders from Chicago and from the nation, but they are especially strong in documenting the evolution of hairstyles and of beauty parlors. The photographs in the Franklin Papers largely pertain to the history of the school, including images of instructional settings, conventions, and alumnae events. A small number of photographs capture Jemison's interactions with black and white civic leaders in Houston.

Newspapers and Other Periodicals

Atlanta Daily World
Beauty Trade
Chicago Defender
Chicago Sun-Times
Chicago Tribune
Ebony Magazine
Houston Informer
Indianapolis Star
Journal of Negro Business
Modern Business
Negro Beautician
Negro Digest
Pittsburgh Courier
SEPIA
Service
Walker News

Articles, Books, and Other Sources

1950–1951 Consumer Analysis of the Pittsburgh Negro Market. Pittsburgh: Pittsburgh Courier Publishing Company, 1951.

Bailey, Ronald W., ed. *Black Business Enterprise: Historical and Contemporary Perspectives.* New York: Basic Books, 1971.

Banks, Ingrid. *Hair Matters: Beauty, Power, and Black Women's Consciousness.* New York: New York University Press, 2000.

Beeth, Howard, and Cary D. Wintz, eds. *Black Dixie: Afro-Texan History and Culture in Houston.* College Station: Texas A&M Press, 1992.

Berger, Iris, Elsa Barkley Brown, and Nancy A. Hewitt. "Intersections and Collision Courses: Women, Blacks, and Workers Confront Gender, Race, and Class," *Feminist Studies* 18 (Summer, 1992): 283–307.

Blanchet, Osceoloa. "The Investigation of Negro Business in New Orleans (1930–1940)," M.A. thesis, Xavier University, New Orleans, 1941.

Boyd, Robert L. "The Great Migration and the Rise of Ethnic Niches for African American Women in Beauty Culture and Hairdressing, 1919–1920" *Sociological Focus* 29 (February, 1996): 34–45.

Brand, Peg Zeglin, ed. *Beauty Matters.* Bloomington: Indiana University Press, 2000.

Bullard, Robert D. *Invisible Houston: The Black Experience in Boom and Bust*. College Station: Texas A&M Press, 1987.

Bundles, A'Lelia Perry. *On Her Own Ground: The Life and Times of Madam C. J. Walker*. New York: Scribner, 2001.

Burrows, John H. *The Necessity of Myth: A History of the National Negro Business League, 1900–1945*. Auburn, Ala.: Hickory Hill Press, 1988.

Castone, Toni. "The History of Dr. Marjorie Stewart Joyner," undated typescript in the Marjorie Stewart Joyner Papers, box 24, ca. 1983.

Chafe, William H., Raymond Gavins, and Robert Korstad, eds. *Remembering Jim Crow: African Americans Tell about Life in the Segregated South*. Center for Documentary Studies of Life behind the Veil Project. New York: New Press, 1991.

Cobbins, Sam. "Industrial Education for Black Americans in Mississippi, 1862–1965." Ed.D. thesis, Mississippi State University, 1975.

Cummings, John et al. *Negro Population in the United States, 1790–1915*. U.S. Bureau of the Census. Washington, D.C.: G.P.O., 1918.

Dailey, Jane Elizabeth, and Glenda Elizabeth Gilmore. *Jumpin' Jim Crow: Southern Politics from Civil War to Civil Rights*. Princeton: Princeton University Press, 2000.

Daniel, Pete. *Lost Revolutions: The South in the 1950s*. Chapel Hill: University of North Carolina Press and the Smithsonian Institution, 2000.

Dickerson, Debra. "Racial Fingernail Politics," *U.S. News Online*, April 14, 1997, pp. 1–4, and http://www.usnews.com/usnews/issue/970414/.

Drake, St. Clair, and Horace R Clayton. *Black Metropolis: A Study of Negro Life in a Northern City*. 2 vols. Revised and enlarged ed. New York: Harper, 1962.

DuBois, W. E. B., ed. *The Negro Artisan*. Atlanta University Publications No. 7. Atlanta: Atlanta University Press, 1902.

————. *The Negro in Business*. Atlanta University Publications No. 4. Atlanta, 1899.

Erickson, Ethel. U.S. Department of Labor, Women's Bureau. Bulletin No. 133. *Employment Conditions in Beauty Shops: A Study of Four Cities*. Washington, D.C.: G.P.O., 1935.

Eskew, Glenn T. "Black Elitism and the Failure of Paternalism in Postbellum Georgia: The Case of Bishop Lucius Henry Holsey," *Journal of Southern History* 58 (November, 1992): 637–66.

Feagin, Joe R. *Living with Racism: The Black Middle-Class Experience*. Boston: Beacon Press, 1994.

Fleming, Walter L. *The Freedman's Savings Bank: A Chapter in the Economic History of the Negro Race*. Westport: Negro Universities Press, 1970, reprint of the 1927 University of North Carolina Press edition.

Franklin, Nobia Anita. *Madame N. A. Franklin's Improved System of Hair Culture*, 4th ed. Houston: Webster Printing, 1921.

Gaines, Jean Foley. "An Evaluative Analysis of Job Opportunities for Negro Students of Business Education in Houston, Texas." M.B.Ed. thesis, University of Colorado, 1956.

Gilmore, Glenda Elizabeth. *Gender and Jim Crow: Women and the Politics of White Supremacy in North Carolina, 1896–1920*. Chapel Hill: University of North Carolina Press, 1996.

Gordon, Edith E. *Establishing and Operating a Beauty Shop*. Washington, D.C.: G.P.O., 1946.

Graham, Lawrence Otis. *Our Kind of People: Inside America's Black Upper Class*. New York: HarperCollins, 1999.

Grimes, Pearl E., and Linda T. Davis. "Cosmetics in Blacks," *Cosmetics and Cosmetic Surgery in Dermatology* 9 (January, 1992): 53–68.

Grossman, James R. *Land of Hope: Chicago, Black Southerners and the Great Migration*. Chicago: University of Chicago Press, 1989.

Harmon, J. H., Jr., et al. *The Negro as a Business Man*. Washington, D.C.: Association for the Study of Negro Life and History, 1929.

Henderson, Alexa Benson. *Atlanta Life Insurance Company: Guardian of Black Economic Dignity*. Tuscaloosa: University of Alabama Press, 1990.

Hill, Ruth Edmonds, ed. *Black Women Oral History Project*. 10 vols. Arthur and Elizabeth Schlesinger Library on the History of Women in America, Radcliffe College. Westport, Conn.: Meckler, 1991).

Hine, Darlene Clark. *Black Victory: The Rise and Fall of the White Primary in Texas*. Millwood, N.Y.: KTO Press, 1979.

———. *The Black Women in the Middle West Project: The Michigan Experience*. Ann Arbor: Historical Society of Michigan, 1990.

———. *Black Women in White: Racial Conflict and Cooperation in the Nursing Profession, 1890–1950*. Bloomington: Indiana University Press, 1989.

"History of United Beauty School Owners and Teachers Association, Alpha Chi Pi Omega Sorority and Fraternity, Greek Letter Beauticians, International, National Local Chapters, and Their Activities." 3d ed., n.p., n.d., MSJP, box 3.

Hope, John. "The Negro and Business," pamphlet, n.p., ca. 1930.

Horton, Myles, and Paulo Freire. *We Make the Road by Walking: Conversations on Education and Social Change*. Philadelphia: Temple University Press, 1990.

Jones, Ruth S. *Practical Preparation for Beauty Culture: A Curriculum for Schools, Manual for Teachers, Handbook for Operators, and Textbook for Students*. New York: Prentice-Hall, 1939.

Kelley, Robin D. G. "We Are Not What We Seem": Rethinking Black Working-Class Opposition in the Jim Crow South," *Journal of American History* 80 (June, 1993): 75–112.

Kenzer, Robert C. *Enterprising Southerners: Black Economic Success in North Carolina, 1865–1915*. Carter G. Woodson Series in Black Studies. Charlottesville: University Press of Virginia, 1997.

Kwolek-Folland, Angel. *Engendering Business: Men and Women in the Corporate Office, 1870– 1930*. Baltimore: Johns Hopkins University Press, 1994.

Lasky, Kathryn. *Vision of Beauty: The Story of Sarah Breedlove Walker*. Cambridge, Mass.: Candlewick Press, 2000.

Litwack, Leon F. *Trouble in Mind: Black Southerners in the Age of Jim Crow*. New York: Knopf, 1998.

Mark, Vernice. *History of the National Beauty Culturists' League, Inc., 1919–1994*. 2d ed. Detroit: Harlo Press, 1994.

Marks, Carole. *Farewell — We're Good and Gone: The Great Black Migration.* Bloomington: Indiana University Press, 1989.

Meyerowitz, Joanne. "Beyond the Feminine Mystique: Reassessment of Postwar Mass Culture, 1946–1958," *Journal of American History* 79 (Mar., 1993): 1455–82.

Mississippi Independent Beauticians Association. *Beautician's Guide and Yearbook, 1948.* Greenville, Miss., 1948.

Nelson, Jill. "The Fortune That Madame Built," *Essence,* June, 1983, pp. 154ff.

Oak, Vishnu V. *The Negro Newspaper.* The Negro Entrepreneur, vol. 1. Yellow Springs, Ohio: Antioch Press, 1948.

———. *The Negro's Adventure in General Business.* The Negro Entrepreneur, vol. 2. Yellow Springs, Ohio: Antioch Press, 1949.

Osthaus, Carl R. *Freedmen, Philanthropy, and Fraud: A History of the Freedman's Savings Bank.* Urbana: University of Illinois Press, 1976.

Papers of Project to Study Business and Education among Negroes. Robert W. Woodruff Library, Atlanta University Center.

Peiss, Kathy. *Hope in a Jar: The Making of America's Beauty Culture.* New York: Henry Holt, 1998.

Pettet, Zellmer Russell, and Charles Edward Hall. *Negroes in the United States, 1920–32.* U.S. Bureau of the Census. Washington, D.C.: G.P.O., 1935.

Pierce, Joseph A. *Negro Business and Business Education: Their Present and Prospective Development.* New York: Harper, 1947.

Pitre, Merline. *In Struggle against Jim Crow: Lula B. White and the NAACP, 1900–1957.* College Station: Texas A&M University Press, 1999.

Plitt, Jane R. *Martha Matilda Harper and the American Dream.* Syracuse: Syracuse University Press, 2000.

Ponder, Janace Pope. "SEPIA." M.A. thesis, North Texas State University, 1973.

Quinn, Leah. "Shop Owner Was an Icon of Beauty in West Austin," *Austin American Statesman,* January 4, 2001.

Randle, James Patrick. "The Nouveau Black Middle Class of Houston: Social Arenas and Self-Identity. M.A. thesis, University of Houston, 1994.

Robinson, Gwendolyn. "Class, Race and Gender: A Transcultural Theoretical and Sociohistorical Analysis of Cosmetic Institutions and Practice to 1920," Ph.D. diss., University of Illinois–Chicago, 1984.

Rooks, Noliwe. *Hair Raising: Beauty Culture and African American Women.* New Brunswick: Rutgers University Press, 1996.

Schroder, David. *Engagement in the Mirror: Hairdressers and Their Work.* San Francisco: R. & E. Research, 1978.

Scranton, Philip, ed. *Beauty and Business: Commerce, Gender, and Culture in Modern America.* New York: Routledge, 2001.

Shaw, Stephanie. *What a Woman Ought to Be and to Do: Black Professional Women in the Jim Crow Era.* Women in Culture and Society. Chicago: University of Chicago Press, 1996.

Sheehan, Arthur T. *Black Pearl: The Hairdresser from Haiti.* London: Harvill Press, 1956.

Silverman, Robert Mark. "The Effects of Racism and Racial Discrimination on Minority

Business Development: The Case of Black Manufacturers in Chicago's Ethnic Beauty Aids Industry," *Journal of Social History* 1 (Spring, 1998): 571–27.

Simkins, Francis B. "The Everlasting South," *Journal of Southern History* 13 (August, 1947): 307–22.

Sitkoff, Harvard. *The Struggle for Black Equality, 1954–1992*. Rev. ed. New York: Hill and Wang, 1993.

Stanley, Autumn. *Mothers and Daughters of Invention: Notes for a Revised History of Technology*. New Brunswick: Rutgers University Press, 1995.

State of New York. Department of Labor, Division of Women in Industry and Minimum Wage. "Report of the Industrial Commissioner to the Beauty Shop Minimum Wage Board, Relating to Wages and Other Conditions of Employment in the Beauty Shop Industry, New York State," March, 1938.

Texas Cosmetology Commission. *A Staff Report to the Sunset Advisory Commission*. Austin, 1991.

U.S. Department of Labor. Bureau of the Census. *Historical Statistics of the United States Colonial Times to the Present*. Bicentennial Edition, Part 1. Washington, D.C.: G.P.O., 1975.

———. Bureau of Labor Statistics. *Occupational Outlook Handbook*. 1980–81 ed. Washington, D.C.: G.P.O., 1980.

Walker, Juliet E. K. *The History of Black Business in America: Capitalism, Race, Entrepreneurship*. New York: Twayne, 1988.

Weare, Walter B. *Black Business in the New South: A Social History of the North Carolina Mutual Life Insurance Company*. Urbana: University of Illinois Press, 1973.

White, Deborah Gray. *Ain't I a Woman? Female Slaves in the Plantation South*. New York: Norton, 1985.

———. *Too Heavy a Load: Black Women in Defense of Themselves, 1894–1994*. New York: W. W. Norton, 1999.

Willett, Julie A. *Permanent Waves: The Making of the American Beauty Shop*. New York: New York University Press, 2000.

Winegarten, Ruthe. *Black Texas Women: One Hundred and Fifty Years of Trial and Triumph*. Austin: University of Texas Press, 1995.

Wolf, Naomi. *The Beauty Myth*. New York: Morrow, 1991.

Index

Page numbers appearing in *italics* refer to illustrations.

122–23, 134, 136, 156; in Houston, 69, 75; and white-collar occupations, 150–51. *See also* beauty schools; training

electricity, 12, 31

employment. *See* occupational options

entertainment, 44

entrepreneurs. *See* businesses, African American

European trip, 57–58

examinations, 8, 31, *103, 133*

family life: Jemisons, 77–80, 116–17, 131–32, 137–38; and traveling sales career, 36–37, 43–44

Feeney, Gladys, 115–16

finger waving, 31, 82

Fook, Ann Douglas, 51

franchising, 28, 41, 45

Franklin, Abbie (Mrs. J. H. Jemison), 66. *See also* Jemison, Abbie Franklin

Franklin, Nobia (Mrs. N. A.), 21, 29, 30, 64–67

Franklin School of Beauty: admissions policies, 81–82; civil rights and integration effects on, 132–36; curriculum, 82–84, 126–27; decline of, 141; development of, 71–75; employment for graduates, 85–88; Jemison's management of, 89–93, 98–99; leadership changes, 138–40; licensing process, 84–85; move to Houston, 5, 67–71; Nobia's creation of, 64–67; Pilgrim Building move, 107–9; student life, 80–81, 91–92, 93–98, 114–23, 136; WWII school operations, 109–13, 114–17

Freeman, N. F., 90

Freeman's Bank, 10

G. I. Bill, 117–18, 120

Garnett-Abney, Grace, 10–11, 36

gas stoves, 31

gender norms: and dealing with men while recruiting, 38; and inequalities in Walker Company, 25–26, 36–37, 43; restricted employment options for women, 8; and self-esteem for women in beauty culture, 145–46

Godfrey Manufacturing Company, 50

golf course integration, 125

government assistance, 120, 150

Graham, Billy, 125

Great Depression, 46–49, 151

Greene, Lorenzo J., 108–9

grooming, hair. *See* hairdressing

hairdressing: African American dominance in, 10; African American preferences in, 11, 15–16, 31–32, 85–86, 140; chemicals for, 16, 17, 18–19,

21, 31; electricity effect, 12; hair growers, 16–17, 21, 22; hair-relaxing lotions, 135; heated tools, 17, 19, 23, 25, 30, 36; marcel techniques, 31, 36, 82–83; as profession, 7; sanitation procedures, 25, 29, 50, 68, 89. *See also* beauty culture

hair dryers, 31

hair growers, 16–17, 21, 22

hair pullers, 25, 36

Hair Refining Tonic and Bronze Beauty Vanishing Cream, 18

hair-relaxing lotions, 135

Harlem, 32

Harper, Martha Matilda, 28, 30

head wrapping, 16

health considerations: Franklin school health testing, 90; sanitation procedures, 25, 29, 50, 68, 89; and traditional black hairstyles, 16

heated hair devices, 17, 19, 23, 25, 30, 36

Hicks, Jessie Mae, 114

High Brown Face Powder, 20

high schools, 122–23, 134, 136, 156

Hi-Ja Chemical Company, 18

Holmes, Margaret, 17, 152–53

Holsey, Lucius Henry, 16

home-based beauty culture, 11, 14–15, 16, 146–47

hotel industry, 153–54

hot-oil treatments, 19

Houston, Tex.: African American business community, 68–70, 76, 138; African American newspaper, 18, 74; Franklin School move to, 5, 67–71; golf course integration, 125

Houston Informer and Texas Freeman, 18, 74

identity politics, 3, 4, 6, 145–46, 152

Illinois (licensing), 27

independence, economic: beauty culture as road to, 5, 6–7, 8, 13, 153; from white employers, 3, 147, 151, 152, 153

Indianapolis, Ind., 12, 22

inspections, 84–85, 100, 125–26

integration: and African American social status, 140–41; effect on beauty schools, 132–36, 155–56; golf courses in Houston, 125; Houston businesses, 138; pros and cons for African Americans, 144–45

inventions: blurred lines of, 21; capital issues and promotion of, 32–33; and cosmetics competition, 22; Franklin's lack of patents, 66; hairdressing tools, 23; Joyner's surrender of, 41

Irving, Gertrude, 90–91

Jackson, Andrew F., 50

James, Ollie Mae, 74–75

ISBN 1-58544-244-5